Managing Commercial
Bank Funds

Emmanuel N. Roussakis

The Praeger Special Studies program—utilizing the most modern and efficient book production techniques and a selective worldwide distribution network—makes available to the academic, government, and business communities significant, timely research in U.S. and international economic, social, and political development.

Managing Commercial Bank Funds

PRAEGER SPECIAL STUDIES IN U.S. ECONOMIC, SOCIAL, AND POLITICAL ISSUES

Praeger Publishers   New York   London

Library of Congress Cataloging in Publication Data

Roussakis, Emmanuel N
  Managing commercial bank funds.

  (Praeger special studies in U.S. economic, social,
and political issues)
  Bibliography: p. 172
  Includes index.
  1. Bank investments.   2. Bank loans.   I. Title.
HG1616.I5R68   1977   658'.91'33212   77-4380
ISBN 0-03-021966-3

PRAEGER PUBLISHERS
200 Park Avenue, New York, N.Y. 10017, U.S.A.

Published in the United States of America in 1977
by Praeger Publishers, Inc.
789 038 987654321

Printed in the United States of America

Dedicated to the cause of a free Cyprus

PREFACE

This study deals with a key aspect of banking, the management of commercial bank funds. Had the banks been operating in a static world, it would have been a rather easy task to provide a set of given rules and formulas to guide the performance of this function. However, the environment in which a commercial bank operates is a dynamic one. This very fact renders the management of bank funds an art. As the economy evolves and changes, a bank must continuously reappraise the management of its funds and adapt to existing means, if it is to survive and achieve its objectives.

Numerous works have discussed bank funds management. Some have treated the subject as part of the overall bank management function; while others have treated it independent of such function. The former have dealt with the subject very cursorily, and the latter, in great detail. My general reliance has been upon those works that addressed the problem in the broadest terms; my concern has been to cover the basic areas of consideration in the management of bank funds without becoming heavily involved in the details of such management. A different approach would have created a text much longer and, perhaps, more burdensome. The basic issues of bank funds management have been emphasized because, once bank executives understand such issues, details of the operating considerations can easily evolve.

Those who write in this field owe an intellectual debt to Professor Roland Robinson for his pioneering work on the subject a number of years ago. Beyond this source, I have found especially stimulating and helpful the writings of two professionals: Roger Lyon's *Investment Portfolio Management in the Commercial Bank,* and Howard Crosse's *Management Policies for Commercial Banks.*

A moral debt is due to all my professors for their contributions to my development and growth. Of special significance have been the contributions of Xenophon Zolotas, University of Athens; J. B. Blayton and B. Wapensky, Graduate School of Business Administration, Atlanta University; Jan Tinbergen, College of Europe, Bruges; and Leon Dupriez and Louis Duquesne de la Vinelle, Catholic University of Louvain. My appreciation goes also to Dr. V. W. Henderson, the late president of Clark College, for having encouraged me in my academic pursuits.

In the preparation of this study, I have been given significant assistance by professors J. Fulton and R. Moses. Important help at various points was additionally given by professors G. Kalogeras and E. Kuehn. Acknowledgment is also due to Dr. John Hampton who read the manuscript and made many constructive comments.

Finally, less tangible but no less important to the long process of bringing this book to completion has been the support and encouragement, expressed in so many ways, of my wife.

CONTENTS

LIST OF TABLES AND FIGURES

INTRODUCTION

Commercial banks constitute the core of a nation's financial system. They are the depositories for the funds of numerous individuals, business units, and the government itself. Through their lending and investing activities they provide substantial financing to all major sectors of the economy—the household, business, and governmental sectors. By extending credit to these segments of the economy, they facilitate the flow of goods and services from producers to consumers and affect the financial activities of the government. They provide a sizable portion of the money supply in the form of demand deposits, and are the means through which monetary policy is effected. All these add up to one thing: no other financial institution contributes more markedly to the successful functioning of a nation's economy than does its commercial banks.

Efficient management conditions a commercial banking system's capacity for meeting a nation's economic needs and goals. Indeed, it is efficient management that underlies the effectiveness of commercial banks in meeting the demands of the society and hence in stimulating the development and growth of the economy. It is essential therefore that bank management be prudent, safe, and profitable if it is to have a strong and adaptable banking system capable of meeting the needs of a growing society. This book is an inquiry into the management of commercial bank funds, with the analysis centered around the individual bank.

Management of the bank's funds is one of the most important aspects of bank management. None of the commercial banking functions can achieve its maximum potential profit for the bank unless the funds management function is efficiently planned and executed. The management of the bank's funds is the pivotal catalytic function that brings together policies in the areas of loans, deposits, investments, and capital, and relates each to the other so that decisions in one area reinforce those in each of the other areas. Funds management is thus the coordination of the commercial banking functions in such a manner as to optimize the bank's profit performance consistent with the constraints imposed on it by law, regulation, and the interests of its community.

As in any other type of business organization, the ultimate function of management rests upon the bank's board of directors. The board, which is elected by bank stockholders, has the ultimate responsibility for formulating bank policy and establishing the managerial framework within which such policy is to be executed. In the formulation of a sound and flexible policy, the board is assisted and guided by the bank's senior management. And as the object of this policy is the efficient utilization of commercial bank funds and the optimization of bank profits, top management's role is to provide directors with an accurate picture of the bank's goals and requirements. Bank liquidity requirements, ability to accept risk based on capital adequacy (solvency), the bank's income performance (profitability), and an appraisal of the market's position and outlook comprise the major parts of this picture. Based on these considerations the board assesses the position of the bank and establishes policy directives for funds management for the ensuing period. And as long as these policy directives, along with the necessary procedures for their implementation, are in a written form, they clearly delineate the nature and limits of both responsibility and authority. Once established, these policies must be periodically reviewed and adapted to changing conditions so that optimal results can be achieved.

The book has been written with the objective of providing professionals and students alike with a description and an analysis of the problems faced in the management of bank funds. In principle, these problems can be easily identified and rationally considered. In practice, however, solutions are anything but watertight. Indeed, in the real world in which the banker operates, application of the relative principles discussed in this book becomes an exercise in informed judgment. The principles therefore presented must be viewed as the guidelines that will assist the banker in the systematic evaluation of the relevant facts. This book does not provide the final answers, as these vary among banks, and even for the same bank these would vary over a period of time.

It is the author's hope that this book will stir the interest of professionals and students of banking both in this country and other parts of the world, especially Western Europe. The financial climate in which European banks have been operating has changed significantly since the early 1960s. The striving of the European economies toward industrial development and economic growth has led to a general state of tightness. New competitive factors have emerged in the financial community in the form of increased foreign bank branches. Banking philosophy has been in the process of development in response to changing needs and tastes of customers. The introduction of the bank credit card, for example, is an innovation that will significantly influence consumer credit. The expansion of the European Economic Community into a nine-country membership promises to add further momentum to the forces of change generated by its initial establishment. Lastly, the trend in the European Economic Community is to benefit from the U.S. experience and introduce a banking framework in many respects similar to that in existence in the United States. Specifically, the Commission of the European Economic Community has issued or drafted banking directives for compliance by the member states that aim at standardizing banking services, establishing uniform banking regulations and controls, and generally at providing a common framework for the exercise of banking throughout the community. In fact, the Commission is even considering the introduction, in the not too distant future, of a deposit insurance scheme functioning along the lines of the Federal Deposit Insurance Corporation. It is therefore the author's hope that understanding of the experience gained by U.S. banks in the management of bank funds will prove itself beneficial to the European banker in his rapidly changing environment. The present study, then, is offered as a work in applied economics in the framework of U.S. banking.

From an organizational standpoint, the material is centered around three subjects: the sources of commercial bank funds, the objectives of portfolio management, and the pattern and distribution of assets in the portfolio to satisfy these objectives. This last subject is discussed in Chapters 3, 4, and 5. Because of the quasi-public character of commercial banking, pertinent laws and actions by regulatory bodies are given due consideration throughout the book.

Managing Commercial
Bank Funds

A commercial bank has access to three sources of funds: invested and senior capital, deposits, and borrowing. Specifically, when a bank sells stocks and senior debt instruments, accepts deposits, or borrows, it is thereby provided with funds that enable it to acquire earning assets—that is to say, to grant loans and make investments. Interest earned on these loans and investments provides the principal source of earnings out of which the bank meets the operating expenses involved in attracting and servicing deposit accounts and in managing its loans and investments. Residual earnings accrue to the bank's owners.

The sources of bank funds constitute the right-hand side of a bank's balance sheet as opposed to the left side, which shows the assets that a bank owns, that is, the uses to which a bank puts available funds. Unlike the situation in other businesses, however, the right-hand side of a bank's balance sheet is made up overwhelmingly of liabilities and only to a much lesser extent of capital. Indeed, a closer look at the funds sources reveals that banks rely heavily on debt to finance the acquisition of bank assets, which in fact are but the debts of others—the federal government, state and local governments, businesses, and individuals. This situation has earned banks the reputation of being dealers in debts.

Bank reliance upon each of the sources of funds and the extent of such reliance are neither incidental nor a matter of an attitude such as "the more funds the better." Instead, it is a matter of policy, developed by the board of directors of each individual bank. Indeed, it is the responsibility of the board to develop policies that will provide answers to such questions as how much funds are needed and in what proportion in each of the various forms.

We shall attempt below to examine the nature and characteristics of each of the sources of bank funds as well as the extent and form of bank reliance upon each source.

CAPITAL

Types and Postwar Growth of Bank Capital

Toward the end of 1976 there were about 14,650 commercial banks operating in the United States. Their total capital amounted to over $73 billion as compared to $7 billion at the onset of World War II (1941). This tenfold expansion in bank capital throughout the postwar period resulted generally from increases in the capitalization of already existing banks rather than the establishment of new ones during the period.[1]

As with other businesses, capital is legally necessary to establish a bank and keep it as a going concern. A bank's capital or stockholders' equity is made up of a number of accounts, each of which has certain features that distinguish it from the others. Traditionally, commercial banks raise capital by issuing shares of common stock. Unlike other companies in the United States, banks usually sell their authorized shares of common stock at the time of organization. The total of these shares is shown in the bank's capital stock account. Shares are carried in this account at par value, and the total par value of all shares constitutes the capital of the bank as stated in the bank's charter. Aside from the paid-in capital stock, however, a bank's capital structure includes also the surplus account, the undivided profits account, and the capital reserves.

It should be noted that while bank stocks have a par value, newly opened banks almost always operate initially at a loss, and therefore bank capital stocks are sold at a premium over par value, which provides the bank a surplus to prevent the impairment of its capital before earnings develop. After the bank establishes itself, this account may be further increased by action of the bank's management, by transfers of past earnings that have been retained by the management. The transfers of past earnings are made out of the undivided profits account—an operating account that includes current as well as accumulated earnings that have not been paid out as dividends, transferred to surplus, or placed in one or more of the reserve accounts that banks keep for specific purposes. Finally, a portion of the funds accounted in the undivided profits account may be allocated to one or more reserve accounts to take care of some contingency or expected event. Examples include a reserve for the anticipated retirement of preferred stock or for an expected court settlement. Reserve accounts may also be established so that uncommon losses will not encroach upon the bank's surplus and undivided profits. Classical examples of such accounts are the reserve for loan losses and the reserve for security losses, both of which technically are asset valuation reserves rather than equity reserves. These reserve accounts have traditionally provided a ready outlet for the charge-offs of losses, and especially loan losses, thereby sparing the bank unnecessary disclosures or any sense of embarrassment.*

The importance of each of these accounts in bank equity capital is shown in Table 1. As shown in this table, throughout the 1960s and in the 1970s the basic sources of equity capital have been common stock issuance, surplus, and undivided profits. A closer look at the evolution of each of these items would reveal that between 1961 and 1975 much of the increase in equity capital actually came from undivided profits, which during these years expanded by fivefold. What this means is that the bulk of equity capital throughout this period was derived from bank earnings rather than the issuance of common stocks. A number of reasons are likely to have been responsible for this development. For some banks it may have been the cost involved in marketing new issues of common stock; to others, the earnings dilution or control dilution effects of such issues.

Marketing new issues generally involves certain costs usually referred to as flotation costs. These involve the costs of underwriting and distributing the new issue, and are generally higher for the issues of smaller and less-known businesses because of the greater risk involved in marketing such issues. Since these expenses are relatively large and fixed, the cost percentage runs higher on small issues. Clearly then, for most small banks, and for that matter for small businesses in general, sale of common stock entails a disproportionate cost as compared to the retention of earnings, which is the most convenient and least expensive way to provide additional equity capital. And if the sale of additional common stock is essential, it is usually a small group of interested local investors that provides a ready outlet. This helps explain why the common shares of most of the country's banks are held by a relatively small number of stockholders, and hence the absence of an active market for these shares. Consequently, only a limited number of banks would be in a position

---

*There has been a growing pressure upon commercial banks for fuller disclosure especially of their loan losses. Much of this pressure has been mounted by the Securities and Exchange Commission (SEC), the Internal Revenue Service, and bank regulatory agencies, and stemmed from the large loan losses sustained by banks in the 1970s.[2]

TABLE 1
Equity Capital Accounts, All Insured Commercial Banks, 1961–75
(millions of dollars)

Year	Total Equity Capital	Preferred Stock	Common Stock	Surplus	Undivided Profits	Equity Reserves
1961	22,101	15	6,585	10,798	4,157	546
1965	28,252	40	8,508	13,465	5,438	802
1966	29,963	62	8,857	13,999	6,166	880
1967	32,021	87	9,254	14,983	6,611	1,087
1968	34,518	91	9,773	16,174	7,420	1,061
1969	37,578	103	10,529	17,461	8,427	1,058
1970	40,475	107	11,138	18,073	10,146	1,011
1971	43,949	92	11,811	19,896	11,135	1,015
1972	48,275	69	12,854	21,528	13,012	812
1973	53,721	66	13,846	23,593	15,362	854
1974	59,028	43	14,789	25,313	17,970	912
1975	64,309	48	15,565	26,713	21,182	800

Note: Details do not add to total because of rounding.
Source: Federal Deposit Insurance Corp., *Assets and Liabilities* (Washington, D.C.: Federal Deposit Insurance Corp., 1965–75).

4

to have their stocks traded in the over-the-counter market or on a national stock exchange.* In fact, this is encountered only among the large banks.

In some banks equity financing is avoided because of the dilution in earnings that it entails. For a small bank whose stock is closely held, issuing new shares of stock to outsiders means giving more owners the right to share in income. In other words, new stockholders acquire equal rights with existing stockholders to share in the net profits of the bank.

In other instances equity financing is avoided because it would involve dilution of control, since the sale of common stock extends voting rights or control to the additional stockholders who are brought into the bank. Clearly, in closely held banks, existing stockholders are unwilling to share control of the bank's operations with outsiders. Thus, the potential dilution of earnings and/or control has in many cases caused existing stockholders to veto the sale of new shares of common stock.

It follows then that undivided profits have played a major role in the growth of equity capital in the postwar years. Taken together with all other types of equity capital—preferred and common stock, surplus, and contingency reserves—these accounts have jointly contributed in a more than fivefold expansion of equity capital in the 1951–75 period. Throughout this period banks relied heavily on equity capital to provide for the growth in capital funds. Simultaneously, however, there has been a growing shift by banks to other nonequity sources of capital—reserves for loan losses, and capital notes and debentures, also known as senior capital.

As stated earlier, reserves for loan losses represent earnings earmarked as valuation reserves against possible loan losses. The importance of this source for commercial banks is illustrated in Table 2. Thus, at the end of 1975, earmarked reserves against bad-debt losses, for all insured commerical banks, amounted to $8.6 billion. If one considers that these reserves in 1951 amounted to only $814 million, it is obvious that in the span of 25 years these reserves increased 10.6 times.

---

*The banking industry has a tradition against listing its stocks. The reason given for this was that banks were afraid that a falling market price on their stocks would lead depositors to think that a bank itself was in danger and, thus, would cause a run on the bank. Some basis for such fears may have existed before the creation of the Federal Deposit Insurance Corporation (FDIC) in 1935, but the fear is no longer justified. The other reason for banks not listing has to do with reporting financial information. The exchanges require that quarterly financial statements be sent to all stockholders; banks have been reluctant to provide financial information. With bank regulatory agencies requiring public disclosure of additional financial information, it is expected that banks will increasingly seek to list their securities on exchanges. A notable first in this respect occurred when the Chase Manhattan Bank was listed on the New York Stock Exchange in 1965.

TABLE 2
Capital Accounts and Reserves for Loan Losses, All Insured Commercial Banks, 1961–75
(millions of dollars)

Year	Reserves for Loan Losses	Total Capital	Capital Notes and Debentures	Equity Capital
1961	2,606	22,123	22	22,101
1965	4,011	29,905	1,653	28,252
1966	4,337	31,693	1,730	29,963
1967	4,733	34,006	1,984	32,021
1968	5,216	36,628	2,110	34,518
1969	5,886	39,576	1,998	37,578
1970	5,999	42,566	2,092	40,475
1971	6,151	46,905	2,956	43,949
1972	6,624	52,368	4,093	48,275
1973	7,527	57,839	4,117	53,721
1974	8,377	63,287	4,259	59,028
1975	8,655	68,716	4,408	64,309

Note: Details do not add to total because of rounding.
Source: Federal Deposit Insurance Corp., *Assets and Liabilities* (Washington, D.C.: Federal Deposit Insurance Corp., 1965–75).

In their practice of maintaining loan-loss reserves, banks have been encouraged both by regulatory authorities and the Internal Revenue Service. Up until 1969, banks were allowed to make additions to the reserve for loan losses out of pretax earnings until these reserves amounted to 2.4 percent of the eligible loans. As a result of this stipulation, loan-loss reserves grew significantly and far in excess of actual losses (that is, between 1950 and 1968, out of $8.8 billion placed in reserves, net loan charge-offs amounted to only $3.2 billion). In 1969, however, the Internal Revenue reduced this allowance to 1.8 percent of eligible loans, indicating that after succeeding adjustments through 1987, such reserves would be justified thereafter only up to the average of actual losses sustained over the most recent six-year period.[3] Clearly, the legislative reduction of the amount of pretax earnings permitted to be transferred to the reserves for loan losses, will affect adversely, over the years, the importance of this source of capital. Barring any legislative changes in this respect, banks will have to rely in the future increasingly on some of the other sources of bank capital.

Another important source of nonequity funds for commercial banks has been debt capital. Specifically, since the early 1960s banks have been increasingly relying on capital notes and debentures to provide for the growth in bank capital funds. The spectacular expansion of this source is shown in Table 2. Thus, as indicated in the table, between 1961 and 1975 the value of capital notes and debentures outstanding increased from a mere $22 million to $4.4 billion.

Up until the early 1960s, bank issuance of capital notes and debentures (unsecured bonds), constituted a rare occurrence. Their use had been generally discouraged by the comptroller of the currency* to such a degree that virtually no national bank had issued such securities since the 1930s. Although such securities are considered entirely acceptable capital instruments in other industries, the attitude of the comptroller had been that they were inappropriate for banks. Apparently this attitude stemmed from the days of the Great Depression when distressed banks had to sell such issues to cope with financial difficulties. The issuance of such securities was thus viewed in subsequent years as a reflection on the soundness of a bank.[4]

After the middle 1950s, however, there was growing pressure from the banking industry as a whole for permission to issue senior securities. The breakthrough at the national level came in the form of a December 1962 ruling

---

*This office, established in the Treasury Department by the National Bank Act of 1864, generally controls the operations of national banks throughout the country (that is, grants charters to national banks, maintains a corps of examiners for the periodical examination of national banks, decides on national bank mergers).

from the then comptroller of the currency (James J. Saxon) that gave national banks more flexibility in the management of their capital account. National banks were now allowed to issue preferred stock, capital notes, or debentures as part of their ordinary course of business activities in raising capital. The funds thus obtained were to be viewed as a portion of unimpaired capital for purposes of calculating lending limits on unsecured loans to any one borrower. These issues, moreover, in the event of liquidation, were considered to be subordinate in priority of payment to payment in full of all deposit liabilities of the bank. Certain limitations were imposed in the ruling, notably that the principal amount of preferred stock and debentures outstanding at any particular time had to be added to all other indebtedness of the bank (both short- and long-term) in determining compliance with the existing rule that total indebtedness could not exceed the sum of 100 percent of the bank's paid-in capital stock plus 50 percent of the surplus.

Many banks have taken advantage of these provisions. As shown in Table 1, for example, a number of banks have made use of preferred stocks as a financing instrument; at the end of 1975, the value of preferred stocks outstanding amounted to $48 million, which represented a threefold increase over the corresponding figure in 1961.

Clearly, the contribution of preferred stocks in the capital structures of commercial banks has been insignificant compared to other sources. To some extent this has been due to the continued association of preferred stocks, both by present-day bankers and investors, with distress financing. Another reason is the hybrid character of preferred stocks in relation to bonds and common stocks. Thus, unlike bond interest, preferred stock fixed dividend payments are not tax deductible, which makes the cost of such funds equal the full percentage amount of the preferred dividend. On the other hand, unlike common stock dividends, preferred stock dividends are most frequently of a cumulative nature—that is, all past preferred dividends must be paid before any payment of common dividends. These disadvantages may, of course, be lessened through a convertibility feature that permits conversion into common stock at a predetermined price, at the option of the preferred stockholder.

Although bank issuance of capital notes and debentures was also associated with the distress financing of the early 1930s, the present-day attitudes of bankers and investors have changed significantly enough to make the issuance of such debt instruments more acceptable in bank capital structures. Thus throughout the 1960s and in the 1970s, a great many banks have sold debentures to raise additional capital. This route was favored by the banks for several reasons, one of which is that subordinated debentures are considered capital by the banking regulatory agencies. The holders of such debt do not participate in earnings beyond the stated interest rate on the debentures. Thus, the equity position of common stockholders in the bank is not diluted, yet the bank has obtained additional capital with which to expand profitably its operations.*

Banks may raise, and often have raised, capital with issues of convertible subordinated debentures. These securities are like the subordinated debentures except that they give the holder the opportunity to trade his debenture for stock at some time in the future at a specified price. Because such issues offer the investor the attractive feature of interest payment protection plus the opportunity to convert at some time in the future to common stock and thus participate in all future earnings, the interest rate on such debentures is generally lower than for those without a conversion feature.[6] That makes convertible security issues desirable from the bank's point of view. Moreover, since they offer a bank an opportunity to obtain permanent capital at less dilution than if stock were issued immediately, convertible issues have been used extensively, and will continue to be employed.

Beyond the issuance of subordinated debentures, national banks have also been making use of the provisions for capital notes. Thus since the early 1960s several banks have issued capital notes of relatively small denominations, which they have sold directly to bank customers. In other instances, such notes have been placed with the major correspondent banks of the issuing bank. Capital notes are generally issued for various sums and are of varied maturities.

As a result of the above provisions, total bank capital has experienced substantial growth. From 1961 to 1975, total bank capital rose from $22.1 billion to $68.7 billion, which represented an increase by three times. Much of this growth resulted from the increase in equity capital. Though such capital continues to be the major component of commercial bank capital structures, increasingly promising is the role of debt capital. Authorization for issuing of debt capital initially to national banks and subsequently to state banks by their respective regulatory authorities (comptroller of the currency and state agencies) is creating new perspectives in the growth of bank capital.

It is also apparent that bank capital can no longer be treated as a single and homogeneous item. Such treatment would have been possible maybe earlier in this century, but certainly not today. Management is now confronted with different forms of bank capital and even different ways of raising a given

---

*In the mid-1960s several of the large New York City banks sold millions of dollars' worth of subordinated debentures at an interest cost of 5 percent—at that time a very high rate of interest —and prompted widespread predictions by financial commentators of subsequent regret by the bankers. In retrospect, such sales were extremely wise moves, which permitted expansion with safety for those banks at an interest cost that was modest in comparison with the 8.5 percent prime rate of the late 1960s or the 12 percent that prevailed in July 1974.[5]

form of bank capital. Choice of the form of capital, of the amounts needed in each of the various forms, and of the way of raising it have important implications for bank profitability. It is in this regard that the term capital management is often used today. It means concern over the way in which capital, like other bank funds, can best be acquired and managed.

Functions of Bank Capital

The functions of capital in commercial banking are quite different from those in most other enterprises. The high degree of financial leverage* encountered in commercial banking gives a different importance to the functions performed by bank capital. Capital can be examined from various points of view—that of the bank itself, that of its depositors, and of its stockholders. What all three approaches have in common, however, is their basic concern over how safe and sound a bank may be.

The initial function of bank capital is to finance (provide funds for) fixed investments, such as building, furniture, machinery, equipment, and supplies necessary to establish a bank as a going concern. Once this operational function has been fulfilled (and despite its importance for the bank as a going concern), it gives way to two more basic functions of capital. From the depositors' point of view, capital's function is to provide a margin of protection for their claims in the event of liquidation. Clearly, capital plays an even more important role in the daily operations of a bank. In the broadest sense, it protects the depositors and any other creditors by providing the security with which to take sensible business risks. In other words, capital performs the function of a guarantee or safety fund against any losses arising from the lending, investing, and all other activities incidental to commercial banking. Capital, then, serves to maintain the institution as a going concern.

From the stockholders' point of view, the function of bank capital is to achieve a sufficient yield in order to meet operating costs and net a fair return to its owners. With possible rare exceptions, the suppliers of bank capital are indeed motivated solely by the desire to own a good investment. They do realize, of course, that the nature of business entails special obligations essential to the public welfare, and are in sympathy with the conduct of the business in a manner compatible with the bank's obligations to its customers, the

---

*Financial leverage is defined as the ratio of total debt to total assets. In the case of commercial banks such ratio is high. As indicated later, in connection with deposits, 81.5 percent of total bank assets are financed by deposits.

community, and the nation. They are nevertheless properly insistent upon the protection of their investment (through sound planning and administration) and upon a rate of return that is as great as that which they could obtain from comparable investment elsewhere. More specifically they invest in the stock of a bank for the same reasons that they choose to invest in the shares of any other business enterprise, namely, to obtain a competitive return on their funds with the hope of appreciation in the value of their stock. Unless this return is obtained they would have no reason for wishing to continue to supply capital to the bank. An unprofitable bank is after all an unhealthy bank and cannot survive. The profit motive of bank shareholders is, therefore, both proper and unavoidable so long as banking is supported by private means.

The protection function of bank capital is considered to be of primary significance. Indeed, if a bank is to continue as a going concern, its capital must inspire sufficient confidence among depositors. For unless such confidence exists a bank will not be able to retain existing deposits and to attract new ones.

Such has been traditionally the role of bank capital. Indeed, throughout banking history bank capital had almost no other purpose than the protection of depositors.* Since 1962, this function of equity capital has been shared by debt capital. With debt securities subordinated to the claims of depositors, debt capital actually serves the same protective function as equity capital. By the same token, the other functions of bank capital are served by debt as well as by equity.

The adequacy of bank capital and hence the safety of commercial banks has been the concern of state and regulatory authorities throughout the banking history of this country. To make sure that banks maintain adequate capital as a condition of deposit insurance and to reinforce this safeguard afforded by capital, state and bank supervisory authorities have seen fit to interfere to a varying extent in banking affairs. U.S. financial history is characterized by a number of periods of unrestrained bank expansion and individual bank abuses, which led to bank failures, with resulting losses to depositors and holders of bank notes. In order to avoid the destabilizing effects of bank failures, the need became apparent for regulatory intervention to supplant the judgment of the individual bank in matters relating to capital adequacy. This intervention has taken the form of state laws and banking regulations that establish criteria for warding off and preventing bank insolvency. These criteria consist of minimum

---

*Many years ago Walter Bagehot wrote that "the main source of the profitableness of established banking is the smallness of the requisite capital. Being only wanted as a 'moral influence,' it need not be more than is necessary to secure that influence."[7]

capital requirements for the organization of a new bank* and norms to ensure thereafter prudence in bank operations.

With the general public basically unversed in this field, the supervisor's judgment has become over the years especially decisive for a bank's continued existence. Thus, today it is among supervisory authorities that a bank must inspire sufficient confidence as to its adequacy to withstand whatever strains may be placed upon it. In a closely supervised private banking system, it is the supervisory appraisal of capital adequacy that determines whether and under what conditions a bank may continue to exist. If capital is considered adequate by examining supervisory authorities it would be satisfactory for the general public.[8]

Consequently, an adequate capital position plays an important role in the safeguarding of supervisory and public confidence in the operations of a bank. In the words of an eminent writer on the subject, bank capital adequacy may be viewed as a factor:

> ... perhaps the most important factor, in maintaining the confidence a bank must enjoy to *continue* in business and prosper. The essential function of bank capital, in other words, is to keep the bank open and operating so that time and earnings can absorb losses; to inspire sufficient confidence in the bank on the part of depositors and the supervisor so that it will not be faced with costly liquidation.[9]

Over the years, several standards or ratios have been developed as to the amount of capital that is considered as necessary for the safe and efficient operation of a bank. These are helpful in analyzing the capital adequacy of an individual bank. Such ratios, however, should not be considered an end within themselves. Conformity to or divergence from the statistical norm should not be interpreted in an absolute manner. The inquiry should always go beyond the quantitative evidence and to an examination of the ingredients from which the ratio is derived.

Figure 1 shows the trends in four conventional capital ratios for all insured commercial banks, from 1935 through 1975. As shown, these ratios have declined considerably from their prewar levels. In the 1950s and 1960s, changes were very modest. Assets, both risk assets and nonliquid assets, have grown faster than capital, with the result that capital has declined as a precentage in relation to each of these two quantities. The same thing held true for

---

*Minimum capital requirements for national banks are fixed by federal regulations, and are in accordance with the population of a bank's head-office city and the number of branch offices. State requirements on capitalization are in most instances similar.

FIGURE 1

Conventional Capital Adequacy Ratios, All Insured Commercial Banks

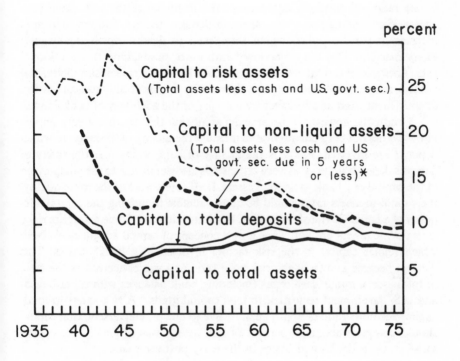

percent

*Available only from 1940 through 1972.
Source: Federal Deposit Insurance Corp., *Annual Reports* (Washington, D.C.: Federal Deposit Insurance Corp., 1935–1975). Data based on June 30 figures.

the earlier relationship of capital to either total deposits or total assets; however, in the immediate postwar years and through the 1950s the trend to either quantity was modestly upward, leveling off in the 1960s.

As is apparent, all these ratios relate capital to a number of key magnitudes in the balance sheet of commercial banks. At various periods of time, many claims were made that each of these ratios was the best index for measuring a bank's capital adequacy. The earliest such claim dates as far back as the turn of the century and refers to the ratio of capital to total deposits. A minimum deposits-to-total-capital-accounts ratio of approximately ten to one, or conversely, that capital should comprise about 10 percent of total deposits, was developed early in the twentieth century and was considered up until World War II a satisfactory requirement for the safety of depositors. During the war years, however, supervisory authorities realized that the ten-to-one ratio was seriously hampering bank financing of the war. Bank purchases of government securities, through deposit creation, had led to a rapid increase in bank deposits, which threatened to narrow down significantly safety margins. This led supervisory authorities to abandon this traditional rule. The ratio of capital accounts to deposits had the virtue of simplicity, and for this reason it has been extensively used by commercial banks and is frequently mentioned as a satisfactory measure of the adequacy of bank capital.

Gradually, however, it became apparent that this tool has a very important weakness. It does not attempt to measure the quality of the assets in which deposits are invested. For it is the quality of bank assets that the safety of deposits depends upon. This very criticism is also applicable to the comparison of the capital of a bank to its total assets. If all assets were of the same quality, the capital-to-assets ratio would be quite valuable in judging the capital adequacy of a bank. Obviously, however, this is not the case. Some assets are risky assets while others are not. Thus a new concept of capital adequacy evolved, which relates capital to the risk factors involved in a bank's assets. This concept became known as the risk asset ratio and was conceived as the ratio of total assets, minus cash items (including bank balances with other banks) and U.S. government securities, to total capital funds.* A risk-assets-to-total-capital-accounts ratio of approximately five to one or, conversely, that capital should comprise about 20 percent of risk assets, was originally considered satisfactory in the United States in the early postwar years.

Before long, students of the subject saw the necessity of defining risk assets more accurately. Specifically, the inclusion of government securities in the riskless asset category was criticized by some on the grounds that though these assets are free of the risk of default (the risk that interest or principal will be

---

*This formula received wide publicity when the New York State Bankers Association, to establish an objective standard for banks to meet, published a study in March 1952 on capital adequacy criteria. Since then, it has also been known as the New York State Bankers Association capital formula. For banks that did not measure up to this standard on the initial screening, a secondary calculation was suggested. In the secondary test, banks could also delete all obligations guaranteed by the U.S. government, obligations of the U.S. government agencies, short-term obligations of New York State, and loans secured by any of these obligations or the cash surrender value of life insurance.

defaulted as they come due), their prices are nevertheless subject to market fluctuations as a result of changes in the market rate of interest. In other words, these assets are not free of the interest rate risk (the risk that interest rates will change, causing the market values of securities to change). This led to the definition of risk assets as all assets less cash items and government securities due in five years or less. The obvious reason for this definition is the liquid nature of government securities maturing up to five years. In other words, these securities are considered to be of a relatively short-term nature and, therefore, as closely approximating a riskless character. By contrast government obligations of over a five-year maturity are not excluded from risk assets, on the grounds that they are susceptible to interest rate risk. The newly defined ratio became known as the capital-to-nonliquid-assets ratio.

Another definition of risk assets that has been put forward, and one generally considered to be more realistic, is total assets less cash, securities of the U.S. government and federal agencies, and loans insured and guaranteed by the federal government and agencies of the federal government. This approach, known as the adjusted-risk-asset ratio, includes in the riskless asset category all loans insured and guaranteed by governmental agencies since these are virtually free of risk.* In other words, should the debtors experience financial difficulty, the governmental agencies—and behind them the government itself—would be liable for the repayment of the loans. This definition of risk assets was widely employed in the United States and heavily relied upon by supervisory authorities in passing judgment upon a bank's capital adequacy. Indeed, on the basis of the adjusted risk asset ratio, a bank was not considered undercapitalized by supervisory authorities if the relationship between its risk assets and capital was not greater than six to one; a six-to-one relationship was considered satisfactory by examining authorities. The calculation as it now appears in Federal Reserve examination forms is reproduced in Figure 2.

The adjusted risk asset ratio, though an improved test in appraising capital adequacy, has its shortcomings. It fails to take into consideration the varying degrees or shades of risk associated with the different risk assets. Moreover, in the riskless asset category, it fails to allow for some degree of risk which, though small, is nevertheless present in some of these assets. For example, no allowance is made for the interest rate risk in federal government and agency securities of longer maturities.

---

*The intent of the government insurance and guarantee program is not to displace banks as lenders but to make certain private debts more attractive to them by virtue of government guarantee or insurance of these debts. Of the governmental agencies that insure and guarantee loans made by banks and other financial institutions to private borrowers, most widely known are the Veterans Administration (VA), the Federal Housing Administration (FHA), and the Commodity Credit Corporation.

FIGURE 2

Adjusted Risk Asset Ratio

Total assets .... $ _____

Deduct:

Total estimated losses .... $ _____

50% of assets classified Doubtful .... _____

Cash and due from banks .... _____

U.S. Treasury securities .... _____

Securities of U.S. Government agencies and corporations .... _____

Public Housing Authority obligations (local issues) .... _____

Federal funds sold .... _____

Securities purchased under resale agreement* .... _____

Loans or portions of loans—

Secured by obligations of U.S. Treasury or U.S. Government agencies and corporations ...... _____

Secured by Public Housing Authority obligations (local issues) .... _____

Insured under the Higher Education Act .... _____

Insured under Title I of the National Housing Act .... _____

Insured under Titles II and VI of the National Housing Act .... _____

Guaranteed under the Servicemen's Readjustment Act .... _____

Guaranteed by the Small Business Administration .... _____

Insured by Farmers Home Administration .... _____

Secured by hypothecated deposits .... _____

Secured by dealers' reserves required by agreement .... _____

Federal Reserve Bank stock .... _____

Income collected, not earned .... _____

    Total Risk assets .... $ _____

RATIO OF CAPITAL TO RISK ASSETS IS 1 TO _____ .

Source: Board of Governors of the Federal Reserve System.

16

To meet these and similar objections in capital adequacy ratios, efforts were directed in developing refined methods of measuring capital adequacy. Of these methods, two deserve consideration and comment because of their contribution to the problem of measuring capital adequacy. These techniques are that of the Federal Reserve Bank of New York and that of the Board of Governors of the Federal Reserve System. Unlike the previous formulas, which consider all risk assets—that is, all assets other than those characterized as nonrisk—in the same general classification, these new formulas assume that all risk assets do not possess the same degree of risk; in other words, that the exposure of bank assets to risk shades all the way from a considerable loss potential to virtually no risk. To develop, therefore, a realistic appraisal of an individual bank's capital adequacy, these formulas go on to allow for varying capital requirements against a bank's different assets. Specifically, the formulas segregate bank assets according to the amount of risk involved and allocate to each category of assets a specified percentage, which, based on the given dollar value of each category, would determine the capital requirement needed to support the risk inherent in each category of assets. The sum of the individual capital allocations against risk assets would represent a bank's total capital requirements. These, compared against the actual capital position of the bank, would determine whether the bank has a deficiency or excess in its capital.

The analytical method of the New York Federal Reserve Bank, developed in 1952, is shown in Figure 3. As portrayed, bank assets are generally divided into six categories or classifications, obviously a more selective basis than a sheer distinction between risk and nonrisk assets. The first asset classification includes riskless assets against which, clearly, no capital is required. And though some element of money risk is present, it is actually small enough to be readily absorbed by earnings. The second classification is designated as minimum risk assets and includes loans and investments that have less than normal credit risk or that may be readily sold, though sometimes at a discount from the face value. Here a requirement of 5 percent of these minimum risk assets is suggested.

The third classification, designated as normal risk assets, represents portfolio assets with normal or usual banking risks. It includes all the remaining loan portfolio not adversely classified by bank examiners and the rest of the grades (Baa or above) of investment securities (other than U.S. obligations) with maturities of longer than five years. The capital requirement suggested against this category is 12 percent.

The fourth classification involves substandard assets—that is, assets that require close and careful attention because of the degree of risk of nonpayment. Clearly, these assets involve more than a normal banking risk due perhaps to the insufficiency of security, to an unfavorable business experience or record of the borrower, or to a weak financial condition revealed in borrower's periodic reports. Because of the risk involved a 20 percent capital allocation is suggested.

FIGURE 3

Capital Adequacy–New York Federal Reserve Bank
Method of Analysis

ASSET CLASSIFICATION	Capital Requirement Percent	Amount
Riskless Assets		
Cash and due from banks	————	
U.S. Government securities due within 5 years	————	
Other comparable assets (e.g. Federal Funds Sold)	————	
	———— –0–	
Minimum Risk Assets		
U.S. Government securities due 5 years or more	————	
Other investment grade securities due within 5 years	————	
F.H.A. insured and guaranteed portion V.A. mortgages	————	
Insured modernization loans	————	
Loans secured by passbooks	————	
Loans secured by U.S. Government securities	————	
Loans secured by cash value of life insurance	————	
Short-term loans to municipalities	————	
Money market loans (broker's loans, commercial paper, short-term commodity loans, etc.)	————	
Loans guaranteed by U.S. Government or Agencies	————	
Other comparable assets	————	
	———— 5%	$————
Normal Risk Assets		
Balance of investment grade securities	————	
Other loans	————	
Other Assets	————	
	———— 12%	$————
Substandard Assets		
Loans so classified	————	
Other real estate	————	
Other securities except stocks and defaulted bonds	————	
	———— 20%	$————
Workout Assets		
Real estate not used for bank premises	————	
Stocks	————	
Defaulted bonds	————	
Doubtful assets	————	
	———— 50%	$————
Fixed Assets		
Bank premises	————	
Furniture and fixtures	————	
	———— 100%	$————
Total Required Minimum Capital		$————

Source: Federal Reserve Bank of New York.

A higher percentage of capital requirement, 50 percent, is applied against a fifth classification known as workout assets. These include loans classified by the examiner as doubtful, defaulted securities, capital stocks, and real estate assets, which banks may not legally acquire in the course of business except through foreclosure in satisfaction of previously contracted debt. Management is expected to dispose of such assets as promptly as possible provided that the bank is able to realize the full potential value of these assets.

The final classification involves assets classified as loss and such fixed assets as bank premises, and furniture and fixtures. These fixed assets are not regarded as investment in the traditional connotation of the word but rather as essential tools to carry out the banking business and hence should be provided by the stockholders. Such assets provide little protection to depositor and in the event of liquidation they are not as readily salable. Hence a full 100 percent capital allocation is suggested.

Against the above capital requirements a bank's total capital funds (including bad debt reserves) are compared. If the bank's capital is in the range between 100 and 125 percent of capital requirements, capital adequacy would be a matter of supervisory judgment; if capital is less than 100 percent, capital adequacy would be questioned, while at over 125 percent it seldom would.

The capital analysis formula adopted in 1956 by the Board of Governors of the Federal Reserve System is somewhat more complex. Initially the formula required varying amounts of capital for ten different categories of assets, ranging from 0.5 percent for short-term government securities to 100 percent for fixed assets. Moreover, a liquidity test was incorporated to relate the liability structure to the asset holdings, entailing additional capital requirements for banks with higher proportions of less liquid assets. This formula was revised and expanded in 1972 and, as shown in Figure 4, it now requires separate capital calculations for over 25 different categories of assets, total assets, and trust department gross earnings. Separate calculations must be made to determine the capital requirement due to credit risk, market risk, and the liquidity available from various assets. In addition, there is a requirement for the calculation of adjusted capital structure as a percentage of total assets, of risk assets, and of total deposits; and also for the calculation of adjusted equity capital as a percentage of total assets, of risk assets, and of total deposits.

Of the various standards of capital adequacy described, no uniformity exists among supervisory authorities as to the analytical approach emphasized in bank examination. In fact, national bank examiners, on the basis of new guidelines issued by the comptroller's office, have moved away from formal analysis and reliance on capital ratios. Instead, the following factors were listed by the comptroller's office as ones to be considered in assessing the adequacy of capital:

FIGURE 4

Capital Adequacy—Board of Governors Method of Analysis

FORM FOR ANALYZING BANK CAPITAL
(Amounts in thousands of dollars)

BANK ——————————— CITY ——————————— STATE ———————

IDENTIFICATION:

ABC 2				
File	District	State	Bank	Exam. Date Yr. Mo. Day

LIQUIDITY CALCULATION / MEMORANDA

	Amount Outstanding	Per Cent	Calculation	MEMORANDA
Demand deposits, IPC		35		(a) "Other liabilities" and "Loans: Consumer instalment" are shown net of:
Savings deposits		25		Dealers reserves .... ———
Time deposits, IPC, under $100,000		30		
Time deposits, IPC, $100,000 & over		80		Income collected but not earned .... ———
Deposits of banks		80		(b) "LIQUIDITY AVAILABLE FROM ASSETS" is to be aggregated only until it equals "TOTAL LIQUIDITY CALCULATION."
Other deposits		80		
TOTAL DEPOSITS				(c) "Cash assets" are shown net of:
Borrowings		100		Required reserves .... ———
Other liabilities (a)		100		(d) "TOTAL ASSETS" are shown net of assets classified as:
Special factors: ———		100		Doubtful .... ———
TOTAL LIQUIDITY CALCULATION (b)				Loss .... ———

	AMOUNT OUTSTANDING	CAPITAL CALCULATION CREDIT RISK		CAPITAL CALCULATION MARKET RISK		LIQUIDITY AVAILABLE FROM ASSETS (b)	
		Per Cent	Amount	Per Cent	Amount	Amount	Aggregate
(1) PRIMARY RESERVE							
Cash assets (c)		0	0	0	0		
Federal funds sold		0	0	0	0		
(1) TOTAL			0		0		
(2) SECONDARY RESERVE							
Commercial paper & bankers acceptances		1		1			
Securities maturing under 1 year:							
U.S. Treasury		0	0	*			
Government agencies		0	0	*			
State, county & municipal		0	0	*			
Other Group 1		0	0	1			
(2) TOTAL							
(3) MINIMUM RISK ASSETS							
Securities maturing 1-5 years:							
U.S. Treasury		0	0	*			
Government agencies		0	0	*			
State, county & municipal		2		*			
Other Group 1		2		8			
(3) TOTAL							
(4) INTERMEDIATE ASSETS							
Securities maturing 5-10 years:							
U.S. Treasury		0	0	°			
Government agencies		0	0	*			
State, county & municipal		3		*			
Other Group 1		3		15			
Loans specially secured or guaranteed		3		15			
(4) TOTAL							
(5) PORTFOLIO ASSETS							
Securities maturing over 10 years:							
U.S. Treasury		0	0	*			
Government agencies		0	0	*			
State, county & municipal		5		*			
Other Group 1		5		25			
Loans: Real estate		5		25			
Consumer instalment (a)		5		25			
All other		5		25			
(5) TOTAL							
(6) FIXED, CLASSIFIED & OTHER ASSETS							
Bank premises		50					
Furniture & fixtures; other real estate		100					
Group 2 securities		50					
Groups 3 & 4 securities		100					
Assets classified substandard		20					
Accruals & other assets		0	0				
(6) TOTAL							

* See reverse side for securities computations which take account of quality, yield and narrower maturity ranges.

(7) TOTAL CAPITAL CALCULATED FOR MARKET RISK

(8) TOTAL CAPITAL CALCULATED FOR CREDIT RISK

(9) TOTAL ASSETS (d) — 2

(10) TRUST DEPARTMENT GROSS EARNINGS — 200

(11) SPECIAL FACTORS:

(12) TOTAL CAPITAL CALCULATION (sum of lines 7 through 11)

(13) ADJUSTED CAPITAL STRUCTURE[1] & CAPITAL STRUCTURE INDEX (Adjusted capital structure divided by line (12)) ...... $————— —————%

(14) ADJUSTED EQUITY CAPITAL[2] & EQUITY CAPITAL INDEX (Adjusted equity capital divided by line (12)) .... $————— —————%

CAPITAL RATIOS

Adjusted capital structure as a percent of:

total assets ————%; total assets minus primary reserves, U.S. Treasury and Agency securities ————%; total deposits ————%.

Adjusted equity capital as a percent of:

total assets ————%; total assets minus primary reserves, U.S. Treasury and Agency securities ————%; total deposits ————%.

[1] and [2] Footnotes appear on reverse side.

20

NOTES REGARDING FORM FOR ANALYZING BANK CAPITAL

A thorough appraisal of the capital needs of a particular bank must take due account of all relevant factors affecting the bank. These include the characteristics of its assets, its liabilities, its trust or other corporate responsibilities, and its management—as well as the history and prospects of the bank, its customers and its community. The complexity of the problem requires a considerable exercise of judgment. The groupings and percentages suggested in the Form for Analyzing Bank Capital can necessarily be no more than aids to the exercise of judgment.

The requirements indicated by the various items on the form are essentially "norms" and can provide no more than an initial presumption as to the actual capital required by a particular bank. These "norms" are entitled to considerable weight, but various upward or downward adjustments in requirements may be appropriate for a particular bank if special or unusual circumstances are in fact present in the specific situation. Such adjustments may be entered under "Special factors" indicated on the Analysis Form.

The requirements suggested in the Analysis Form assume that the bank has adequate safeguards and insurance coverage against fire, defalcation, burglary, etc. Lack of such safeguards or coverage would place upon the bank's capital risks which it should not be called upon to bear.

* **SECURITIES COMPUTATIONS** which take account of quality, yield and narrower maturity ranges. For determining market risk take the following steps:

1. Distribute the bank's holdings of U.S. treasury, U.S. Agency and State and Political Subdivisions in the following matrices:

Years Over Through	U.S. Treasury Avg. Cpn. Rate[1]	Par	Book	U.S. Government agencies and corporations Avg. Cpn. Rate[1]	Par	Book	States and political subdivisions Avg. Cpn. Rate[1]	Par	Book
1	$	$		$	$		$	$	
1　2									
2　5									
5　10									
10　20									
20									
Totals	$	$		$	$		$	$	

Years Over Through	U.S. Treasury Avg. Cur. Mkt. Yld.[2]	Market[2]	U.S. Government agencies and corporations Avg. Cur. Mkt. Yld.[2]	Market[2]	States and political subdivisions Avg. Cur. Mkt. Yld.[2]	Market[2]	HIGH YIELDS U.S. Treasury	U.S. Government agencies and corporations	States and political subdivisions
1	$		$		$		7.75	8.21	5.02
1　2							7.78	8.23	5.11
2　5							7.82	8.29	5.32
5　10							7.64	8.39	5.65
10　20							7.30	7.98	6.08
20							7.07	8.12	6.43
Total market value	$		$		$				

[1] Average coupon rate. The preferred method is to obtain by computing actual annual coupon income generated by securities in a given cell and dividing such annual coupon income by the par value of the cell. In the alternative, the average coupon rate may be imputed as described below.

[2] (Not necessary to complete if average coupon rate is known.) Average current market yield (approximate yield base for market value shown) may be obtained from actual knowledge of yields used to obtain above market value or by selecting a single investment issue for each cell that is representative of that particular cell, e.g., for State and political subdivisions with maturities of from 10-20 years, select a medium grade issue maturing in 15 years or as close to 15 years as is available. Divide the market value of the issue by par value and locate the resultant value in the **Comprehensive Bond Value Tables** under the coupon rate of the issue selected and trace across to maturity yield. Enter maturity yield under "Avg. Cur. Yld." above. If information concerning the individual securities comprising each cell is unavailable, enter market yields obtained from a general review of rates prevailing at or near the time of pricing.

2. Price the securities in each cell to yield at the high yield rate set forth in the high yield matrix. Note: Price as though each cell was a single issue using average coupon rate and total par value. Assume maturities for each cell as follows: 1—(1 year); 1-2 (1½ years); 2-5 (3½ years); 5-10 (7½ years); 10-20 (15 years); 20 (25 years [except assume 20 years for U.S. Agencies]). Note: If bank has a concentration of lower quality municipal securities add about 50 basis points to high yield for "States and political subdivisions".

3. Determine the amount of maximum probable market depreciation in each cell by subtracting the market value obtained from step 2. above from the book value of securities. Enter actual figure for maximum potential market loss in the appropriate market risk column, combining where necessary in order to conform to distribution as appears on the front of the Form. If computations show potential market appreciation enter zero for market risk.

Method for Imputing Coupon

Par value + Market value = Assumed price
Locate assumed price in the Comprehensive Bond Valuation Tables assuming a coupon equal to average current yield. Trace the price to the yield to maturity column in the tables. **The yield to maturity is the imputed average coupon rate of that particular cell.** (Note: Owing to the restraints of the table size the yield may have to be interpolated; a more precise method for obtaining the yield may be achieved by utilizing the mathematical equation for determining such yields.)

Note: If the above data are unavailable and as an alternative but less desirable method, the following percentage charges may be used:

All securities maturing under 1 year, 1 per cent; 1-5 years, 8 per cent; 5-10 years, 15 per cent; over 10 years, 25 per cent.

[1] Adjusted capital structure—Total capital accounts plus reserves on securities and loans minus assets classified loss and 50 percent of assets classified doubtful.
[2] Adjusted Equity Capital—Adjusted capital structure minus debt capital.

Source: Board of Governors of the Federal Reserve System.

1. The quality of management;
2. The liquidity of assets;
3. The history of earnings and the retention thereof;
4. The quality and character of ownership;
5. The burden of meeting occupancy expenses;
6. The potential volatility of deposit structure;
7. The quality of operating procedures;
8. The bank's capacity to meet present and future financial needs of its trade area, considering the competition it faces.

As is apparent, each of these factors relates, in one way or another, to the various kinds of risk that a commercial bank is exposed to. Beyond these qualitative factors, however, emphasis is placed upon the growth rate of earnings and assets in attempting to appraise capital adequacy. Obviously, if a bank's earnings and assets are not growing, such a bank is more susceptible to risk than one that enjoys a growth record.

Other regulatory agencies have to a certain extent followed suit. Indeed, the official statements of such agencies have been worded very carefully so as to dispel the idea that exclusive reliance is placed on ratios or formulas in determining capital adequacy. In fact, these agencies (that is, the Federal Reserve and state authorities) have made every effort to incorporate in their analytical or statistical methods consideration of qualitative factors similar to the above. Clearly such an approach is more realistic than sheer abandonment of the use of formulas, as was the case with national bank examiners. Indeed, it would seem difficult to appraise capital adequacy and convince management of the objectivity of examiner judgment without reliance on some analytical or statistical method. It appears, therefore, that some use of capital ratios or formulas is inevitable, even as a rule of thumb for examiners in screening the capital positions of banks.

Whatever the analytical approach of supervising agencies may be and however effective their moral suasion, the basic responsibility for capital adequacy lies with the board of directors and the top management of each individual bank. Bank management owes, not only to itself but to the depositors and the economy as a whole, a careful appraisal of all the risks facing the bank to ascertain the adequacy of bank capital. This holds especially true for those banks that continue to cling to some arbitrary rule-of-thumb approach in the determination of the adequacy of bank capital. Sound management dictates a continuous self-analysis of bank assets in an effort to predict and minimize losses. However imperfect the above formulas may be in measuring the adequacy of bank capital, they are nevertheless far more reliable than mere intuitive judgment. Used with this understanding, these formulas have some value in determining portfolio policy. More specifically, they determine, on the basis of a particular asset structure, whether a bank's capital is underemployed or overemployed. Obviously, it is in the bank's interest to avoid having an underemployed capital position just as it is to avoid an overemployed or overextended one. If the capital is underemployed, a more liberal portfolio policy may be pursued. In other words, such a capital position would permit the acceptance of an equivalent increase in risk in the bank's asset structure. This extension in risk would take place in the bank's loan or investment portfolio in the form of a more liberal lending or investing policy. On the other hand, if the bank's capital position is overextended, it can follow either of two procedures: it can attempt to raise additional capital to cover the risk involved in its asset structure, or it can so manage the structure of its assets as to reduce the risk involved to a level consistent with its present capital.[10] In essence, the second alternative suggests that a conservative asset-management policy is a feasible, and perhaps a superior, substitute for additional capital. Object of such a policy would be the bank's investment portfolio and the risks inherent in it. Indeed, since lending constitutes a bank's primary function, a conservative asset-management policy should aim at reducing the risks implicit in the bank's investment portfolio in order to effect a compensating reduction in the bank's aggregate risk exposure. Portfolio risk reduction would be thus implemented in the employment of all new funds, maturing funds, and proceeds from profits realized on portfolio transactions.

Over the years, the use of capital adequacy ratios (that is, capital to risk assets and to nonliquid assets) for the commercial banking system as a whole has been markedly down. Yet, the system is considered less vulnerable to serious trouble now than it ever was. A number of reasons help to explain this. In the first place, banking has become far more sophisticated in its policies and practices. As banks obtained more experience in the employment of bank funds, they gained more confidence in their ability to design sound asset portfolios. Then, too, depositor safety is more effective today. For a number of years, stockholders were subject to what is referred to as double liability, that is, an additional assessment, up to the par value of the stock owned, to cover losses, should they occur. Today, however, depositor protection is provided by the FDIC, which insures depositor funds up to $40,000 per account.*

---

*The FDIC is an agency of the federal government whose operating income is derived from assessments on the deposits of the insured banks. Its functions with respect to bank failures may be classified into preventive and remedial. In the framework of the former, the FDIC examines and supervises the insured banks, lends funds to or buys assets from banks in distress, makes deposits to such banks, and arranges for their merger or consolidation with financially healthier banks; in the latter case, it pays off insured depositors in accordance with their deposit balances and up to $40,000 per account.

By offering such insurance protection the FDIC has reduced the likelihood of depositor distrust in banks and the consequent danger of panics and bank runs. Finally, there has been a radical change in the economic environment in which banks operate. Fiscal and monetary policies are now more flexible and effective in alleviating or counteracting business cycles.

It was noted above that one of the most important reasons behind an adequate capital position was the safeguarding of supervisory and public confidence in the operation of a bank. Though a necessity, adequate capital does not by itself assure the safety of commercial banking:

> Adequate capital, of course, is not a substitute for sound lending and invest-ing policies; it cannot take the place of experienced and progressive manage-ment or a well-conceived program of control, profit planning and audit. It can only provide assurance to the public, the stockholder and the supervisor that the bank has the strength and the wherewithal to survive circumstances and conditions which the best management can never foresee. In a real sense, the provision of adequate capital is the price of the private enterprise banking system in the United States.[11]

DEPOSITS

Deposits are the most important source of bank funds. At the end of 1975, deposits accounted for approximately 81.5 percent of total bank liabilities and capital—which means that 81.5 percent of total assets are financed by deposits. The value of deposits increased greatly over the years, from $71 billion in 1941 to $786 billion in 1975. The postwar growth of deposits for all commercial banks in the United States is illustrated in Figure 5.

In every study on money and banking it is fully expounded that in the commercial banking system as a whole, the volume of deposits depends pri-marily upon the volume of the system's reserves and the amount of credit—in the form of loans and investments—extended by banks on the basis of these reserves. That is to say, when banks have incentives to expand their earning assets and the public is willing to borrow (through loans and debt securities), desposits are created; by contrast, when earning assets are reduced, the depos-its of the banking system are affected accordingly. Thus, the line of causation in the banking system runs from the assets side to the liabilities side of the balance sheet. In other words, assets give rise to liabilities. For the individual bank, however, the line of causation is reversed. That is, liabilities give rise to assets. Indeed, an individual bank first must attract deposits and then put them to work. As this study is examining the sources of funds available to an individual bank, deposits will be studied from the perspective of the individual bank.

FIGURE 5

Principal Liabilities and Capital Accounts of Commercial Banks
(billions of dollars)

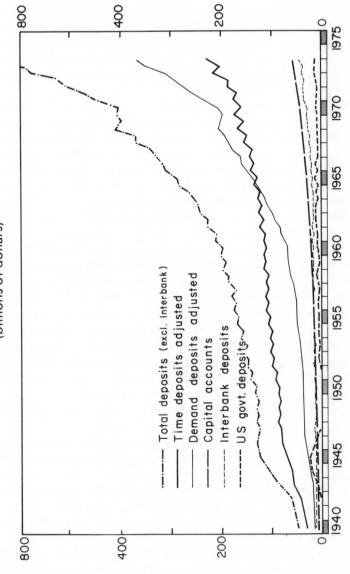

Total deposits (excl. Interbank)
Time deposits adjusted
Demand deposits adjusted
Capital accounts
Interbank deposits
US govt. deposits

Source: Board of Governors of the Federal Reserve System, *Historical Chart Book* (Washington, D.C.: Federal Reserve System, 1974).

Attracting Deposits

It is apparent that a commercial bank's deposit policy is the most essential policy for its existence. Put in another way, the growth of a bank depends primarily upon the growth of its deposits. The volume of funds that management will use for creating income, through loans and investments, is determined largely by the bank's policy governing deposits. When that policy is unduly restrictive, growth is retarded; conversely, when that policy is liberalized, growth is accelerated.

Bank policy in respect to deposits is clearly reflected in the option exercised by customers in using retail or wholesale banks, a choice limited mainly to banks located in large urban financial centers. Retail banks cater to large numbers of customers who have small means, as well as to business interests; but the wholesale banks have as customers elements representing large means and often having large sums on deposit with such banks. One is catholic in its approach to attracting clientele, the other eclectic.

Retail banks serve more largely than do wholesale banks the needs of the mass market, which today, with constantly rising standards of living, tends to demand increasingly varied banking services. Retail banks enjoy a natural syndrome: new depositors, swelling the ranks of the old, demand wider services; the banks, in turn, expand their services and thus accelerate their growth. Profits and growth are more likely to ensue from wider circles of depositors and from meeting their demands for services. A concomitant development also occurs: by serving the maximum number of persons, retail banks have closer ties with the communities in which they are located, and are recognized as contributors to the development of their communities. The rewards of a bank's community service are great.

Bank policy as regards deposits may be shaped by factors other than whether the bank serves a select or a mass clientele. Most banks today, whatever their type, sense the importance of creating for their customers attractive and inviting surroundings. The mausoleum atmosphere that formerly marked the interiors of banks has given way to bright appointments and an air of cheerfulness. An attendant development has been that bank employees have dropped their old airs of reserve and today appear warm and friendly. Pleasant surroundings and cheerful employees in banks today together tend to attract new depositors, without in the least impairing the bank's efficiency.

Closely allied to attractive surroundings and friendly employees as influences on bank deposits is easy accessibility of the bank and of its services to the public. Sharp increases in urban population and accelerated movements of population from inner-city to suburban areas have combined to lead large urban banks to open growing numbers of branches located in neighborhood and suburban shopping centers. This diffusion of banking services through branches has made banking transactions both simpler and more inviting for bank customers; branch banking enables customers to escape many of the tensions born of inner-city traffic congestion, paucity of parking facilities, and the general headlong tempo of doing business in a city's downtown financial area. The branch bank in a neighborhood or suburban plaza will have ample parking space, and customers can transact their banking business in a much more relaxed environment. Customers at the branch bank have a more easy access to officials for transactions requiring consultation, spend usually less time is queues at tellers' windows, and, if they are motorists, find drive-in banking facilities more readily available than at an inner-city bank.

New bank deposits often derive from public attitudes toward bank officials. Where a bank's officials are thought indifferent to, or aloof from, a community's problems, the public tends to shun that bank. Recognition of this fact has caused bankers to identify themselves and their institutions more closely with the concerns of the communities that they serve; bank officials serve on boards and committees of community organizations, encourage new industries to locate in their community, stimulate the growth of small businesses, and through all such activities evince the bank's interest in the well-being of individuals and of the corporate community of which it is a part. In short, civic consciousness among bankers, the understanding that what is good for the community is also good for the bank, tends to attract new accounts and the utilization of banking services through loans and investments.

It is no overstatement to say that new deposit accounts are frequently the result of the types of services offered by banks. Banking is highly competitive; banks offering better and more diversified services have advantages over those whose services are limited. Nowhere is this more true than in the United States. Commercial banks in this country have been advertising extensively in all media emphasizing the range of services available to the public. Calling themselves full-service banks, they offer the widest range of banking services available anywhere under a single roof. This multiplicity of services is made available through specialists who can lend maximum aid to clients who seek counsel and finances. Banks still perform the roles that banks carried out a century ago: they are today, as then, safe depositories for customers' funds, they continue to provide for the transfer of funds, and they still maintain credit facilities for their clienteles. But today's bank will offer services hardly dreamed of by bankers of a half-century ago. Hence, it is not surprising to discover a bank today dispensing general information to clients, that is, on domestic or foreign markets, on acquisitions, on tax matters, as well as handling the clients' personal affairs through trust and fiduciary arrangements. Services vary, of course, from bank to bank, one institution serving special needs of its community that may differ markedly from the needs of another community. But one thing seems to determine what specific services a given bank may make available to its customers: the peculiar needs vocalized by customers on the one hand, or sensed and made provision for by bankers on the other hand. This had led some banks to become known as oil banks, textile banks, electronics banks, and the like. Eventually other companies in an industry seek a relationship with these specialized banks because they know that the intricacies of their particular business will be understood by the banks and that their needs will be adequately served.

The interest rate that a bank pays on time accounts is another factor influencing the size and growth of these accounts. Though this factor may not be the decisive one in the decision of all savers to save, it undoubtedly cannot be dismissed lightly. The existence of other competing financial institutions and the rates paid by them has been an important element in the growth of commercial bank time deposits. Yet, the fact that banks hold large amounts of such deposits testifies to the effectiveness of bank marketing techniques.

The efficiency of bank policy in attracting new deposits depends to a large extent upon the level of economic activity. Bank deposits increase in periods of prosperity and decline in periods of recession. Individual banks may represent departures from aggregate experience, but most of them would tend to feel the same effects. A period of prosperity is chacterized by relatively high levels of employment, a rising consumer spending on durable goods and houses, and a strong demand for credit by businesses and individuals. Banks are generally more liberal in their lending activities and a feeling of optimism prevails in the economy. On the other hand, during periods of adverse economic conditions bank deposits fall to a lower level than that of a period of prosperity. A period of recession is characterized by rising unemployment, a cutback in consumer spending, and a slackening business demand for credit, which makes banks seek investment outlets.

Although a local economy tends to reflect the total economy of which it forms a part, there may be some characteristics of a local economy that cause sharp fluctuations in a local bank's deposits. Any two given types of economy, for example, an industrial and an agricultural, will have within themselves differences in the factors that govern bank deposits. In fact, even economies of one type are bound to have within themselves differences in the factors that govern bank deposits. In general, in an agricultural economy with a single cash crop, deposit declines will be greater during the spring months as money must be spent for seeds, fertilizers, and other production expenses. By contrast, deposit buildups will be greater when crops are harvested and sold. If there are crops harvested twice a year (that is, in the spring and in the fall), deposits show less fluctuation, and instead of one high point for deposits during the year, there will be two such points. Thus, deposits are generally more stable in a farming economy that is characterized by diversification than in one that has a single cash crop; in such diversified economies, there would be more than one high point for deposits during the year. An economy that depends on the raising of cattle for market will cause bank deposits to rise, chiefly when cattle are sold, whereas one that depends on dairying will tend to have much steadier bank deposits throughout the year.

Industrial communities, too, experience deposit fluctuations, some more than others. Deposits will fluctuate less in a community that enjoys diverse industries than in one that has a single industry or several of the same kinds of industry. In the latter case, there is the danger that a falling demand for that particular product, or a shortage in raw materials originating outside the community, will have consequent effects upon local bank deposits. In such an instance, the industry and its employees, local merchants, and the population of the community will generally suffer, and deposits in the community's banks will correspondingly slacken off. Similarly, if the industry is cyclical in nature or likely to suffer frequent fluctuations in its tempo of activity, there will be consequent ups and downs in the local banks' deposit patterns.

Nature and Classes of Bank Deposits

Let us now examine the nature and classes of bank deposits. Deposits constitute the largest category of bank liabilities. Deposits in general indicate moneys that have been left with or lent to the bank. The depositors—individuals, business firms, and governmental bodies—entrust these funds to the bank with the clear understanding that they retain the right to request withdrawals as needed and that the bank will honor their demand promptly. A bank's deposit liabilities are therefore fixed sums subject to payment at a time and under conditions agreed upon when the deposits are made. It is essential that the bank observe scrupulously its obligations to depositors if it is to continue as a going concern. Clearly then, it is only by assuming deposit liabilities that banks can obtain the bulk of their working funds. However paradoxical this may seem, it is nevertheless true. A bank is probably the only type of business entity that prides itself on its liabilities. The fact that the total volume of earning assets that a bank can own is directly related to the total of its deposit liabilities outstanding provides banks with a strong inducement to constantly strive to increase their deposit liabilities.

Banks have always held deposit liabilities but they never succeeded in managing these liabilities as they do today. Banks have always been pleased to receive deposits, and most of them have been making a continuing effort to solicit such deposits from various sources. Since the early 1960s, however, banks have been increasingly trying to influence the volume of certain kinds of deposits they receive to bring about desired shifts in their deposit structure. Traditionally, the deposit structure of a commercial bank has been thought to be determined primarily by the depositors, and not by bank management. This traditional view is now being increasingly challenged. Deposits, however, are but one aspect of the bank liabilities that management has been attempting to significantly influence through deliberate policy actions. The other aspect is nondeposit liabilities; that is, liabilities of a nondeposit, or money market, nature that are incurred at the bank's own initiative. This new approach for influencing liabilities through management policy actions, is generally called liability management and is an aspect of the overall funds management of a commercial bank. As such, it is a corollary to capital management. Liability management is concerned only with those liabilities that can be influenced in significant amounts through management policy actions.[12]

Liability management banking was originated in the early 1960s by large banks in New York City that were at the time coming under strong double pressures: a growing demand for loans as the economy was experiencing recovery from the 1960–61 recession, plus an inadequate growth of demand deposits at these banks. The liability management strategy involves choosing the source of financing to be used (that is, choosing between deposit financing and nondeposit financing), determining the amounts needed, and obtaining the funds at the lowest possible cost with the least risk exposure. Cost considerations are usually the first step in determining the source of funds. Risk is the other consideration involved in the use of funds; it refers to the danger that rates may fall sharply while the liability is outstanding. Clearly it is difficult to judge in advance what difficulties may lie ahead, but should the rates fall sharply, the bank is obligated to continue paying interest at the higher rate assumed when the liability was issued. There would be a paper capital loss because the value of the liability rose (just as there would be a paper loss if the value of a bank asset declined).

Deposit financing will be discussed below and nondeposit, or money market, financing, in the following section.

Deposits at commercial banks are maintained for a variety of purposes. They may serve as working cash balances available for use in making payments or as a liquid form of investments that will yield over a period of time a certain return or idle funds accumulated for some specific purpose. Typically, the depositor who wishes to use his account for transaction purposes carries a demand deposit, and the depositor who wishes to accumulate savings or earn a yield carries a time or savings deposit. In practice, however, there are many exceptions to this general rule: some demand deposit accounts lie relatively idle while frequent withdrawals are made from a number of time and savings accounts.

Demand deposits constitute a homogeneous category of deposit accounts, unlike time and savings deposits. In technical parlance, the phrase time and savings deposits is a broad concept encompassing three distinct categories of deposit accounts: savings deposits, which are evidenced by a passbook issued to the deposit holder(s) and in which the bank records additional deposits or withdrawals as these occur; time certificates of deposits (usually referred to as CDs), which are evidenced by a formal, and usually negotiable, receipt issued for funds left with the bank for a specified period of time and which are payable upon surrender of this receipt properly endorsed; and open-account time deposits, which are covered by written contracts that do not permit their owners to withdraw all or any part of these deposits before maturity date established when the funds are deposited. Unlike the first two types of time and savings deposits, the third type is quantitatively unimportant and quite heterogeneous as to the variety of the accounts included.*

There are three basic differences between demand deposits and time or savings deposits. With demand deposits, withdrawals may be made on demand. In the case of withdrawals from time or savings deposits, however, the depositor is required to give the bank at least 30 days' notice, although with saving accounts, banks seldom enforce this requirement. Holders of CDs may of course sell them at any time. If no buyer is available, however, banks are usually willing to repurchase a CD from a buyer before maturity.

A second basic difference is that demand deposits can be used directly as money; that is, a demand depositor can pay for goods and services by writing a check for the amount due. Funds held in savings or time deposits must first be converted into currency or into a demand deposit before they can be used for making payments. A natural consequence of this difference is that demand deposits are generally more active than time and savings deposits, and hence they entail a higher cost of handling for a bank. A look at the nature and purpose of each of these two categories of deposit accounts, as discussed above, would be sufficient to convince one of the cost inequalities involved. Time and savings deposits, for example, would have normally a smaller turnover than demand deposits and consequently involve the banks in considerably less work and expense. From this it follows that the operating cost of handling time deposits is generally small. By contrast, demand deposits, which constitute the major component of this country's money supply, have a higher turnover. It is commonly estimated that 90 percent of the dollar value of money transactions in this country are settled by checks. Moreover, it has been established that in 1971 alone, nearly 24 billion checks were written, transferring trillions of dollars around the country. Assuming that these checks were written during business days, the 1971 estimate corresponds to some 95 million checks per business day. Projections for 1980, assuming a 7 percent increase per year in the number of checks written, estimate that 40 billion checks will flow through the commercial banking system.[13]

---

*This category includes a large diversity of deposit accounts. One type of deposits included are the so-called club deposits. These are short-term deposit plans offered by banks to induce savers to deposit regularly a stated amount of money. The understanding is that within a specified period of time there would be deposits large enough to enable the depositor to meet his bills, that is, at Christmas, or for his vacation. In accordance with the nature of the anticipated expenditure, these plans have been known as Christmas Club Savings, Vacation Club Savings, Tax Club Savings, and so on. Other types of deposits included are some interbank and U.S. government interest-bearing deposits, and accounts accumulated for payment of personal loans. This assortment of accounts makes this category quite heterogeneous vis-a-vis the other two categories.

Therefore, this turnover of demand deposits renders the servicing of such deposits a time-consuming and expensive process. The handling of checks drawn by depositors, the collection of checks drawn on other banks and brought in for deposit, and the keeping of records entail expensive supplies and equipment, and the services of bookkeepers, all of which involve a substantial cost for the bank. Then, too, time and savings deposits provide a greater volume of loan funds than do demand deposits of the same amount because of the lower cash reserves required, both by law* and by operating necessity,† against time deposits. In addition, time and savings deposit accounts permit the employment of larger proportions of these funds in less-liquid and higher-yielding assets (longer-term loans and investments) than is true for demand deposits.

A third distinguishing factor is that banks are allowed to pay interest on time and savings deposits but not on demand deposits. Prohibition of interest payments on demand deposits has its origin in the depression years and, specifically, it was provided for in the Banking Act of 1933. This act also provided for ceilings on the maximum rates payable by banks on time and savings deposits. The object of these measures was to strengthen the banking system by eliminating cutthroat competition for deposits among banks. The reasoning was that the ensuing lower interest expenses, vis-a-vis profits, would permit banks to strengthen their capital positions and reduce the necessity of making high-yielding loans and investments in which the credit risks were large.

However plausible these provisions may have appeared at the time, their continued existence is no longer justified. As stated above, this law was enacted during the depression years and as such it reflects much of the determination so characteristic of that era to establish a sound banking structure. However, since that time, economic conditions have changed significantly. Rigid banking rules have since been introduced and the supervisory and regulatory structure of the banking industry materially strengthened. Also, the capital adequacy concept has since evolved and acquired new dimension. On the other hand, these measures, by fostering certain inequalities, have been responsible for misallocation of resources in the economy.

---

*Member banks of the Federal Reserve System are required, according to Regulation D, to maintain with the Federal Reserve Bank reserves which vary according to the type and size of bank deposits. Generally, reserves against time and savings deposits range from 3 to 10 percent of such deposits, while against demand deposits, and depending upon the designation of the bank, they range from 10 to 22 percent for reserve-city banks or 7 to 14 percent for other banks.[14]

†Operating reserves held by most banks against their time and savings deposits are usually substantially less than those for demand deposits.

The immediate effect of the prohibition of interest payments on demand deposits has been to limit the importance of these deposits as a source of loanable funds. This has led banks to develop methods of offering a yield to demand deposit holders as a means of attracting such deposits. In other words, it has led them to engage themselves in a nonprice competition to attract demand deposits. This yield has taken many forms. It is a common practice, for example, among banks to vary interest rates charged on loans to large corporate borrowers in accordance with the size of the balances maintained in their checking account; that is, the larger the balance, the lower the interest rate charged. In other instances reduced service charges are applied to accounts with large balances, and some banks have gone as far as to waive service charges entirely to attract demand deposits. Still others have introduced premiums in an effort to boost their new accounts. A few large banks have made it a practice to assist corporate treasurers in investing corporate funds in the money market.

With many large depositors, and especially business firms, increasingly concerned with conserving their use of demand deposits, some large banks have been stressing prompt collection and payment services to lure these depositors. Such services are made possible in a number of ways, that is, through direct arrangements with the Federal Reserve Banks in other districts or with major-city correspondent banks, altogether bypassing the Federal Reserve System; through use of special carrier services to major cities to ensure faster collection than can be afforded by mail; and through locked-box arrangements.* The more economical use of demand deposits made possible by these banks, however, affected the velocity of demand deposit turnover. What this means is that with demand deposits used more actively, the level of such deposits fluctuated more rapidly and widely with adverse effects upon bank liquidity.

The economic effects of the prohibition of interest payment on demand deposits have been given important recognition. A presidential commission established in 1970—known as the Hunt Commission—to study the structure, operation, and regulation of the financial system of the country, recognized the need for reviewing the interest rate prohibition. The bill that evolved out of its recommendations provided for the abolition of this prohibition after a

---

*Under a locked-box plan, local and regional payments on company billings are sent directly into a post office box placed under the control of the collection bank, thereby saving important time in the collection and clearing of these items. If the billing company is located in another city, once the checks are cleared, the local bank remits the funds by wire to the company's bank of deposit. Through such a method, collection time can be reduced by one to five days. Examples of freeing funds in the amount of $5 billion or more by this method have been cited by firms.

certain transitional period; the reasoning behind this was that the prohibition had caused certain dislocations in the economy and that an immediate change would have disturbing effects. Out of this bill came the Financial Institutions Act of 1975, which was passed at the Senate level and is currently awaiting ratification by the House. In this act it is stipulated that interest on demand deposits—unless delayed by the Federal Reserve System until January 1, 1980 —is permitted for all national banks and thrift institutions, effective January 1, 1978.[15] Of similar nature have been the recommendations made by the Financial Institutions and National Economy (FINE) Study, currently being considered by the House, and which seek a major restructuring of the nation's banking industry.[16]

Both of the above measures also recommended the removal of interest rate ceilings on time and savings deposits after a period of five and one-half years. As mentioned earlier, ceiling rates on these deposits had their origin in the Banking Act of 1933 and have been known as the Federal Reserve Regulation Q.* From the early 1930s through the early 1950s, however, the effects of this regulation were hardly felt by commercial banks. For one thing, ceiling rates were well above the going rates of interest. Indeed, the lack of adequate demand for loans and the volume of excess reserves held by commercial banks in the 1930s and 1940s had led a great many banks to discourage time deposit growth by paying minimum rates on such deposits.† From the early 1950s on, however, this situation started changing significantly as the result of the rapid growth of postwar credit demand. As pressures for loanable funds increased, banks were led to offer ceiling rates on time and savings deposits and thus to feel, for the first time, the effects of Regulation Q. As the rates paid by competitive financial institutions—savings and loan associations, mutual savings banks, and credit unions—were free from similar regulation, banks soon found themselves at a competitive disadvantage in attracting time and savings deposits.

After due consideration of the situation, the Federal Reserve System revised upward, in the middle of 1957, the interest rate ceiling on bank time and savings deposits. Since then, ceiling levels have changed on several occasions throughout the 1960s and in the 1970s. In these and in other instances the symptoms were the same; during periods of high business activity and

---

*The Federal Reserve System has introduced such regulation for its member banks. The FDIC has adopted this regulation, thereby extending it to those insured banks that are not members of the Federal Reserve System. Finally, the various state authorities have introduced similar regulations for nonmember and noninsured banks.

†It has been estimated that from 1929 through the early 1950s, time and savings deposits grew at only half the rate of demand deposits, with consequent implications upon the share of commercial banks in the assets of all financial institutions.[17]

interest rates the banking industry was experiencing shortages of funds as a result of the "price control" imposed by Regulation Q.

Though revision of Regulation Q improved the competitive position of commercial banks, this regulation nevertheless affected the flow of funds and the allocative functioning of the money market mechanisms. During periods of tight money conditions it encouraged the loss of funds and their flow toward other nonbank financial intermediaries or directly to the users of funds. This phenomenon, known as disintermediation, occurred in a number of instances (that is, in 1959, in 1966, in 1968–70, and in late 1973). This inability of commercial banks to compete effectively for funds induced them to innovate and develop sources of financing. The earliest and most important of such sources was of a deposit nature and involved the CD; other sources were of a nondeposit nature (that is, the Eurodollar financing) and shall be discussed in the next section.

The CD was basically the answer to some large metropolitan commercial banks to the pressures they were experiencing in the early 1960s. Specifically, these banks found themselves at the time under pressure on the one hand from a growing demand for loans, as the economy was recovering from the 1960–61 recession, and on the other from an inadequate growth of deposits. This slow growth was due primarily to the increasingly sophisticated cash-management techniques of their major depositors, large corporations, and the ability of these firms to economize on their demand deposit balances despite rising sales. Thus in an attempt to arrest the slowdown in their deposit growth and recapture some of the lost deposits, these banks initiated the issuance of CDs.

The CD in itself was not a new instrument. Prior to 1961 a few CDs had been issued but their total dollar value was unimportant because they were of a nonnegotiable form. In other words, as these CDs were of a nonnegotiable form they did not offer corporate treasurers the same options of other money market instruments, that is, Treasury bills. Such CDs had to be held to maturity, when they were redeemable at the issuing bank. It therefore became apparent to New York City banks that to succeed in retaining or in attracting corporate funds, they had to offer an instrument with more liquidity than these CDs or the regular time deposit accounts and yet with approximately the same yield.

When New York City banks announced early in 1961 the acceptance of time deposits in the form of time certificates from corporations, they provided for the full negotiability of these instruments. A government securities dealer had agreed to make a secondary or trading market for these new instruments by matching together buyers and sellers. This fact converted the CD from a private arrangement between banker and depositor to an open-market instrument, a financial claim enjoying wide acceptance because of unquestioned soundness of the issuer, ease of transfer, and nearness to maturity. Shortly thereafter, many other commercial banks throughout the country began to bid for time deposits by offering negotiable CDs while additional security houses began to make markets in the instruments.

The issuance of CDs enabled commercial banks to compete actively with other money market instruments for the funds of individuals, businesses, and government, thereby accelerating the growth in time deposits. In mid-1975, the value of outstanding negotiable CDs issued by the so-called weekly-reporting banks (which include the largest banks in the country) approximated $81.5 billion compared to about $1 billion outstanding in 1961. Of the $81.5 billion, $27.7 billion, or 34 percent, was issued by large New York City banks while $53.7 billion, or 66 percent, was issued by other large banks throughout the country. The acceptance of the new money market instrument by corporations has been spectacular.

The most popular maturities of CDs are three, six, nine, and 12 months, although some have been issued for up to ten years. The large majority of banks that have issued CDs have done so in small denominations ranging from $1,000 up to $100,000. Small denomination CDs are issued in a variety of forms to meet the needs and tastes of various types of customers. A popular form is the savings certificate, which is customarily issued for a definite period, that is, three years. For interest-conscious savers this is a more attractive alternative to passbook savings because of the higher rates of interest involved. Consumer savings certificates are of a nonnegotiable nature and hence held to maturity by the owner and refunded with another CD of the bank. The CDs for which a secondary market exists and that qualify as money market securities are issued by the largest banks in the country. These CDs are typically issued in denominations of $500,000 or $1 million and are actively traded. Small and large denomination CDs are now issued by several thousand banks throughout the country, adapted according to each bank's needs and the economic characteristics of the market served. Purchaser-holders include not only businesses, but also savings banks, state and local governments, foreign agencies, individuals, and other economic units.

Banks typically post the rates they are offering for CDs of various maturities and may adjust these rates daily or even hourly. Whenever a bank needs or desires funds with a particular maturity, it raises the rate to make it competitive with rates on CDs issued by comparable banks. When the bank has obtained sufficient funds, it lowers the rate and keeps it noncompetitive until it desires to obtain additional funds. The CD is thus an excellent example of the liability management strategy discussed earlier. By varying the interest rate offered on CDs, a bank is now in a position to change its deposit structure in accordance with management objectives. At the same time CDs offer an additional degree of liquidity for a commercial bank. Instead of liquidating assets in the course of its operations to obtain funds, a bank now has an alternative; it can elect to use CD financing.

Although CDs have strengthened the competitive position of commercial banks, they are not beyond regulatory control. Indeed, though CDs are considered to be money market instruments, issuing banks have been subject to the same provisions of Regulation Q that provide for ceiling rates on time and savings deposits. Regulatory ceilings have had disruptive effects on the orderly development of the CD as a money market instrument. Such was, for example, the case in the years 1968–70 when the pursuit of a tight money policy by monetary authorities made money market rates move above the existing ceiling rates on CDs. As the Federal Reserve authorities had decided not to raise such ceiling accordingly, the issuing banks could only watch helplessly as holders of CDs redeemed them at maturity and turned to other higher-yielding instruments, as did those who might otherwise have bought CDs. The ensuing decline in CDs of some $14 billion was undesirable from the standpoint of the orderly development of the secondary market for CDs, although it may have been defensible from the standpoint of the monetary policy.

In 1973, regulatory interest rate ceilings were removed for large denomination CDs; that is, for those of over $100,000. The 1973 decision of the Federal Reserve to exempt large denomination CDs has contributed to the increased stability in the market for such CDs. As of April 30, 1976, the value of the large CDs outstanding for all insured commercial banks amounted to $76 billion, or 35 percent of the total market, while $142 billion, or 65 percent of this market, was made up of small denomination CDs. Large denomination CDs were issued by 8,719 insured banks while in the issuance of small denominations CDs, 14,347 banks were involved—which is tantamount to saying that virtually all insured banks issued small denomination CDs. When taken together, small and large CDs amounted to $218 billion and made up approximately 55 percent of all insured banks' time and savings deposits.[18] Removal of the regulatory rate on small CDs as provided by the Financial Institutions Act, will have important impetus upon the future growth of this instrument and the size of its market.

Interest rates on demand deposits and removal of Regulation Q for commercial banks do not exhaust the anticipated effects of the Financial Institutions Act. The objective of this act is more ambitious and stretches into the functions of other financial institutions, and hence into the structure of the very financial system. The intended impact of this act is increased competition among financial institutions by elimination of unnecessary and outdated regulation that prevents the integration of the financial system of the country. Increased competition would reduce the cost of financial services as well as expand the scope of the services offered. This is expected to occur through removal of the old lines of demarcation in the activities of these institutions and hence by permitting them to compete in each other's traditional lines of financial services. Thus for banks, as we saw, interest rates on demand deposits are reinstituted and ceiling rates on time and savings deposits removed. On the other hand, savings and loan associations, credit unions, and mutual savings banks are permitted to offer typical banking services such as checking accounts, interim financing of properties, and consumer loans. Moreover, they are permitted to invest in corporate bonds and commercial papers. The broadening of the investment and financing opportunities of deposit institutions has a price—elimination of the preferential tax treatment thus far enjoyed and equalization with commercial banks' taxation and reserve requirement provisions.

The elimination of traditional lines between these institutions and commercial banks extends beyond their operative aspects and into their supervisory and regulatory structure. The Financial Institutions Act proposes a single regulatory agency that would assume the responsibility of the comptroller of the currency and the regulatory and the supervisory functions of the Federal Reserve, the FDIC, the Federal Home Loan Bank Board, and the National Credit Union Administration. A natural corollary of such an agency's functions would be the regulation of nationwide branching.

We are thus on the verge of important changes in the functioning and the regulatory framework of deposit institutions. Though government regulation has been formally the initiating force, important impetus has been given all along by basic market forces. In other words, much of this change is traced to public pressure on the demand side of the market and to competition on the supply side. Market influence is a natural and continuous process in a dynamic society. As society evolves and changes, institutional arrangements must change with it.

Change is usually resisted at the time it is implemented and is always uncomfortable for some time. Judging in retrospect the evolution and current state of the financial market since yesteryear, it is only reasonable to assume that increased competition will in turn increase the effectiveness of this market in its function of allocating funds among different borrowers and sectors of the economy.

The effects of these proposed financial reforms are expected to be of signal importance. The process of change will be set into motion once the Congress enacts the proposed reforms. Growing evidence at this time suggests that House action on the proposed reforms will be deferred until the 95th Congress convenes. This means that the proposed reforms will have to be reintroduced in the Congress sometime in 1977. Clearly, it is too early at this time to predict the fate of the Financial Institutions Act, but some forces are at work that will contribute to the adoption of at least some of its provisions. The concept of equality in competition among thrift institutions is definitely a force that allows a considerable degree of optimism concerning the adoption of some of the provisions of the proposed reforms, as is also the idea of a more effective monetary policy through extension of reserve requirements to all thrift institutions. The need for additional government revenues and opposition to tax loopholes are forces that act against continuation of the preferential tax-treatment status and in favor of institutional equality in taxation. The idea of convenience and the needs of the public also favor the broadening of the powers of all financial institutions. Last, but not least, the parallel and yet more far-reaching objectives pursued by the House, in the framework of the FINE study, are adding important momentum to the need for enacting financial reforms.

BANK BORROWING

Banks have begun to obtain increasing percentages of their total financing through borrowing. In fact, at times borrowings of all commercial banks have equaled or exceeded commercial bank capital. As of September 29, 1976, for example, the borrowings of all commercial banks amounted to $77.5 billion and capital to $73.1 billion. This is all the more impressive if we consider that at the end of 1968 borrowings were about one-fourth the size of bank capital.

The type of debt financing we are concerned with here is incurred by a commercial bank at its own initiative. Such financing is of a nondeposit nature and offers a bank the possibility to raise funds for short periods of time. Liabilities of this type, with one exception (Federal Reserve credit), are known as money market liabilities because they are generally purchased or acquired by paying a competitive price for them in the money market. The management of these funds is part of the broader liability management concept mentioned earlier in connection with deposit financing. Money market liabilities constitute an additional source of funds available to a bank and hence an alternative for adjusting bank liquidity positions. The availability of alternatives generally contributes to the greater safety of deposits and the increased efficiency of the commercial banking systems.

Until the late 1960s, borrowing was a negligible component of bank financing. The subsequent tight money conditions were especially instrumental in the development of this source. For, it was under these conditions that banks began to increasingly rely upon financing through nondeposit arrangements. Of the instruments available for bank borrowing, two have been in existence for decades and are still used very extensively. But changing conditions led banks to develop more versatile tools, and new ones continue to appear as banks become more adept to liability management. In this section we will consider both the traditional and the more recently developed tools that banks use in liability management.

One source that banks can use to raise supplementary funds is repurchase agreements. Under a repurchase agreement, commonly referred to as RP, a bank (borrower) sells securities out of its portfolio to a buyer (lender) with a commitment to repurchase them at a specified date at a stated price. The securities involved in the transaction are usually obligations of the federal government or its agencies, or of the state and local governments. The buyer is protected from the risk of market fluctuations in the value of the securities since the agreement commits the bank to purchase them back and specifies a repurchase price that equals the original sale price plus the interest earned by the buyer during the period of the agreement. The interest paid to the buyer is determined by the going market rate for repurchase agreements. The period covered by such an agreement may be one day or several days, or, if the agreement is one without a fixed maturity, it may be terminated at any time at the convenience of the seller or buyer. In effect, the transaction represents a loan to the bank from the buyer, with the security serving as collateral.

The use of repurchase agreements as a discretionary source of bank funds received important impetus during 1969 as the result of an intensified loan demand. Thus the volume of securities sold by commercial banks under repurchase agreements rose rapidly throughout the year, reaching a level of $4 billion by mid-1970, before declining subsequently to lower levels.*

Occasionally, banks may turn to one or more of their correspondent banks (in adjoining or larger cities) to borrow the funds needed. Such borrowing is generally considered an accommodation extended to smaller banks that are not members of the Federal Reserve System, in the framework of correspondent relationships. Most frequently, however, banks borrow from each other through the federal funds market. This source has been available to banks for a considerable length of time and is still used to a great extent by both large and small banks. "Federal funds" is the term applied to the excess balances that member banks carry in their reserve account with the Federal Reserve Bank. These are usually borrowed by banks who need to supplement their legal reserves on a temporary basis. It is precisely this need for immediate credit by reserve-deficient banks that has created the market for excess reserve funds. The borrowing and lending of excess reserves, usually called "purchase" and "sale" of such funds, results in a more efficient utilization of the reserve base by the commercial banking system than would be possible without the existence of such an arrangement. The transaction itself is in essence a one-day loan for which the borrower pays one day's interest. The operation generally involves a reciprocal exchange of checks. The lending bank (seller) draws a check on its reserve account at the Federal Reserve Bank, which it gives to

---

*Banks have since been very active in the market for repurchase agreements, though largely in the capacity of a lender to security dealers financing their inventories of government securities. Banks find such arrangements an attractive outlet for their excess funds since they usually provide a slightly higher return than do one-day loans to other banks in the federal funds market. The dollar value of such financing to dealers outstanding in June 1976 amounted to $3.3 billion.[19]

the borrowing bank (buyer) for clearance. The borrowing bank reciprocates by giving the lending bank a similar check on its reserve account for the same amount plus interest for one day, with that check to be cleared the following business day. Thus the borrowing bank's legal reserve balances increase that particular day, but decrease the following day. Though a one-day transaction, the operation can be repeated daily with the borrowing bank varying the amount of its purchase in accordance with the short-run changes in its needs.[20]

The largest volume of funds is traded in multiples of $1 million. However, with the growing participation of smaller banks, an increasing number of transactions are conducted in much smaller amounts as well.[21] The total volume of federal funds purchases has increased significantly. Net interbank federal funds purchases by large commercial banks, for example, rose from $9.5 billion on December 31, 1969, to $46.8 billion by the end of September 1976. Gross trading in federal funds is obviously much larger than net purchases. For instance, in the week ending September 29, 1976, net purchases by large commercial banks were $46.8 billion compared to gross purchases by the same banks of $62.5 billion.[22] Gross purchases clearly cover all transactions in federal funds including a two-way transaction. Such a transaction occurs when an individual bank purchases and sells funds the same trading day. This move may be dictated by variation in a bank's federal reserves experienced in the course of the same business day.

The rate of interest paid on federal funds is largely determined by the rate at which banks are able to borrow from the Federal Reserve System (discount rate). However, when reserves are plentiful and demand for federal funds is slack, the funds may trade for long periods at rates considerably below the discount rate. Since the 1960s, federal funds have traded above the discount rate because some banks have sought to use this market as a permanent source of funds while others have been willing to pay a premium to avoid borrowing at the Federal Reserve window even on a temporary basis.[23]

One of the provisions of the 1962 ruling by the comptroller of the currency with respect to bank senior debt capital provided that it was within the corporate powers of a national bank to borrow for general banking purposes by issuing unsecured promissory notes of short-term maturity. Immediately after this ruling was made, several large-city banks began to offer such notes to tap short-term funds.[24] Bank interest in the issuance of these notes stemmed basically from the fact that these were looked upon as nondeposit obligations. As such, they were exempted from a number of supervisory regulations: they were not subject to provisions on ceiling interest rates (Regulation Q); no reserves were required against such notes; and they were not part of the bank's deposit base upon which FDIC assessments were calculated for deposit insurance premium payments.

The use of short-term notes, however, was rendered uneconomical for banks in 1966. During that year, Federal Reserve authorities ruled that these note issues constituted time deposits and were therefore subject to all the provisions applicable to such deposits.

Banks have been able to circumvent existing regulation and obtain the necessary funds from the open market through bank holding companies. In other words, a bank can tap market funds by having the bank's holding company issue its own short-term open-market obligations, known as commercial paper. Congress and various states have specified conditions under which banks may form a parent corporation—a holding company—to own bank stock and to engage in business operations including some that a commercial bank would be prohibited form entering into directly. Leasing, sales of computer services, and similar matters can be handled by a bank holding company. Also, the holding company can issue commerical paper. Typically, the funds acquired by the issuance of commercial paper to the public by the holding company are in turn used to acquire loans and investments from the subsidiary bank. So far as the banking organizations as a whole (holding company plus bank subsidiary) is concerned, the result of commercial paper issuance is the same as in the case of direct bank-issued obligations. As far as the investors are concerned, the holding company's paper is regarded as being an issue of at least equal quality compared to issues of promissory notes by the bank itself. The holding company's physical assets may be virtually nil but it owns the stock of the commercial bank.

In other cases, banks have formed independent companies, not holding companies, and these companies have sold paper in the market, and then bought loans and investments from the commercial bank. The two techniques are analogous, although the legal aspects differ.

Large commercial banks have become an important factor on the borrowing side of the commercial paper market through their parent corporations. On June 30, 1976, commercial paper issued by these corporations amounted to $8.0 billion, which accounted for 16 percent of the $50.0 billion outstanding on that date.[25]

Another source of funds that commercial banks have turned to occasionally for short-term borrowing has been the Eurodollar market.* Eurodollars are deposits, denominated in U.S. dollars, placed with banks outside the United

---

*The origin of the Eurodollar market is usually traced to two banks owned by Russia: The Narodny Bank in London, and the Banque Commerciale pour l'Europe du Nord located in Paris. The Russians feared expropriation of their dollar deposits at U. S. banks in the event of a political deterioration in U.S.-Russian relations, so they began selling their dollar balances to others. The cable address of the Banque Commerciale pour l'Europe du Nord is "Eurobank" and bankers soon began calling dollar deposits there Eurodollars and the market that was developed, the Eurodollar market.

States (including branches of U.S. banks abroad), where the local currency is not dollars. Eurodollar deposits arise when the owner of a demand deposit in a U.S. bank transfers ownership of that deposit, to a bank outside the United States in exchange for a deposit in the foreign bank denominated in dollars. Thus, the foreign bank or U.S branch acquires the customer's dollar claim and offers in exchange a Eurodollar deposit account. The foreign bank or U.S. branch may in turn lend its dollar claims against the U.S. bank, at the going market rate of interest, to another bank or, depending upon the case, to its home office in the United States. In the latter case, the transaction enables the home office to raise the supplementary funds needed.

U.S. businesses are large depositors in the Eurodollar market, and they may borrow dollars from banks abroad. Commercial banks also may make deposits in the Eurodollar market or they may solicit deposits through their branches abroad. In fact any economic unit holding a substantial deposit in a U.S. bank is a potential supplier of Eurodollars. Most Eurodollar deposits are interest-bearing time deposits of relatively short maturity, but maturities may be extended to five years, and interest may also be paid on demand deposits.

Borrowing from the Eurodollar market is an option available almost exclusively to the largest U.S. banks, which maintain banking offices overseas. The Eurodollar market has been especially important during periods of tight money conditions. Such was, for example, the case in 1966 when banks, because of the prevailing monetary stringency, found themselves unable to issue CDs at the going rates of interest and decided instead to seek funds in the Eurodollar market. Thus between January and December 1966, liabilities of U.S. banks to their foreign branches rose from $1.7 billion to $4.0 billion. Then again in 1969, when demand for bank credit far outdistanced the ability of banks to supply it, borrowings by U.S. banks from their foreign branches rose throughout the year, from $6 billion in January to nearly $13 billion in December.[26]

Clearly, if the Eurodollar market had not been available as a source of funds, banks would have been forced to borrow even more heavily than they did from domestic sources, and stresses upon the Federal Reserve Banks or the money market would have been even greater than they were. The Federal Reserve can inhibit bank use of this market, however, and since 1969 it has applied reserve requirements against Eurodollar deposits,[27] at rates varied from time to time, as a means of influencing the total volume of such liabilities outstanding. The imposition of reserve requirements on such borrowings has made it unlikely that Eurodollars will again be an important source of funds for U.S. banks.

The sale of or participation in loans is another important source of funds utilized by banks. The sale of loans may occur when banks located in areas where the demand for loans is slack make their ample funds available to banks located where loan demand is high. Alternately, a bank may sell a loan or invite other banks to participate in a loan, because it is too large for the bank to handle alone. For some banks, originating and selling loans (that is, mortgage loans) has developed into a business in itself. These banks usually maintain the servicing of such loans thereby preserving customer relationship and ensuring at the same time a source of additional income.

The sale of loans and participations is frequently handled by larger-city correspondent banks. Participation in loans with correspondent banks benefits both sides. Specifically, correspondent participation in local loans is a method of bringing additional funds into the community. On the other hand, large banks, by allowing their smaller correspondents to participate in loans that they originate, make it possible for such banks to conserve their loanable funds. The practice of loan participation with correspondent banks has been gaining widespread acceptance among banks. Indeed, in recent years, a growing number of banks have placed loan participations with correspondents, as suggested by relative data.[28]

Commercial banks that are members of the Federal Reserve System have an extra source of borrowing, their regional Federal Reserve Bank. This source of funds has been available to commercial banks since the inception of the Federal Reserve System. Although Federal Reserve credit extensions are not properly a money market instrument, they are nevertheless treated here since they constitute an alternative source of bank borrowing. Federal Reserve loans to member banks take the form of discounts, often called rediscounts, and advances. If the commercial bank resorts to a rediscounting transaction, it offers for discount at the Federal Reserve Bank negotiable instruments that it has already discounted for its customers. In effect, the borrowing bank sells to the Federal Reserve Bank its own customers' notes, drafts, and bills of exchange and is itself liable to the Federal Reserve Bank if the original maker defaults on the maturity date of the instrument. But the commercial bank may elect to obtain a direct advance from the Federal Reserve Bank on its own promissory note, pledging as collateral some acceptable asset. Both transactions differ only in form, since both have the same effect of increasing the commercial bank's reserve balances at the Federal Reserve Bank.

Most borrowing from the Federal Reserve Banks takes the form of advances rather than rediscounting. Securing funds by means of an advance is generally believed to be a simpler and more flexible tool than rediscounting in correcting imbalances in the reserve position. One reason for this preference is that banks are frequently unable to provide the financial statements and other information routinely required by the Federal Reserve Bank about the individuals or companies liable for paying the rediscounted instrument on maturity. More important, however, banks frequently want to borrow for only a limited number of days, and eligible paper of the right amount and the right maturity may not be readily available.

Borrowing from the Federal Reserve, however, is not an automatic right. Federal Reserve credit is extended to commercial banks only when seasonal or exceptional developments have created unexpected depletion of reserves. These developments may proceed from national, regional, or local circumstances. In such instances, Federal Reserve Bank resources are readily available to the commercial bank whose reserves aré thus impaired. Continuous use of Federal Reserve credit, especially in consecutive reserve-adjustment periods, is generally discouraged unless it is associated with efforts to correct the situations that have motivated such borrowing. Clearly then, Federal Reserve borrowing facilities are not intended to be used regularly as a reserve-adjustment instrument in the management of a bank's reserve position.[29]

The prevalence of the above circumstances, however, is not the sole determinant of the volume of commercial bank borrowing from the Federal Reserve. Traditional dislike for operating on borrowed funds is also an important element. As might be expected, sensitiveness to indebtedness varies from bank to bank. Indeed, for certain banks, borrowing from the Federal Reserve may be considered as a last resort while for others it may just be a matter of managerial policy to avoid such borrowing altogether. The latter attitude holds especially true among small banks, which are very sensitive about listing borrowings in their published statements.

Perhaps even more important than the prevailing attitude and disposition of commercial banks toward operating on borrowed funds, however, is the very cost of Federal Reserve borrowing or the discount rate. In administering its discount facilities the Federal Reserve is guided by two objectives: to provide temporary funds and assist commercial banks in adjusting their reserve positions; and to influence prevailing economic conditions in a manner that will be inducive to economic growth, price stability, and a high level of employment. Of these two objectives, the pursuit of the latter one is, of course, predominant since the discount mechanism constitutes one of the instruments of monetary control. In other words, the level of the discount rate is determined on the basis of the general credit policy pursued. When monetary authorities pursue a policy of tightening credit, the discount rate may be set at or above the short-term market rates of interest, thereby bidding up the cost of money and rendering unprofitable any commercial bank borrowing from the Federal Reserve in meeting reserve deficiencies. Conversely, when monetary authorities pursue a policy of easing credit, the discount rate will be lowered as part of this policy. At this phase of policy, however, the lowering of the discount rate is not an effective aspect of control because commercial bank reserve positions are eased and banks have no need to borrow funds from the Federal Reserve.[30]

Member bank borrowings from the Federal Reserve System have fluctuated over the years. Borrowings are generally greatest when money is tight, and their level is often taken as an indication of the degree of tightness in credit

FIGURE 6

Short-Term Interest Rates
(percent per annum)

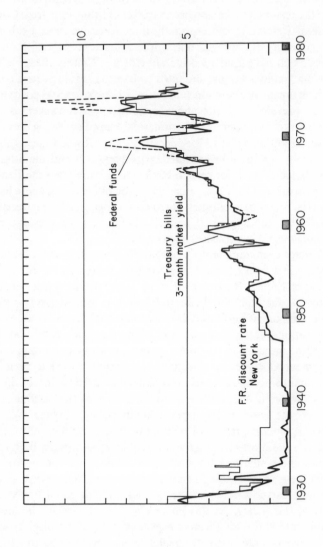

Source: Board of Governors of the Federal Reserve System, *Historical Chartbook* (Washington, D.C.: Federal Reserve System, 1976)

markets. Substantial borrowing thus occurred in 1969 and again in 1973, but reached an unprecedented level in mid-1974 when it rose to $3.4 billion.[31] Considering the high degree of monetary restraint, the volume of borrowing indicates the relatively low level of the discount rate during this period as compared to the cost of alternative reserve-adjustment media.

The tightness in the credit markets, and its effect on interest rates during the years 1969 and 1973–74, is illustrated in Figure 6. As shown in this figure, interest rates, reflecting the prevailing money market conditions, rose substantially during these years, surpassing all previous levels. A closer look at this figure shows the relatively lower level of the discount rate duing these years. Note, of course, that the discount rate is not a natural market rate but an administered rate altered accordingly by Federal Reserve authorities to conform with prevailing money market rates. The other rates illustrated are market-determined rates and, as can be seen, they have been highly volatile. This is especially true for the federal funds rate. As stated earlier, federal funds transactions are affected by the reserve position of individual banks. As most banks wait to adjust their reserve positions with the Federal Reserve Bank later on in the day when their reserve needs become apparent, the federal funds rate would exhibit important volatility from one day to another. This volatility is especially accentuated as the reserve settlement period draws to a close. Banks that did not adjust their reserve positions earlier during the period would be actively engaged in the market to avoid any deficiency in their reserves with the Federal Reserve Bank, and consequently the penalties involved.

The rate of U.S. Treasury bills is also included in the figure because Treasury bills are by far the largest money market instrument. At the end of August 1976, $161 billion in Treasury bills was outstanding, with maturities stretching up to one year. As they constitute short-term debt obligations of the U.S. government, they are a popular money market instrument among U.S. government agencies, Federal Reserve Banks, and such private investors as thrift institutions, insurance companies, commercial banks, and state and local governments. [32] Commercial banks rank at the top of the private investors list because of the high degree of liquidity that this instrument possesses.

Of the wide variety of money market instruments reviewed in this section, some are tailored to specific needs—for example, repurchase agreements—while others serve a more general purpose—for example, Treasury bills. The best single indicator of conditions in the money market is frequently regarded to be the going rate on federal funds. The considerable growth of the federal funds market and the frequency of transactions involved have enabled changing conditions in the money market to be transmitted much more quickly throughout the country. Indeed, with banks from coast to coast actively involved in the purchase and sale of funds, the effects of money market developments are felt by the different regions of the country.

SUMMARY

In summary, this chapter has examined the sources of commercial bank funds. Bank funds are derived from that portion of the bank's original capital that is not needed for construction of physical facilities to house the banking operations, from senior debt capital, and from additions to retain earnings. More important, however, they are derived from bank deposit and nondeposit, or money market, liabilities. In the former case these are made up of demand deposits, and time and savings deposits competitively attracted and retained; in the latter case, such liabilities are incurred at the bank's own initiative and they include Federal Reserve credit and such money market liabilities as borrowing federal funds and Eurodollars, entering into repurchase agreements, and marketing bank-related commercial papers.

In the employment of these funds banks are guided by a number of considerations. Thus, the objectives of funds management in a commercial bank are to provide adequate liquidity; exhibit the degree of prudence appropriate to an institution entrusted with the funds of others; maximize earnings for the stockholders; and meet the legitimate financing needs of the community or market served. These objectives have a dominant influence on a bank's asset structure. To this issue we turn in the following chapter.

NOTES

1. *Federal Reserve Bulletin* (October 1976): A14.

2. See, for example, "Fuller Disclosure for Banks—At Last," *Business Week* (April 19, 1976):74–76; and "The Used-Lot Dealers," *Forbes* (July 1, 1976): 62–64.

3. *Standard Federal Tax Reporter,* 9 vol. (Chicago: Commerce Clearing House, 1976), vol. 4, paragraph 3458.01.

4. George W. McKinney, Jr., "New Sources of Bank Funds: Certificates of Deposit and Debt Securities," *Law and Contemporary Problems* 32 (Winter 1967): 85–86.

5. *Federal Reserve Bulletin,* op. cit., p. A26.

6. McKinney, op. cit., p. 97.

7. Walter Bagehot, *Lombard Street: A Description of the Money Market,* 8th ed. (London: Kegan Paul, Trench, & Co., 1882), p. 245.

8. Roland I. Robinson and Richard H. Pettway, *Policies for Optimum Bank Capital* (Chicago: Association of Reserve City Bankers, 1967).

9. Howard D. Crosse, *Management Policies for Commercial Banks* (Englewood Cliffs, N.J.: Prentice-Hall, 1962), p. 158.

10. Roland I. Robinson, *The Management of Bank Funds,* 2d ed. (New York: McGraw-Hill Book Co., 1962), p. 436.

11. Crosse, op. cit., p. 186.

12. G. W. Woodworth, "Theories of Cyclical Liquidity Management of Commercial Banks," in *Banking Markets and Financial Institutions,* ed. Thomas G. Gies and Vincent P. Apilado (Homewood, Ill.: R. D. Irwin, 1971), p. 158.

13. Federal Reserve Bank of New York, *The Story of Checks,* 5th ed. (New York: Federal Reserve Bank, 1972).

14. *Federal Reserve Bulletin,* op. cit., p. A7.

15. U.S. Congress, Senate, Committee on Banking, Housing and Urban Affairs, *Financial Institutions Act of 1975: Senate Report 94–487,* 94th Cong., 1st sess., November 18, 1975.

16. U.S. Congress, House, Committee on Banking, Currency and Housing, "Discussion Principles Concerning the Role of Our Financial Institutions in the National Economy," *Congressional Record,* 94th Cong., 1st sess., November 6, 1975.

17. For the trend in the growth of bank time and savings deposits vis-a-vis that of other financial institutions since the turn of the century, see Raymond W. Goldsmith, *Financial Intermediaries in the American Economy Since 1900* (Princeton: Princeton University Press, 1958).

18. *Federal Reserve Bulletin,* op. cit., p. A26.

19. Ibid., p. A36.

20. Wesley Lindow, "The Federal Funds Market," *Bankers Monthly* (September 1960): 20–22.

21. Ibid., p. 26.

22. *Federal Reserve Bulletin,* op. cit., pp. A18–A21.

23. For an excellent analysis of the operation of this market, see Board of Governors of the Federal Reserve System, *Trading in Federal Funds* (Washington, D.C.: Board of Governors of the Federal Reserve System, 1965).

24. McKinney, op. cit., p. 98.

25. *Federal Reserve Bulletin,* op. cit., p. A25.

26. *Federal Reserve Bulletin,* (December 1971): A88.

27. Effective September 1969, banks that were members of the Federal Reserve System and had foreign branches were required to maintain a 10 percent reserve against foreign branch deposits. See, for example, *Federal Reserve Bulletin,* August 1969, p. 657.

28. Robert E. Knight, "Correspondent Banking. Part I, Balances and Services," *Monthly Review,* Federal Reserve Bank of Kansas City (November 1970); "Correspondent Banking. Part II, Loan Participations and Fund Flows," *Monthly Review,* Federal Reserve Bank of Kansas City (December 1970).

29. Karl R. Bopp, "Borrowing from the Federal Reserve Bank—Some Basic Principles," *Business Review* (Federal Reserve Bank of Philadelphia), June 1958, pp. 5–6.

30. On Federal Reserve credit see also Board of Governors of the Federal Reserve System, *The Federal Reserve System—Purposes and Functions,* 6th ed. (Washington, D.C.: Board of Governors of the Federal Reserve System, 1974), pp. 70–77.

31. *Federal Reserve Bulletin* (September 1975): A2.

32. *Federal Reserve Bulletin* (October 1976): A35.

CHAPTER
2

OBJECTIVES OF
PORTFOLIO MANAGEMENT

The nature of a bank's liabilities, together with the thin layer of equity on which a bank operates, renders the employment of bank funds a factor of primary significance. More specifically, available resources must be used in a manner that will permit the bank to attain a number of objectives. This leads naturally into a discussion of the basic objectives of bank portfolio management and hence the factors that affect the general character and composition of commercial bank assets.

First, a bank's portfolio policies should be so designed as to enable the bank to meet liquidity requirements without exposing itself either to embarrassment or to unusual pressure; in other words, maintain the degree of liquidity necessary to meet deposit withdrawals and increased requests for loans upon demand.

Another consideration that must govern portfolio policies is that the greatest part of a bank's liabilities is subject to withdrawal either on demand or after very short notice. Bank portfolio policies must therefore be guided by prudence; that is to say, bank lending and investing would be meaningful only when undertaken where there is almost complete assurance that the principal will be returned. Another way of stating this objective is that the bank has specific liabilities, and the bulk of its assets must also take the form of specific claims that are reasonably protected against risk. Clearly, asset quality, and hence solvency, considerations are in the foreground of this objective.

In addition to the maintenance of liquidity and solvency, bank policies should be geared toward achieving sufficient income on bank portfolio so that operating costs can be met and the bank can continue profitably as a going concern.

To attain these objectives commercial banks must achieve a certain pattern and distribution of their assets. Hence portfolio management may be said to refer to a bank's determination of what constitutes the best distribution of assets in its quest for liquidity, solvency, and income. Here precisely lies the difficult task of a bank's funds management. Attaining these ends means in fact solving the basic conflict between liquidity and solvency on the one hand and income on the other. This conflict arises from the inverse relationship of the former attributes to the latter. Indeed, the nearer an asset is to cash, the more remote is the possibility of potential losses to the bank from default or market risks. Such a highly liquid—and hence safe—asset, however, would yield a relatively lower income over time than a less liquid and riskier asset. In other words, the rate of return on assets tends to vary inversely with their degree of liquidity and safety. In a final analysis, this conflict in the employment of bank funds boils down to a conflict between liquidity and profitability. "The art of commercial banking," wrote Roland I. Robinson, "is solving this basically conflicting requirement: that of being safe and yet profitable."[1]

As might be expected, the solving of this conflict rests entirely upon each bank's management. It is a matter of individual judgment based upon experience and knowledge. Hence no two banks would solve this conflict the same way and the composition of their portfolios would vary accordingly.

LIQUIDITY

A basic objective of portfolio management is the maintenance by a bank of sufficient liquidity to meet varied demands for funds. More specifically, a bank must maintain highly liquid assets in sufficient amounts to meet deposit withdrawals as well as legitimate loan requests. The maintenance of liquid funds against deposit demands has been termed by some analysts "deposit liquidity"[2] or "protective liquidity,"[3] as distinguished from "lending liquidity"[4] or "portfolio liquidity,"[5] which applies to the maintenance of liquid funds for meeting the community's additional loan demands. Therefore, for a bank to develop a comprehensive liquidity policy, it is necessary to determine the combined liquidity requirements for both of these types of demands for funds. For this purpose it is essential that we examine first each of these demands separately.

As stated in the preceding chapter, the bulk of bank liabilities consists of contractual obligations to pay to the public fixed amounts on demand or after very short notice. The fact that a bank must honor its depositors' withdrawal requests as efficiently as possible dictates for the bank a certain type of liquidity policy in the employment of these funds. In other words, the nature of bank liabilities makes it essential that the resources of a bank be managed in such a way as to provide the means for meeting demands for funds as they are made. This obligation constitutes the most immediate and compelling necessity confronting the management of a bank. Indeed, failure to remain in a position to meet such demands as they are presented leaves management with no alternative but to close out the bank. The maximum of liquidity would, of course, be attained through the maintenance of all bank assets in the form of cash. However, the impracticability of such a measure is obvious. Even with its assets entirely in cash and thus with no investment or loan expenses, a bank would still incur major costs of operation. For, however liquid and safe cash may be, its profitability is nil. Under the circumstances the service charges for maintaining deposit accounts would be so inordinately high as to discourage customers from placing their funds with the bank.

In determining a bank's policy toward maintaining liquidity, management must consider the behavioral pattern of deposit accounts. As might be expected, all deposit accounts do not exhibit the same behavioral pattern. Indeed, due to a number of factors and differing situations, deposit accounts do not move in the same direction and at the same time or with the same velocity. It may be argued, of course, that fluctuations of individual accounts or a group of accounts may be offset by changes in other accounts or a group of accounts. Yet a bank cannot depend on that possibility. For banks, for example, located in communities importantly subject to the economic effects of one industry, such as resort and agricultural areas, deposit accounts would not be productive of their own offsetting changes nor of even nominal changes. And rightly so, since changes in depository accounts would move in the same direction and at about the same time. Indeed, if the industry suffers, so will its workers and local merchants—all undoubtedly bank customers—and bank deposits will decline. Conversely, if the industry prospers, bank deposits will build up.

It follows that whatever the type or classification of deposits may be, that is, whether they are called demand or time, or whether they are of private or public ownership, what matters for the bank is the likelihood that any specific deposit, or group of deposits, may be drawn down within a relatively short period of time. In view of this, potential deposit withdrawals and hence demands for funds, may be classified into "those which (a) will surely occur, (b) those which might but are not certain to occur, and (c) those which are unlikely to occur, but under certain circumstances, could possibly occur."[6] This classification of deposit withdrawals in accordance with the likelihood of their occurrences has a direct bearing upon the liquidity of the assets a bank must employ. It is sufficient to say at this point that the greater the likelihood of such withdrawals, the higher should be the liquidity of the assets employed.

A bank's first step in establishing protective liquidity requirements is therefore to determine the likelihood of deposit withdrawals. Stated differently, a bank must determine the volatility of its deposits. There are no absolute rules or methods of determining deposit volatility. Past experience and knowledge of the community or markets served would contribute toward a better sense of judgment, which coupled with a systematic analysis of the deposits themselves should serve as guidelines in the determination of the probable behavior of the accounts and hence of bank liquidity provisions against deposit withdrawals.

Rather than a detailed analysis of each deposit account, management may group accounts together and analyze such groupings separately. In this case, of course, the criterion for such groupings would be the degree of volatility of deposit accounts. It will usually be found that the major portion of a bank's deposit volatility is due to the behavior of the larger accounts, the unexpected or sudden withdrawal of which would cause relatively heavy pressures upon the liquidity position of a bank. In the demand deposit area, large deposit accounts are more susceptible to wide fluctuations than all other demand deposit accounts because their holders do not usually leave them idle for long periods of time. But in the time deposit category, too, large accounts are responsible for most fluctuations. More specifically, the large time open accounts, savings accounts, and CDs are likely to account for most of the fluctuations in the time deposit area. Indeed, there are instances when the vulnerability of these accounts may match, if not surpass, that of large demand deposits. This would hold true especially during a period of economic expansion when interest rates are rising and bond prices declining. It is during these periods that holders of large savings accounts, but holders of CDs mostly of less than $100,000 denominations, generally seek outlets offering more remuneration for their funds than banks are willing or permitted by law to pay.

In computing liquidity requirements against large deposit accounts, bank management must first separate the large accounts from all other accounts in each class of deposits.* Once this is done, a semimonthly figure may be established for the aggregate of the large accounts category, in each class of deposits. A similar figure may be derived, however, for the rest of the accounts in each class of deposits, which may now be grouped into a separate category. Management may then proceed to chart separately the aggregates established for each category, in each class of deposits. These aggregates carried back over a number of years would provide management with a historical pattern of deposit behavior by both groups of deposits in the demand, and time and savings areas. An example is illustrated in Figure 7, which shows hypothetical patterns of deposit volatility for the aggregate of large accounts in demand deposits, passbook savings, and time deposits. Clearly, similar patterns may also be established for the complementary category of accounts in each of these classes of deposits. Parallel trend lines may then be drawn through or near the

---

*What constitutes a large account is, of course, a relative matter, which can only be determined by each individual bank's management. Howard D. Crosse mentions, for example, as belonging to the large accounts category all those deposits that are individually equal to one-half of 1 percent of a bank's total deposits.[7]

FIGURE 7
Deposit Volatility

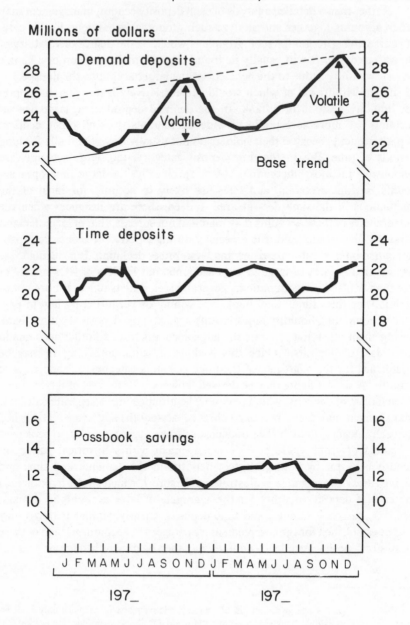

Source: Compiled by the author.

54

high and low points of these plots. The spread between the lines would indicate the maximum liquidity required against these deposits at any given time. The trend line drawn through or near the low points would designate the base or level of nonvolatile deposits. Where a clearly rising or falling trend manifests itself allowance can be made for increasing or decreasing the base level. The amount by which deposits exceed this base line would represent deposit volatility and is a statistical measure of the amount of liquidity required against them. Thus at any given time in the year bank management may relate the actual deposit position of the bank to these plots to determine the amount of liquidity required. By relating the bank's deposit position to historical patterns management may also determine the approximate timing of liquidity requirements.

The amount of liquidity established on the basis of deposit volatility would constitute a bank's first line of liquidity defense. Adjustment to this amount may only be made as to the corresponding percentage of required reserves maintained against such deposits. The reasoning behind this adjustment lies in the fact that deposit withdrawals would release amounts equal to the required reserves maintained against them.

The second line of liquidity defense is related to the withdrawal vulnerability of specific deposit accounts. Indeed, there will be times when a careful examination of certain large or special accounts on an individual basis may require the providing of a larger degree of liquidity protection than that suggested by the analysis. In such instances, detailed knowledge of the specific accounts and their prospective use would greatly aid bank management in determining the liquidity coverage required. A 20 percent liquidity reserve, for example, may be considered satisfactory on the assumption that a bank may be losing one out of five such accounts in the next few years. If so warranted by circumstances, liquidity protection against these accounts may even extend to full liquidity coverage. These liquidity considerations may be applicable both on demand, and time and savings deposits. One such case of an unusual deposit situation requiring a thicker protective liquidity cover was cited above when reference was made to the more aggressive employment of CDs in periods of rising interest rates. A case of full liquidity protection may arise when, for example, the proceeds of a bond issue have been deposited at a bank and are held in demand or time deposits pending accurately timed payments for the financing of a specific project. In instances such as those described above, the culling out of specific deposit accounts and a thorough knowledge of their prospective use would make possible the periodic projections of expected deposit fluctuations in the light of all known factors.

Lastly, as a third line of liquidity defense, an additional amount is recommended as a margin of safety against random or unforeseen circumstances. As is apparent, this would constitute a residual liquidity reserve and may amount to between 5 and 10 percent of all the remaining (nonlarge) deposits. In any case, a bank's willingness and ability to buy liabilities at any time would be an important determinant of the size of this liquidity reserve. The assets that bank management may employ to cover this marginal area, however, can be in the form of slightly less liquid investments, though still readily convertible into cash (that is, securities of a one-to-five year maturity range).

As stated earlier, bank liquidity serves two basic functions—meeting deposit demands as well as requests for funds arising from the community's needs for additional credit. Having examined the former, we may now turn to the latter.

In providing liquidity against potential loan requests, bank management is in a somewhat different position from that applying on deposit withdrawals. What must be observed here is that unlike fluctuations in the deposit demand, increases in loan requests are subject to management control. In other words, it is incumbent upon a bank's management to tighten up lending policies or to altogether refuse to make some loans. The availability of funds exerts important influence upon the decision of bank management. Normally new loan requests should be met from the bank's largest source of loanable funds —the loan portfolio itself through the turnover of loans.

The loan portfolio thus assures a bank's ability to make new loans. The degree of loan portfolio liquidity is, of course, affected by the length of loan maturities. Thus, the longer the maturities of a loan portfolio, the slower will be its loan turnover and hence the lesser its flexibility in meeting day-to-day requests for new loans as these develop.[8] The opposite would hold true if a bank's loan portfolio contains short-maturity loans. Where the new loan demands exhibit a seasonal pattern, it is natural that the flow of loanable funds resulting from periodic loan repayments would be at times short of the loan demands and at other times in excess of them.

To determine the amount of liquidity required against such a seasonal, or normal, loan pattern, the same method as that employed for computing protective liquidity can applied. More specifically, the bank's loan pattern can be depicted by establishing total semimonthly loan portfolio aggregates, which can be charted over a period of time in the past. As was done with deposits, parallel lines may be drawn through the high and low points of these plots to indicate the overall loan trend and the range of liquidity required. Unlike deposit liquidity requirements, however, which are measured against the base line, the amount of loan liquidity required at any time will be determined by the amount by which the graph falls below the upper trend line at any given point. In other words, with the upper trend line representing a maximum or ceiling to which loans may be expected to rise periodically or seasonally, the amount by which loans are below this maximum indicates a rough estimate of loan liquidity requirements at that time. The difference in the measurement of loan as against deposit liquidity requirements is a recognition of the fact that increases in loans make demands upon a bank's liquid position in the same way as do decreases in deposits. A hypothetical pattern of loan demand variation, and hence loan liquidity requirements, is presented in Figure 8.

A bank's loan liquidity requirements as determined above may be supplemented by additional liquidity provisions as protection for unforeseen loan developments. In other words, management may provide for a margin of safety to meet unexpected loan demands. The amount arbitrarily suggested for such a margin may be roughly twice the bank's legal limit for loans.* In a final analysis, however, the amount that should be reserved as a margin of safety would be determined by bank management after careful appraisal of the composition of the loan portfolio.†

FIGURE 8

Liquidity Needs for Loans

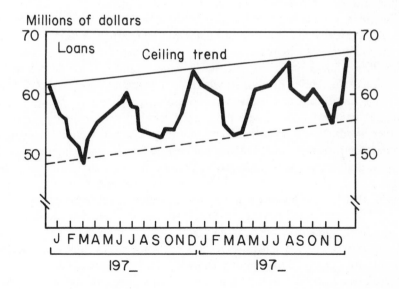

Source: Compiled by the author.

---

*A bank's legal limit for loans is 10 percent of its capital and surplus. Hence, the amount suggested for a bank to maintain is roughly 20 percent of its capital and surplus.[9]

†The loan portfolio of a bank actively engaged in commercial lending would require a relatively large margin of safety since the demand for business loans is usually more susceptible to fluctuations over the business cycle than the demand for consumer or real estate loans.[10]

If the demand for loans has been rising rapidly—as a result, for example, of a bank's aggressive lending policy or of a cyclical rise in business activity —and the management expects this rise to continue, provisions should be made for additional liquidity. In such instances, bank judgment alone can only determine how much additional liquidity should be reserved for the loan portfolio and what the degree of this liquidity should be. The rapidity of the anticipated loan growth will be a basic determinant of the liquidity of the assets employed. Funds reserved for such purposes are usually placed into slightly less liquid investments with their maturities arranged in a laddered form. "The composition and maturity distribution in this portfolio should, therefore, represent the banker's appraisal of the relative degree of liquidity required of the excess of lendable funds over the actual amount lent."[11]

The deposit and loan trends discussed above are a significant tool for bank management in determining the amount of combined liquidity cover that a bank should maintain. The graphic presentation of a bank's deposit and loan fluctuations would provide management with a picture of the similarity or dissimilarity of the two trends and enable it to determine the individual bank's protective and loan liquidity requirements at any particular time. Taken separately, a projected increase in deposits would call for increased protective liquidity while a projected increase in loans would call for decreased loan liquidity. Combining or netting, whatever the case may call for, of projected changes in deposits and loans in order to obtain a picture of the net liquidity requirements would assume a direct relationship between the two trends; in other words, that a potential decrease in loan demand would, through loan repayments, release funds which could be used for protective liquidity, or that a potential increase in deposits would provide loan liquidity. Such an assumption would appear logical only if it were to be assumed that history repeats itself; that is, that historical trends will continue in the same pattern.[12]

The practice of relying on loan portfolio to meet deposit liquidity is considered a questionable banking practice on other grounds, too.[13] For one thing, during a period of depressed economic conditions a bank's loan portfolio would lose much of its liquidity through renewal of outstanding loans and forced loan liquidations. But under normal circumstances, too, it is not advisable that bank management look to loan portfolio as a source of protective liquidity. When a bank grants a loan it is not possible to predict with absolute accuracy whether or not the loan will be repaid as agreed. The willingness and ability of the borrower to repay may change. Thus loans that were considered as good loans when they were made, could well become bad loans in a relatively short period of time. In some instances these loans—usually referred to as problem loans because of the problems they present as far as collections are concerned—may even require resort to the investment portfolio for additional liquidity so that they may be extended on the basis of a workout arrangement.* Hence the need for separate appraisals of the bank's protective and loan liquidity requirements.

It follows then that liquidity requirements must be established separately for deposits and loans. Once these are determined, the two amounts added together would provide the bank's aggregate liquidity requirements. Such requirements would clearly be at a maximum if the bank's loans are down and the deposits are up. For, it is at these times that the future holds the greatest potential increase in loans or decline in deposits, and thus liquidity should be at a peak, so it can be used up in meeting the loan increase in prospect, or the deposit decline that is coming up. On the other hand, requirements would be at a minimum if the position of loans and deposits is reversed. In any case, by allowing additional liquidity for a margin of error or for an extra margin of safety in liquidity estimates, the bank would be prepared for the unexpected in both loans and deposits. This kind of liquidity planning constitutes the foundation of a safe institution that can weather financial turbulence and prosper in the long run.

With liquidity requirements established, the management's next step is to make adequate provisions for the bank's liquidity needs. In other words, management must translate the bank's liquidity requirements into specific assets. A bank's overall need for liquidity may be classified into (1) immediate, for day-to-day operations; (2) seasonal, for deposit shifts and loan demands anticipated in the near future; (3) cyclical or unforeseen, for longer-run deposit shifts and loan demands associated with the business cycle and/or extraordinary developments. Liquidity for a bank's immediate needs can be provided only in the form of cash. Cash is the most liquid form of asset and serves to meet the bank's day-to-day operational requirements. To plan for all other needs, seasonal and cyclical, by adequate cash holdings would require the bank to forego earnings needlessly. It can be just as safe for the bank to invest these funds in highly liquid assets; that is, in assets that with little or no delay or loss of capital can be converted into cash and yet generate for the bank some income.

------

*As implied by the term, a workout arrangement is a process in which the bank works with the borrower for the repayment of the loan instead of resorting to and exhausting every legal means to enforce collection. Such arrangement is not a legal device; it might be described as an austerity program imposed upon borrowers who have been desirable customers of the bank in the past, with their consent and cooperation. Depending upon the case, the steps may include bank advice on varied aspects of business policy to affect the borrower's earning capacity, the bank's active participation in the business, extending or redrawing the loan contract, and advancing additional funds to place the borrower in a stronger financial position.

For the liquidity needs outlined above, funds management should be able to look, respectively, to primary reserves, which are made up of cash and would therefore enable a bank to meet its legal and day-to-day operational requirements; and secondary reserves, which are made up of liquid investment assets and would be held for protective and loan liquidity requirements. Secondary reserves would be divided into seasonal and cyclical to allow for cash needs likely to occur and for those that are remote or less likely but possible. Secondary reserves are the bank's reservoir of near-cash assets that are used to recreate the primary reserves when the latter are drawn down in meeting deposit withdrawal demands. A detailed discussion of both the primary and secondary reserves is undertaken in the following chapter where the actual employment of bank funds is discussed.

SOLVENCY

The maintenance of liquid assets of sufficient amount to meet demands for funds as they are made is, then, one objective of portfolio management. Another is the maintenance of solvency; this is essentially the problem of keeping the realizable value of all assets equal to the value of total liabilities. The former constitutes a short-run objective for bank management while the latter is a long-run objective. Indeed, as we saw, the maintenance of a sufficiently liquid position constitutes the most immediate and compelling obligation of bank management, since failure to meet all claims as they come through would leave management with no alternative but to close bank doors. Solvency, on the other hand, would ensure the safe and hence continued existence of the bank. Unless this objective is constantly considered, the day will come when the short-run objective of liquidity cannot be met. That is, upon the fulfillment of the immediate objective of liquidity depends the ability of the bank to remain open, but upon the achievement of the long-run objective largely depends the attainment of the immediate one.

The basis of an attack on the issue of solvency is suggested by the statement of the problem. The objective of bank management is to keep assets equal to liabilities; as long as such equality exists, a banking concern is solvent. Since bank liabilities are expressed in fixed amounts of money, it is evident that the causes of insolvency lie in changes in the value of bank assets. Indeed, as stated earlier in connection with capital, if the value of assets declines, but less than the amount of bank capital, then capital is said to be impaired, yet the bank is still solvent. But should the assets decline in value until the margin of bank capital is wiped out, then insolvency exists. It is possible for a bank or banks to be insolvent for a shorter or longer period and still remain in business. A number of banks, throughout their individual histories and in one or more instances, have been temporarily in a position where the current market value of their assets failed to cover liabilities. Yet many of them were able to overcome this situation and gradually restore full solvency. With bank insolvency brought about through changes in the value of assets, it is essential that we turn to an examination of the causes of these changes.

One source of difficulty is the continual exposure of bank employees and officials to large sums of money. It is a problem of surety. Indeed, it is by no means unknown that bank employees and officials occasionally bow to temptation and appropriate some of the bank's funds for themselves. As long as individuals are subjected to the financial, social, and moral pressures of our free society, the possibility of bank losses due to defalcation will be, of course, always present. Yet it is to a bank's interest to take all necessary precautions to prevent, to the extent possible, the losses and embarrassment that result from the dishonest acts of its employees and officials.

A bank may protect itself from loss resulting from defalcation by adequate fidelity insurance, though this type of protection merely shifts the burden from the bank to the insurance company. Many difficulties may be avoided by improvements in bank administration, such as using better protective equipment, clarifying the duties of officers and employees, and improving auditing systems. The last includes continuous checking (preauditing), staff cooperation, and frequent postaudits. The best that can be done, therefore, is to control the opportunities and to shorten the time between commitment of an offense and exposure.

But a much more important source of bank difficulty is assets that do not turn out as expected when initially acquired. In an effort to minimize this possibility, both legal prescription and administrative regulation by supervisory authorities have supplemented the judgment of the individual bank in achieving and maintaining solvency. This is done by laying down a framework within which the bank can exercise its discretion. The restrictions are of two kinds. The first, capital requirements for banks, was discussed in the previous chapter. The other type of regulation relates to the classes of assets that banks may acquire and hold. Some of the major rules on the types of assets that banks may acquire and hold may be here conveniently summarized. Banks may not acquire bonds that are regarded, by the principal rating agencies, as predominantly speculative unless such bonds are acquired by way of compromise of a doubtful claim; they may not own corporate stocks unless these have been acquired as collateral on defaulted loans, in which case such stocks are to be disposed of as soon as can reasonably be done without undue loss;* banks may

---

*About the only stocks that commercial banks in the United States are permitted to own are stocks in their own subsidiaries (that is, in a safe-deposit company, in a real estate concern that has been established to own the bank building), in the Federal National Mortgage Association (a governmental agency that provides a market for housing loans insured by the VA and FHA), in corporations established to engage in foreign banking, and in the Federal Reserve Banks of their respective districts, which is viewed as a condition for membership in the Federal Reserve System.

not grant loans on the security of their own stock, nor buy their own stock in the market since this would in effect reduce their outstanding capital, but such stock can be acquired and held temporarily as it enforces payment on outstanding loans; loans to bank officers may not exceed a stated amount; mortgage holdings may be restricted to a specified ratio of time and savings deposits or capital;* the amount that may be lent to any one borrower cannot generally exceed a set percentage of a bank's capital and surplus, and the same limitation applies to holdings of securities of any one obligor (government obligations are exempt from this restriction).† The purpose of these restrictions is to encourage diversification—to compel it, in fact—and so to reduce the risk of asset depreciation. The rules also serve to strengthen the bank's independence from any one extremely large borrower, and also to prevent the bank's resources from being used directly to advance its officers' personal fortunes. But in spite of these safeguards, asset values do deteriorate. The reason for declines in the value of assets is to be found in the risks inherent in bank portfolios.

The previous discussion on the function and importance of bank capital did not elaborate sufficiently on the risks involved in the banking business. Banks are established for a dual purpose: to provide needed services to the public and to earn adequate income to enable themselves to continue as going concerns. Therefore, taking risks can be said to be the business of bank management. A management that runs a bank on the basis of avoiding all risks or as many of them as possible would lead the bank to stagnancy and inadequacy in serving the community's legitimate credit needs. On the other hand, a management that takes excessive risks, or takes such risks without knowing the extent of them, will sooner or later expose the bank difficulty. During periods of economic expansion banks may seem to take some of the risks in banking without apparent implications, because such risks would be obscured beneath the prevailing economic prosperity; however, with the first serious business recession, the preceding period's unsound banking practices will not fail to generate losses, losses which if too large may be decisive as to a bank's continued existence. Between these two extremes there are different gradations of risk taking. Clearly, the degree of risk to be taken by each individual bank is a matter of management judgment. With this in mind, we may now turn to examining the nature of banking risks.

---

*A national bank may not lend on mortgage more than an amount equal either to its capital and surplus or to 100 percent of its time and savings deposits, whichever is larger. No mortgage loans may exceed two-thirds of property value nor run for more than 20 years; however, these limits do not apply to mortgages with government insurance or guarantee.

†This percentage is commonly restricted, with certain exceptions, to 10 percent of a bank's capital and surplus.

By holding debt contracts as the bulk of their assets, banks expose themselves to certain hazards that are due to the uncertainties of future events. These hazards are the risk of default, or credit risk, and the interest rate risk.[14] The most obvious hazard in banking is the risk of default—that is to say, the possibility that the funds loaned or invested will not be repaid, with consequent loss to the bank. In their lending and investing operations few banks ever knowingly make poor loans and investments. In fact, it is what occurs after a loan or investment is made that will be decisive as to whether it will deteriorate in quality or go into default. Such adverse circumstances are generally unforeseeable. One cannot predict, very far ahead, a borrowing firm's ability to meet promptly and fully its promise to pay interest and repay principal. For example, loans made now with every expectation of their being sound can turn out poorly because of an unexpected business recession that adversely affects the borrower's ability to discharge the debt. Even self-liquidating short-term commercial loans get into difficulties in such periods, and may necessitate many renewals or extensions before repayment is finally made. Similarly, long-term commitments that can now be easily handled by the borrower may become impossible due to a future shift of demand away from his product or service. Or perhaps additional future debt may be incurred that may cast doubt on the borrower's ability to carry the larger volume of debt. For these and other reasons reflecting the uncertainty of economic life, default or the fear of possible default may bring about a fall in the market value of assets.

The risk of default ranges from practically no risk, in instruments such as governmental obligations or the highest grade of corporate debt, through many shadings or gradations of risk. The problem of judging gradations of risk requires a considerable degree of skill. For, as seen above, what may appear to be currently within a borrowing firm's ability to pay may five years later turn out not to be the case. The firm's prospects may have definitely turned for the worse because of such developments as a downturn in economic activity, changes in demand, additional future debt, and threats of war. Thus, the further one looks into the future, the less certain one is about the actual ability of the borrower to carry the debt. Because of this uncertainty element the risk of default, and hence the risk to the quality of bank credit, is ever present. This risk element must be covered in the price of the security, and banks typically buy debt that has only slight chance of default. Thus, the price differentials among various debt instruments, other factors being equal, presumably reflect the risk of default. This in itself presents the management of a bank with a problem. To maximize bank profits the management needs high yields, but these are associated with the riskier opportunities. Thus, skill and judgment are required to evaluate the opportunities open to the bank—for, if the loan or investment is defaulted, not only does income suffer but solvency is also impaired.

Even if there is absolutely no question at all about the debt being repaid along with the interest paid regularly when due, there can still be changes in the market value of assets held. Thus where there is practically no question of the credit standing of the debtor in making present and future payments, fluctuations in the price of debt instruments are dominated by the interest rate risk. This is another type of ever-present risk in banking, and commercial bank exposure to it occurs when customer demand for funds (deposit or loan demand) necessitates the liquidation of the debt instruments held at a loss. A depositor's withdrawal demand is one that a bank must honor promptly; failure to do so would force the bank to go out of business. During periods of decline in economic activity, such as the depression of the 1930s in the United States, withdrawal demands originate mainly from depositors who come on the run to convert their deposits into currency because of distrust in banks generally. The danger of such panics and the accompanying runs on banks have been greatly reduced, if not eliminated, by such banking reforms as the establishment of a deposit insurance system, stricter banking laws, and a greatly improved bank supervision. These reforms have contributed in strengthening the banking structure and the confidence of the public in banks.

Of more significance to banking policy, however, is the depositor withdrawal demand during boom periods. In such instances, depositors tend to draw down their deposit balances to take advantage of outlets for remuneration greater than the bank is willing or permitted to pay for their funds, that is, invest them in money market instruments. Eventually, of course, the checks drawn for the purchase of these securities will be redeposited by their recipients in various banks; however, this flow of deposits from one bank to another would prove embarrassing to the bank that loses them.

But along with depositor withdrawal demand, banks also experience during such periods an even more significant demand for funds, namely, a heavy demand for credit from their customers. This demand provides commercial banks with strong incentives to expand their loan portfolio and hence to increase bank earnings. During such periods, however, monetary authorities rely almost exclusively on bank credit restraint to promote a sustainable rate of economic growth and to counter inflationary pressures. Banks that cannot then obtain funds from other sources (that is, through liability management) on an acceptable cost basis would have no alternative but to resort to their investment portfolio and liquidate securities to meet the extensive credit demands. Such a process of financing additional loan demands is for banks a costly one, especially if the securities liquidated are bonds of intermediate- or longer-term maturity, the prices of which are generally affected by even moderate changes in the level of interest rates.

It may be argued, of course, that a bank could always refuse to grant additional credit. This, however, is not always possible. For example, a bank could hardly afford to refuse to accommodate the loan request of a depositor of long standing who has maintained large balances with the bank. The same would hold true for the loan request of a firm that plays an important role in the growth of the region, or for the request of the local municipality that is interested in the financing of a project that is vitally essential to local welfare. Refusal on the part of the bank to meet these and other similar loan requests could lead to the closing of deposit accounts and the loss of valuable customers.

To protect itself against the losses that would result from the forced sale or liquidation of long-term assets in meeting customer demands for funds, a bank must maintain adequate liquidity. Estimating a bank's liquidity needs, both for the short and intermediate term, was discussed in the preceding section. If the bank's calculations are reasonably accurate there should be no need to dispose of long-term portfolio assets in advance of their maturity because of any demands made upon the bank by depositors or borrowers. With economic forecasting, however, at best an inexact science, there is always the possibility of forced liquidation of bank security holdings in advance of maturity because of customer demands for funds. In some instances, such liquidation may even be prompted by tax considerations (to establish a capital loss, which will be charged against current income). Regardless of the factor that gives rise to the need to sell in advance of maturity, the prevailing level of interest rates in the market will be a critical factor when sale is contemplated.

The general level of interest rates, at any given time, is the product of the interplay of the demand for and the supply of funds in the market. The demand for funds is affected by the level of business activity; it rises when business activity expands and it declines when such activity slackens. The supply of funds, on the other hand, is affected by the monetary policy pursued: a policy of monetary ease (easy money policy) has an expansive effect upon the reserves of the banking system, and hence upon the extension of credit by commercial banks and—through them—by other lenders, while a policy of monetary restraint (tight money policy) has a contractive effect upon the system's reserves and therefore upon credit extension. During periods of monetary ease, market rates generally tend to decline, while in periods of restraint they further increase.

The general level of interest rates, as this is affected by the market demand and supply forces, will determine, at the time of the liquidation, whether or not the market value of the securities owned declines, and hence whether or not capital losses will be sustained. Specifically, the market value of securities moves inversely to changes in the current market rate of interest. Thus, if as a result of market forces, the going rate of interest moves up, the market value of debt instruments calling for fixed payments over time (based on some previous lower rate) will fall. To illustrate this, let us assume that a bond is purchased bearing an interest rate of 6 percent and maturing in 20 years. If the bond is purchased at par (100 percent of face value), its market price would be $1,000. Suppose that subsequent to this purchase, the market rate of interest for comparable quality bonds rises to 8 percent. Clearly the market value of this bond will be affected. What the bond is worth can be determined by the use of the following present value calculations of the lump sum at maturity and the stream of interest payments:

Present value (PV) of the $1,000 maturity value:
$$PV= \$1,000 \ (.215) = \$215$$
PV of the stream of interest payments:
$$PV= \$60 \ (9.818) = \$589.08$$
Hence, bond value $= \$215 + \$589.08 = \$804.08$

Thus as the result of an increase in the going rate of interest to 8 percent, the value of the bond will decline to yield a competitive rate of return. At the price of $804.08 this bond provides an annual rate of return of 8 percent. It follows that a change in interest rates affects inversely the value of a bond with consequent effects upon its yield. A rise in interest rates depreciates the value of lower-interest-bearing bonds, causing their yield to increase, while a decrease in interest rates appreciates the value of higher-interest-bearing bonds, causing their yield to decrease.

This fall in price will be similar for all bonds of similar risk and maturity. If coupon rates of interest differ, market prices will tend to fall accordingly to keep the yields in line with one another. The longer the period that the instrument has before it matures, the greater will be the fall in its market price. This point can be well illustrated by making reference to the above example. Suppose, for example, that the initial purchase included two additional bonds of the same quality and bearing the same interest as the one described above, but of longer maturities. Specifically, let us assume that one of these had a maturity of 25 years, and the other, of 30 years. In such a case, the rise in interest rates to 8 percent will cause the value of the 25-year-maturity bond to decline to $786.50 and the value of the 30-year-maturity bond to decline to $774.48. Clearly, the effect of this rise in interest rates is accentuated by the longer maturity of the debt instrument. By the same token, a decrease in interest rates would cause the value of the longer-maturity bonds to appreciate more than that of the shorter-maturity ones.

Clearly then, the longer the maturity of the securities owned by the bank, the greater the decline in their market value and hence the larger the capital losses to be sustained by the bank, which is forced to convert them into cash.[15] But even if the bank may not have to sell the bonds that have declined in price because of the change in the rate of interest, the bank is not realizing the same amount of income it could be receiving at the higher rate if it had not invested in the bonds it now holds.

The interest rate risk is, therefore, inherent in all contracts calling for fixed payments over time. Consequently bonds that are free of any default risk are still subject to the interest rate risk, since the future level of interest rates is uncertain. This fact could make a case for the loading up of short-term securities by the banks since such securities are insulated from wide fluctuations in value. This is another aspect of liquidity, then. Even a long-term bond may become part of a bank's secondary reserves as it approaches maturity. This means that the realizable price in the event of its liquidation is more certain, and differs from its stated redemption value by only a small amount. But, of course, by loading up on short-term securities the bank precludes much chance of capital appreciation, should interest rates fall.

Consequently, to prevent insolvency and an ensuing closing, a bank's management may take certain precautions, such as limiting investments to government securities that are default free or to corporate securities of the highest grade, diversifying their investment and loan portfolios, administering loans properly, setting up valuation reserves,* strengthening the bank's capital structure so as to provide a cushion between capital stock and deposit liabilities, adopting procedures and purchasing equipment that will discourage embezzlers, and purchasing adequate fidelity insurance. Of these precautionary measures, the importance of adequate capitalization was discussed in Chapter 1, and banks' loan and investment policies will be discussed in Chapters 4 and 5.

INCOME

In addition to maintaining solvency and liquidity, a bank must also achieve a sufficient income on its portfolio to pay operating costs and provide a competitive return on the capital ventured in the enterprise. In the quest for income, management must always keep in mind the need for maintaining liquidity and solvency. In fact, it should never subordinate the need for liquidity and safety to the income function. While income is definitely important, and clearly essential for the successful performance of a continuing banking operation, the aggressive pursuit of income per se, without regard to these other factors, could rapidly precipitate the collapse of the bank. The employment of bank funds must, in the first place, be consistent with the bank's liquidity needs and, secondly, be within the limits of the amount of risk that capital available for the portfolio can bear. Within the confines of these two basic policy considerations, efforts may be directed toward the realization of adequate income. Management has some choice in the way in which income may be sought and also in the way in which profits are used.

---

*As was stated in Chapter 1 in connection with a bank's capital structure, valuation reserves represent earnings earmarked to cover losses resulting from portfolio exposure to bank risks. Valuation reserves are hence offsets to asset accounts and take the form of reserves for losses on bank earning assets, that is, loans and/or investments.

The importance of profits to commercial banks is hard to exaggerate. Profits are a decisive factor for the continued existence of a bank and its success as a going concern. Profits represent the return on the capital funds invested in the bank. In fact it is for this return that shareholders are willing to supply the capital that will enable the bank to fulfill its role as the chief credit-granting institution in the economy. If the return on existing capital is not comparable to the returns on other investments, capital will, in the long run, be attracted to other economic pursuits. Profits moreover constitute an important source of bank capital. It is a common practice of banks to retain a relatively large portion of their earnings for capital additions. To the extent that profits are used for the payment of dividends, they have favorable effects upon the marketability and value of bank shares, thereby rendering it possible for the bank to return to the market and raise additional capital to finance expansion and improvement in banking practices. But depositors, too, benefit from bank profits, as they result in a stronger, safer, and more efficient banking structure by increasing reserves and improving banking services offered. Borrowers also have interest, indirectly, in bank profits. Bank policy of plowing back earnings into equity capital results in a larger capital account and therefore in an increased commercial bank lending and investing ability. Indeed with an increase in the size of capital, banks can make larger loans to any single borrower and invest larger amounts in the securities of any single issuer. Even those economic groups that do not directly use commercial bank services benefit indirectly from adequate bank profits. The reason is that bank profits contribute to the strengthening of the banking structure, which results in the safety of deposits and the availability of credit to the economy, with consequences that are felt throughout it and are reflected in the nation's economic welfare.

Banking is a service business; like many service businesses, its operating expenses are to a large extent fixed, especially in the short run. Thus bank expenses in the short run are not closely correlated with the volume of business done or with the gross profit. With bank costs, therefore, fairly constant in the short run, the maximization of income and minimization of variable costs maximizes profits.

In evaluating assets for income purposes, the basic element to consider is the yield that a bank can expect from the various loan and investment choices open to it. Three factors usually are weighed by management in attempting to estimate the probable yield from some loan and investment opportunity: (1) the likeliest value of gross receipts from a given asset while it is in the bank's portfolio; (2) the variable cost involved in ownership of the asset; and (3) the price or actual cost of procuring the earning asset. Each of these will play a part in management's estimation of the yield from a given asset. Only on the third factor can management have definite knowledge, but regarding the first two factors, only educated estimates are available. Hence, yield is largely conditioned by the accuracy of management's estimates. Let us look more closely at each of these factors in determining yield.

The estimation of the gross receipts obtainable from a lending or an investing opportunity is often a difficult matter. As already noted, a typical debt contract calls for a stated number of payments of some stated sum. In the instance of governmental obligations, fulfillment of the obligation is virtually certain; but in consumer and even business loans, the possibility of default must be weighed in an estimation of the gross receipts that may be obtained. But, as noted earlier in discussing solvency, debt contracts are also subjected to interest rate risk. We have observed then that when a bank purchases securities, it faces the possibility of being forced to sell them in advance of their maturity to meet deposit withdrawals or loan demands. Bankers can never be certain of the future market price obtainable for a security; such price can result in a capital loss on resale if interest rates increase while the security is in the bank's portfolio. Hence, estimate of gross receipts involves both the specified payments as already contracted, and any capital gain or loss if the security is sold prior to its maturity.

Consequently, in estimating the gross receipts obtainable from an earning asset, a distinction must be made between investments and loans. The investment portion of a commercial bank's portfolio includes all those financial assets that are bought and sold in the open market. Hence, investments are marketable debt instruments, to which there is always attached the interest rate risk—the possibility of losing money whenever it may be necessary to sell the instrument. Conversely, the loan portion of a bank's portfolio is made up of nonmarketable instruments. When loans are made a bank is not concerned with the interest rate risk since it cannot and does not plan to dispose of such loans. But it is concerned with the risk of default that is present here. Loans have the advantage of higher gross receipts over investments, but they also entail greater risk. To loan to a high-risk borrower is to increase bank income if all goes well, but to court insolvency if it does not.

It is evident that estimates of gross receipts are subject to wide margins of error. Such estimates are at best subjective based on as much objective fact as possible.*

It is doubtless easier for bank management to estimate the cost associated with ownership of an asset than to forecast the gross receipts of that asset. The larger banks generally have detailed data on the supplementary costs pertaining to expansion of their portfolios through addition of new earning assets,

---

*This argument may be illustrated by citing the experience of one of the largest West Coast banks and one of the country's largest. In 1958, in anticipation of a light loan demand, this bank loaded up on long-term Treasury bonds. It turned out, however, that the private loan demand was quite heavy, and to meet it required the liquidation of practically all short-term governmental obligations and sizable sums of long-term ones as well, the latter at a loss. As the bank's annual report put it, the bank sustained losses in the selling of the long-term bonds to obtain necessary funds to meet the unexpected loan demand.

these costs constituting the bank's variable costs. Banks normally know what it costs to service varied types of loans and investments, whether handling a purchase of government securities, or merely arranging term loans for businesses. Since for a given class of loan or investment the servicing costs are fairly constant regardless of amount involved, the larger the principal sum, the more profitable it is for the bank.

The third factor determining yield on a loan or investment is the price or actual cost of the earning asset, which, as we have observed, is the only concrete factor of the three, the other two being to some extent subjective estimates.

We can now put the above information together and estimate the yield of this asset for the bank. The first step in this respect is to establish a net expected revenue figure. This can be arrived at by deducting from the expected gross receipts obtainable periodically from the asset, while it is in the bank's portfolio, the corresponding variable cost connected with holding the asset. Once the net cash inflow or net expected stream of revenue is determined, the rate of return can be established with the help of a mathematical formula. The easiest way in which this rate of return can be expressed as a simple numerical value is to find the rate of discount that makes the present value of the expected future stream of revenue exactly equal to the cost of the asset. Stated differently, the yield or rate of return is the discount rate that makes the estimated net receipts exactly equal to the known cost of acquiring the asset.

The equation for calculating yield is:

$$V = \frac{R_1}{(1+r)^1} + \frac{R_2}{(1+r)^2} + \cdots + \frac{R_N + M}{(1+r)^N}$$

Here V is the cost of acquiring the asset; R_1, R_2, and so forth represent the net cash flows; r is the unknown internal rate of return; N is the asset's expected life; and M, the principal at maturity. We can illustrate the application of this formula by making reference, for example, to the purchase of a bond. Thus, let us assume that a three-year bond is acquired for $948.62, generating an annual interest income of $60 and at the end of the third year (at maturity) $1,000. The equation would be:

$$\$948.62 = \frac{\$60}{1+r} + \frac{\$60}{(1+r)_2} + \frac{1,060}{(1+r)_3}$$

Solving for r, we find that the rate that makes the total present value of future income equal the cost of the asset is 8 percent.

An approximate yield estimate can be derived by means of a simple arithmetical computation. The formula that may be used in this respect is:

$$\text{Yield to maturity} = \frac{\begin{array}{c}\text{annual dollar} \; + \; \text{annual accumulation or}\\ \text{coupon interest} \; - \; \text{annual amortization}\end{array}}{\dfrac{\text{Current market} + \text{par value}}{2}}$$

Here we can use the information of the example illustrated above and calculate, with the use of this formula, the approximate yield to maturity. The example mentioned a three-year bond acquired at the price of $948.62 bearing a 6 percent rate of interest. Since this bond at maturity will be redeemed for $1,000, the investor will receive an appreciation of:

$$\frac{(\$1,000-\$948.62)}{3} = \frac{\$51.38}{3} = \$17.127 \text{ per year}$$

To determine the yield, we also need to ascertain average investment, which can be established by averaging the cost of the bond ($948.62) and the par value at maturity ($1,000). Using this information on the above formula, we have:

$$\text{Yield to maturity} = \frac{\$60 \; + \; \$17.127}{\dfrac{948.62 + 1,000}{2}} = \frac{77.127}{974.31} = 7.916 \text{ percent}$$

If the bond was bought at a premium, the above calculation would differ in that we would need to amortize the premium on an annual basis and hence charge it off to annual interest income.

In determining the profitability of alternative earning asset opportunities, estimates of such profitability are heavily colored by feelings of optimism or pessimism on the part of the bank. Indeed, the way banks view the future plays an important role in determining the profitability of earning assets and therefore in bank decisions to acquire such assets or not. Thus, though based on objective facts, the estimation of yield involves a partly subjective element—anticipations. When bank expectations are pessimistic, estimates of future revenues would be very conservative and the yields of earning assets would appear low and unattractive. This would lead banks to refrain from acquiring earning assets and instead hold on to their excess reserves. Such a situation would have as its result that bank revenues would decline and fixed costs would undermine net worth. On the other hand, when bank expectations are overly optimistic, future revenues would be estimated very generously and the yields would appear very attractive. In consequence, banks would acquire earning assets. With elements of emotion and intuition underlying such purchases, it is likely that estimates would turn out badly, in which case the result for the bank would be insolvency. Obviously, in any future-oriented decision, elements of risk and uncertainty are invariably present.

The height of the yield has only relative importance in determining commercial bank acquisition of earning assets. In evaluating earning asset alternatives, consideration must also be given to the balancing of short-run profit opportunities against long-run profit maximizing. What this means is that with management having decided in favor of one of the opportunities open to it, it might be necessary to forego the purchase of some other kind of asset. Management usually attempts to balance short-term profit opportunities having the added incentive of safety against those yielding long-term profit but carrying great elements of risk. For example, the choice of management may lie between purchasing short-term government securities and lending locally to a struggling, but promising, young business firm. If the bank purchases the government security, it will earn a definite, though perhaps smaller, return but enjoy relative safety, since it runs no risk of default and a smaller chance of loss if it must liquidate the asset. But over and against this safety factor, management must weigh the long-term opportunity for establishing a continuing credit relationship with the fledgling local business, for the latter will both become a depositor and make use of the bank's varied other services. For after all, the typical bank is intimately tied to its own particular community and the interests of that community. Thus bank loans to local businesses and residents may, in the long run, benefit a bank many times over by increasing its earnings over the years. It follows that by accommodating worthy local customers first, even at the expense, if necessary, of turning down outside borrowers, a bank may be maximizing profits in the long run by incurring greater risks than short-run profit considerations justify. For, the bulk of the bank's deposits and other income producing activities, such as trust accounts, will be due to its serving of local persons and business firms. Clearly then, however inviting the yields of individual assets, the decision to purchase one asset instead of another is frequently based on the long-run benefits the bank may enjoy through exercising its options.[16]

The income performance of a bank constitutes the end result of the portfolio policies pursued. What is true for a bank holds true also for the banking industry as a whole. Figure 9 provides an illustration of the income performance of commercial banks in the United States throughout the postwar period. As shown, the composition of operating income in commercial banks changed dramatically during this period. Thus from 1946 to 1975, income from loans rose from a mere 33 percent to 69 percent of current operating earnings of commercial banks. A record high of 75 percent of such earnings was attained in 1974. At the same time there was a large decline in the share of income derived from security holdings. This change in the relative importance of loan income as against security income in commercial bank earnings reflects essentially postwar shifts in bank holdings of earning assets. The rapid growth in the demand for credit since the end of the war has made bank loans the most important form of banks' earning assets.

FIGURE 9

Current Operating Revenues, All Insured Commercial Banks
(distribution in percent)

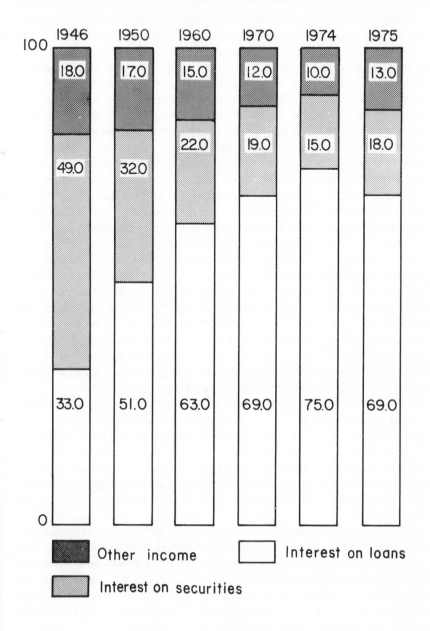

Source: Federal Deposit Insurance Corp. *Annual Reports* (Washington, D.C.: Federal Deposit Insurance Corp., 1946–75).

Second to bank income from loans and securities is income derived from the services banks render. Despite the large number of services banks perform for their clients, the proportion of total operating earnings derived from service charges and other sources has been of declining importance.

Operating expenses for all insured commercial banks, for the 1946–75 period, are shown in Figure 10. Total expenses for these banks increased from 62 percent of current operating revenues in 1946 to 86 percent of such revenues in 1975. Interest on time and savings deposits has grown to be the largest single item of operating expenses. In 1946 this item amounted to 9 percent of current operating revenues, rising by 1975 to 39 percent of such revenues. The growth in the relative importance of this item has been due to the growth in the amount of time accounts held by banks and in the rate of interest paid. With the increased demand for funds in the postwar years and the accompanying increase in rates on loans and investments, banks have been able to pay a higher rate. It appears, because of the intense competition for time and savings deposits, that bank expenses for this item will further increase in the future.

Salaries and wages has been the second largest single item of operating expenses. In 1946 salaries, wages, and fees accounted for 30 percent of operating revenues as compared to 19 percent in 1975. This decrease in the relative importance of salaries was basically the result of the much faster rise in the operating revenues of commercial banks throughout this period. The importance of this item, which in 1975 amounted to $12.6 billion, is characteristic of a service industry. Many of the services offered by banks are of a personal nature and require individual rather than mechanical performance. Credit analysis, trust services, and the investment function require an analysis and judgment that cannot be performed by machines.

Other expenses include a number of items that individually are insignificant but collectively appear relatively important. These include the expense of occupying bank premises—net, furniture and equipment; taxes other than on net incomes (that is, property tax); depreciation; interest on borrowed money; and such miscellaneous items as assessment for deposit insurance, other insurance premiums, supplies, and advertising expenses. This category accounted for 23 percent of current operating revenues in 1946 as compared to 28 percent in 1975.

In arriving at the banks' net income picture, allowance must be made for nonoperating income and expense items. Nonoperating incomes are usually made up of such items as profits on the sale or redemption of securities, recoveries on loans originally charged off, and profits on real estate sold, if any. Nonoperating expenses include loan losses, losses on the sale or redemption of securities, transfers to reserve accounts, contributions to a retirement or pension plan, and losses on forged checks.

The profitability of insured commercial banks is shown in Table 3, where it is compared to that of all corporations that filed income tax returns in the

FIGURE 10

Current Operating Expenses as Percent of Total Operating Revenues,
All Insured Commercial Banks
(distribution in percent)

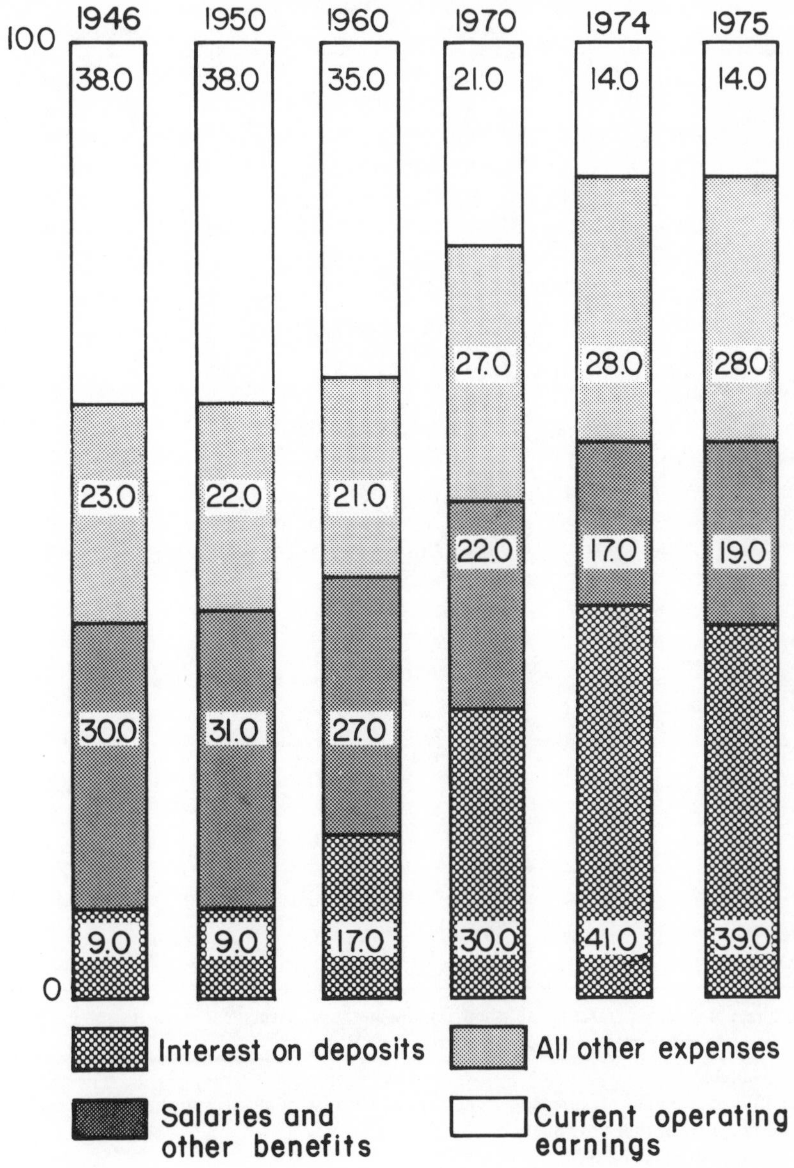

Source: Federal Deposit Insurance Corp., *Annual Reports* (Washington, D.C.: Federal Deposit Insurance Corp., 1946–75).

TABLE 3

Rate of Return on Capital of All Insured Commercial Banks as Against that of Corporations, 1946–75 (percent)

Year	Banks	Corporations
1946	10.0	9.9
1947	8.2	11.3
1948	7.5	11.4
1949	8.0	8.7
1950	8.5	11.3
1951	7.8	9.0
1952	8.1	7.7
1953	7.9	7.5
1954	9.5	7.1
1955	7.9	8.5
1956	7.8	7.9
1957	8.3	7.1
1958	9.6	5.5
1959	7.9	6.5
1960	10.0	7.0[a]
1961	9.4	7.0
1962	8.8	_b
1963	8.9	7.6
1964	8.7	8.4
1965	8.7	9.5
1966	8.7	9.8
1967	9.6	9.0
1968	9.7	8.7
1969	11.5[c]	7.7
1970	11.9	6.8
1971	11.8	7.5
1972	11.6	8.2[d]
1973	12.1	_b
1974	11.9	_b
1975	11.2	_b
Average	9.4	8.3

[a] All preceding years' rates established on the basis of fiscal year data. From 1960 on, rates are established on the basis of calendar year data.

[b] Not available.

[c] Not fully comparable to preceding years' rates because of changes in the form of reporting introduced from that year on.

[d] Based on preliminary data.

Sources: U.S. Treasury Department, Internal Revenue Service, *Statistics of Income: Corporation Income Tax Returns* (Washington, D.C.: Internal Revenue Service, 1946–72); Federal Deposit Insurance Corp., *Annual Reports* (Washington, D.C.: Federal Deposit Insurance Corp., 1946–75).

period 1946–75. Rate-of-return estimates are in both cases established on the basis of the ratio of net profits after taxes to equity capital. On an average basis the return on bank capital throughout this period was 9.4 percent, compared to an 8.3 percent return for all corporations. The return on bank capital invested reached an unprecedented 12.1 percent in 1973, a year in which bank loans grew rapidly with consequential effects upon bank income. The rate of return on stockholders' equity in all corporations showed greater variation in this period than was found in commercial banking. Thus, return to corporate stockholders' equity varied from a low of 5.5 percent to 11.4 percent, while the return in commercial banking varied only from 7.5 to 12.1 percent. Bank profitability was thus relatively more stable than corporate profitability. This does not mean, however, that commercial banking is an industry that does not suffer from cyclical fluctuations. Bank profits are influenced by the business cycle, but a bank's ability to invest in loans when loan demand is high, and in securities when the demand for loans is not great, reduces variability of bank profits. Banking is generally a profitable business. There are very few unprofitable banks, and when unprofitableness does occur, it is more commonly the result of capital rather than of operating losses.

SUMMARY

The emphasis in this chapter has been on the objectives of portfolio management: to provide the bank with liquidity, solvency, and income. These particular objectives are, of course, not unique to banking. Most nonbank businesses pursue the same goals, with liquidity often subordinated to the other two, especially to income. Not so, however, for the commercial bank. The commercial bank is unique in that all of its deposit liabilities, which constitute at the same time the major source of bank funds, are payable on demand or after short notice. If it cannot meet demands for payment it cannot remain in business. Hence the overriding emphasis on liquidity.

The fact that bank funds are derived from fixed value liabilities requires that the bulk of the bank's assets take the form of specific claims that would be reasonably protected against any qualitative or monetary deterioration. This concern constitutes the essence of the solvency objective.

Income must be pursued within the confines of the other two basic policy considerations. A bank's income performance serves as a barometer for both creditors and stockholders of the bank's success as a going concern.

These objectives then determine the pattern and distribution of assets in the portfolio. Portfolio management is thus a matter of combining various classes of assets in order to achieve the optimum balance between liquidity, solvency, and income. Portfolio management is but a variation of the old economic dictum: the allocation of scarce means among competing ends. The issue presented to banks, then, is the familiar one of maximizing profit while providing for liquidity and solvency. The manner in which management goes about in the pursuit of this goal is the ultimate test of its efficacy and success.

The following chapter will examine the means—bank assets—by which management attains the portfolio objectives; the chapter discusses the character and composition of bank assets.

NOTES

1. Roland I. Robinson, *The Management of Bank Funds,* 2d ed. (New York: McGraw-Hill Book Co., 1962), p. 4.

2. Howard D. Crosse, *Management Policies for Commercial Banks* (Englewood Cliffs, N.J.: Prentice-Hall, 1962), p. 134.

3. Roger A. Lyon, *Investment Portfolio Management in the Commercial Bank* (New Brunswick, N.J.: Rutgers University Press, 1960), p. 10. For his usage of this term, Lyon refers to Robinson, who makes extensive use of it when discussing bank liquidity.

4. Ibid.

5. Crosse, op. cit.

6. Ibid., p. 135.

7. Ibid., p. 137.

8. American Bankers Association, Economic Policy Commission, *The Problems of Commercial Bank Liquidity* (New York: American Bankers Association, 1957), p. 2.

9. Crosse, op. cit., p. 140.

10. Ibid.

11. Lyon, op. cit., p. 17.

12. Ibid., p. 19.

13. *American Bankers Association, Economic Policy Commission,* op. cit., p. 3.

14. For an elaborate discussion of the investment risks of default (financial risk) and of interest rates, see Harry Sauvain, *Investment Management,* 3d ed. rev. (Englewood Cliffs, N.J.: Prentice-Hall, 1967), Chapters 6 and 7.

15. For a detailed discussion on how a change in interest rates affects the market prices, and hence the yields, of securities of different maturities, see Sauvain, op. cit., pp. 169–79.

16. This point is effectively developed by Donald R. Hodgman in *Commercial Bank Loan and Investment Policy* (Champaign: University of Illinois, Bureau of Economic and Business Research, 1963).

CHAPTER

3

USES OF COMMERCIAL
BANK FUNDS: ASSET
LIQUIDITY RESERVES

The preceding chapter suggests that bank management must be guided by some sort of order of priorities in the use of bank funds. That is, if a bank is to discharge its community obligations in a satisfactory manner and continue as a going concern, available funds must be allocated on the basis of anticipated requirements of differing degrees of urgency. To do so is implicit in any attempt to provide a rational solution to the fundamental banking problem. The "schedule of priorities" suggested by Robinson indicates that bank funds are used in four basic ways: to maintain primary reserves, to provide secondary reserves, to meet customer demands for funds, and to make open-market purchases of earning assets.[1]

Of top priority in a bank's employment of its funds is the maintenance of adequate primary reserves, that is, of enough cash resources. Primary reserves, or cash assets, enable a bank to meet its legal and day-to-day operating requirements. Nothing else can provide the immediate liquidity of cash holdings. Indeed, these assets are immediately available with no risk of loss whatsoever. But cash holdings generate no income.

Secondary reserves, or protective investments, perform precisely the role suggested by their name. These are assets that yield some income to the bank, but more importantly, they can be converted from an earning asset into cash with little or no delay or loss of principal. These assets are held for protective and loan liquidity requirements that are of a seasonal as well as cyclical nature. In Robinson's words, these assets will provide funds, if necessary, "(1) for likely and indeed almost forecastable cash needs, (2) for remote, unlikely, but possible cash needs."[2] The secondary reserve account is the principal source of liquidity and, as such, its function is to provide funds to meet deposit declines or loan increases. It is a reservoir of near-cash assets that is drawn upon to replenish the primary reserves, when these become depleted.

The first two priorities serve to insure the bank's ability to continue in business by meeting the claims presented to it for payment. After providing for these the bank is able to consider its third priority item, customers' needs for funds. The commercial bank has a basic function to fulfill in making funds available to the local community. Traditionally banks have been primarily direct lenders to their customers. Business firms have been demanding credit to finance their productive and distributive processes; consumers, to finance the acquisition of goods and services for which they will pay at a later date. Through extending credit to customers whose operations and needs are intimately known and understood, commercial banks will tend to have a thorough knowledge of the local market. This advantage of banks over other financial institutions, however, does not extend into transactions in the open market for investments. In this market, financial institutions (that is, insurance companies and trust funds) play a more important role because of the more stable nature of their liabilities and the large investment research staffs they maintain.

The last use of bank funds is in the purchase of investment securities in the open market. If the first three use priorities have not exhausted bank lendable funds, then, to maximize income, the otherwise idle funds are used in the open market purchase of earning assets. The investment portfolio, therefore, is residual in character, although this should not be taken to imply any inferiority in the quality of assets of which it is composed. As a matter of fact, the quality of these assets is for the bank as important as that of the loan portfolio assets. Because the average commercial bank is too small to afford the research staff of other financial institutions, banks resort to quality recommendations made by private rating agencies.

The above discussion reveals that the asset mix owned by a bank is conditioned by a diversity of factors. Some assets are held because they are legally required or because they are necessary for efficient operation; these are a bank's primary reserves, or cash assets. The rest of the bank's assets are income yielding and comprise its loans and investments. Part of these earning assets are held with only secondary consideration given to earnings; these are secondary reserves and are made up basically of gilt-edged open market investments that produce some income but, most importantly, can be readily converted into cash. Hence viewed according to the type of assets held, there is no distinction whatsoever between a bank's loans and investments on the one hand and secondary reserves on the other. But when bank earning assets are viewed according to the function or role fulfilled in a bank's portfolio, then there is a distinct difference. Secondary reserves constitute a bank's protective investment in liquid assets while loans and investments are held primarily for the income they produce. Hence from a functional point of view, the assets held by a bank are divided into three categories: primary reserves, secondary reserves, and loans and investments.

We propose, then, to examine each of these specific categories of bank assets as related to the portfolio objectives discussed in the preceding chapter. In this chapter we shall discuss primary and secondary reserves, and in the succeeding chapters, loans and investments.

PRIMARY RESERVES

Primary reserves, or cash assets, are one of the categories of assets most frequently referred to by bank management, banking regulations, and banking authorities. The term itself is an economic rather than an accounting concept, coined to designate certain ideas about a group of bank assets. Hence the term as such is not to be found in a bank's statement of condition (balance sheet), but it is a key part of the functional balance sheet that stresses the uses of the bank's resources.

As stated earlier, the assets generally designated as primary reserves are those nonearning assets of commercial banks that are in the form of cash or convertible into it on demand. Primary reserves constitute a bank's source of pledgeable assets. Indeed, primary reserves enable commercial banks to fulfill the requirement of the law that they maintain cash reserves against their deposits. One function of primary reserves, therefore, is to meet legal reserve requirements. Another function of primary reserves is to serve as the first line of defense in meeting the withdrawals of depositors; that is, primary reserves ensure the capacity of the commercial banks to meet the withdrawal demands of depositors. Depositors can draw against their deposit accounts, of course, either by demanding hand-to-hand money or by writing checks payable to others. If they demand hand-to-hand money, the bank must pay out of its cash holdings carried in the vault. If they write checks, the bank must use its balances with other banking institutions (the Federal Reserve Bank and correspondent banks) to meet them as they come in for payment through clearing channels (provided, of course, that the clearing balance is "adverse," that is, that the amount of incoming checks on any day exceeds the amount of checks upon which the bank obtains payment from other banks on that day.) These different functions of primary reserves led to the distinction between legal reserves (the cash reserves that the law requires a bank to maintain with the Federal Reserve Bank) and working reserves, which are held in the form of vault currency, cash terms in process of collection, and deposits at other banks, including deposits at the Federal Reserve Bank over and above the amount required by law, that is, excess reserves.

Wherever commercial banking has developed, the need for cash reserves has been universally demonstrated. At first, the size of cash reserves held by commercial banks was merely a product of individual bank experience. The epidemics of bank failures—which occurred in the histories of many nations —proved, however, that banks used to operate beyond the bounds of prudence. This fact led banking authorities in this country to legally introduce prudent liquidity standards to ensure commercial bank ability to meet withdrawals of deposit in cash. Provisions for legally required reserves were thus introduced for the first time in the banking history of the United States in 1864 with the passage of the National Bank Act. These provisions were modified later on with the establishment of the Federal Reserve System in 1914, but the basic idea of requiring banks to maintain cash in some prudent proportion to their deposit liabilities was continued. Observing legally required reserves thus became part of the management of bank funds.

In compliance with this requirement, member banks of the Federal Reserve System are required to maintain at the Federal Reserve Bank of their district a prescribed amount of cash reserves.* Member bank reserve requirements vary according to the designation of the commercial bank and the size and classification of the deposits. The legal limits of reserve requirements are as follows:

	Minimum Percent	Maximum Percent
Net demand deposits, reserve city banks	10	22
Net demand deposits, other banks	7	14
Time deposits, all banks	3	10

Net demand deposits are determined as follows: gross demand deposits minus cash items in process of collection and demand balances due from domestic banks. The current reserve city designations are as follows. A bank having net demand deposits of more than $400 million is considered to have the character of business of a reserve city bank, and the presence of the head office of such a bank constitutes designation of that place as a reserve city. Cities in which there are Federal Reserve Banks or branches are also reserve cities. Banks that do not fall in the above categories are classified as "other banks," and are subject to lower requirements as indicated above.[3] The legal reserves are computed on the basis of deposits outstanding on the bank's books over a short

---

*Reserve requirements of nonmember banks vary considerably both as to amount and nature. Many of the states have patterned their reserve requirements after those adopted by the Federal Reserve, while others have maintained requirements above those for comparable member banks. But important differences exist also as to the composition of reserves. In most cases the reserves of nonmember banks include balances on deposit with other commercial banks, and these funds can be loaned or invested by the correspondent banks. Nonmember bank reserves may even be in the form of government securities.

period of time. Statutory regulations do not permit legal reserves to be depleted for any extended period of time. Indeed, the latitude allowed for deviation from legally required reserves is generally very little and any deficiency in reserves entails considerable financial penalty. Since the law does not permit legal reserves to be depleted for any extended period of time in order to meet demands for cash, required reserves can no longer be considered as a significant source of liquidity and hence a bulwark of protection. "Thus we find the paradox: in practice, a bank cannot depend on its legal cash-reserve requirement to meet deposit shrinkage; this must come mainly from other assets."[4]

In addition to possessing a low degree of liquidity, reserve requirements also involve a loss in bank income. A bank's gross earnings and in turn its net profits are determined both by the amount of loanable and investible funds on hand and the efficiency with which these funds are employed. Clearly, the required maintenance of legal reserves with regulatory authorities is a limiting factor in a bank's supply of loanable and investible funds and hence in a bank's earnings prospects.

The function of legal reserves today is a very basic one. Their existence is now justified not on the grounds of enforcing minimum liquidity standards of managerial prudence, but rather for providing a tool of monetary policy. Indeed, it is now generally recognized that reserve requirements serve primarily as a control device through which monetary authorities can at any time influence the availability and cost of credit. More specifically, by altering upwards or downwards reserve requirements, monetary authorities can effectively decrease or increase the ability of commercial banks to lend and invest, and therefore affect accordingly the volume of bank deposits, the major part of money supply. This manipulation of reserve requirements is, or course, streamlined with the objectives of monetary policy.

With legal reserves a means of monetary regulation, the individual bank must continue to think in terms of having what it has promised to pay its depositor—cash. This is, in the first instance, provided by working reserves.

Banks hold relatively little cash in their vaults to take care of their day-to-day operating requirements. Such cash usually represents only a small percentage of the bank's primary reserves and is held to meet daily requests for currency, that is, for coins and paper money. As might be expected, vault cash requirements vary widely among banks, and at any particular bank such requirements vary from season to season. Experience teaches each bank when the heavy drains come (that is, on an annual, monthly, or weekly basis) as well as the times when a heavy cash inflow may be expected.

Since banks are the public cash depots, management must look at it as a service function not only to keep the cash on hand that regular and exceptional circumstances will call for, but also to keep it in the denominations and form that are demanded. Most banks replenish their cash supplies from the nearest Federal Reserve Bank or branch, though some still get direct shipments from their city correspondents. The size of cash in vault, then, is frequently related to the distance between a bank and its cash source, distance here being measured in terms of the length of time needed to acquire such cash. Large banks located in the country's money markets frequently carry less than 1 percent of their demand deposits in the form of cash in vault, seldom more than 2 percent. This percentage varies widely for banks in other parts of the country, ranging frequently between 2 and 4 percent of demand deposits.

During the early 1960s reserve requirements regulation changed to permit member banks to include vault cash in computing their required reserves. This seemed justified on two counts: currency, which is the main component of vault cash, is chiefly in the form of Federal Reserve notes, which basically is the same as member-bank reserves in the Federal Reserve Banks; also, banks located a considerable distance from the Federal Reserve Banks must hold more vault cash than those closer to their source of new currency.

Although member banks can count vault cash in meeting reserve requirements, they frequently try to minimize these holdings. Not only is it a question of a nonearning asset; it is also a problem of surety (that is, because of armed robberies or defaulting tellers). The least-cash-possible principle has been gaining widespread acceptance among banks. Thus banks with excess vault cash resulting from favorable over-the-counter balances may use them to replenish their reserves with the Federal Reserve Banks or with correspondent banks, to pay off their borrowings from the Federal Reserve Bank, or to increase their earning assets.

Cash items in process of collection include checks, promissory notes, and other matured items deposited at the bank by its customers for collection. While this item looms large in a bank's financial statement, it must not be viewed as a source of bank funds in the same way as are deposits at other banks or coin and paper money. Instead it must be viewed as an offset to similar items that are on their way for collection from other banks. The items are cancelled after collection but other similar items take their place.

The third and most important part of a bank's working reserves are held as deposits with other banking institutions—that is, excess reserves with the Federal Reserve Bank but, most importantly, demand deposits with other banks. The practice of maintaining demand deposits with other banks has stemmed from the need of banks to clear and collect checks drawn on other banks located in distant towns or cities. Indeed, it is this need that has gradually given rise to a reciprocal, or correspondent, relationship between banks. Therefore, a correspondent relationship entails primarily the maintenance of interbank demand deposits for the prompt settlement of the checks handled. The clearing and collecting of checks takes place in accordance with previously made interbank arrangements covering such aspects as credits, minimum balances, fees, and other charges involved. A correspondent relationship may also extend to services other than those associated with the clearing and collecting of checks. Small banks have thus come to benefit from such services as invest-ment counseling, participation in syndicated loans that otherwise would not be available, the taking over by a correspondent bank of loans that are too big for the small bank to handle, guidance for the setting up and handling of special types of loans, and in cases of emergency the availability of a credit refuge. These services render correspondent banking a vehicle for substantial economies of scale especially for smaller banks.

As noted above, deposits at the Federal Reserve Bank over and above legally required reserves are known as excess reserves and reflect a bank's liquidity preference. Some banks feel more secure against unexpected fluctua-tions in their reserve position by maintaining such excess reserves in their account at the Federal Reserve Bank. Other reasons for excess reserves may be the anticipation of rising interest rates above current levels and hence the prospect for higher returns, or to economize on the costs of potential reserve deficiencies.

The relative importance of each of the component items of the primary reserve category is shown in Table 4. As is apparent, cash items in process of collection constitute the largest item, followed by correspondent bank balances with domestic and foreign banks. Clearly the importance of each of the ac-counts shown in this table, and its weight in the primary reserve category, will vary depending upon many factors, including the tightness of the money market and bank practices in regard to the management of the cash assets.

Banks generally seek to hold to a minimum the volume of their working primary reserves in the form of vault cash and deposits at other banks. Because such funds yield no income, the well-managed bank will always seek to hold

TABLE 4

Cash Reserves, All Insured Commercial Banks, December 31, 1975
(in millions of dollars)

Item	Amount	Percent of Total
Currency and coin (cash in vault)	12,355	9.6
Reserves with Federal Reserve Banks (member banks)	26,780	20.7
Demand balances with banks in the United States (except U.S. branches of foreign banks)	32,168	24.9
Other balances with banks in the United States	7,567	5.9
Balances with banks in foreign countries	2,821	2.2
Cash items in the process of collection	47,333	36.7
Total	129,024	100.0

Source: Federal Deposit Insurance Corp., *Assets and Liabilities* (Washington, D.C.: Federal Deposit Insurance Corp., 1975).

no more of them than are necessary to avoid excesses or deficiencies of required reserves. This concern is generally thought of as management of the money position. The objective involved (avoiding excesses or deficiencies) obviously represents an ideal situation and hence a continuing target for bank management. Yet today banks are in a far better position than they ever were in controlling working reserves and minimizing foregone earnings. With Federal Reserve member banks now permitted to count their vault cash as part of their legally required reserves, inefficiency in this area of funds management has been reduced considerably.

Occasional reserve shortages, however, inevitably occur from time to time. Required reserves are affected daily by all the transactions through which payments flow into or out of the bank (that is, clearing and collection transactions, payments for checks and other items presented to the bank, cash receipts and disbursements, transfer of balances, and other direct charges to reserve balances). Those managing the money position must daily be informed of all important transactions that affect the bank's required reserve balances, and take the necessary steps to counteract possible adverse effects of any such transactions. As in other aspects of funds management, here, too, flexibility is essential. There is a choice of alternatives that a bank may employ to adjust a deficiency in its reserve position. Money position management must make decisions and execute transactions in short-term liabilities or in short-term assets. In other words, it is a matter of deciding between using liability liquidity or asset liquidity in adjusting the reserve deficiency. Liability liquidity consists of short-term bank borrowing, which in essence is an aspect of liability management. Thus the bank may borrow from the Federal Reserve Bank or use money market instruments (that is, use repurchase agreements, purchase federal funds, borrow Eurodollars). Asset liquidity, on the other hand, consists of selling short-term assets or using the proceeds of maturing short-term assets to meet liquidity needs. The asset liquidity approach is an important aspect of asset management, which deals with the distribution of funds among the various asset categories. Banks have traditionally relied upon the asset liquidity approach in the handling of their liquidity needs. The choice between using asset or liability liquidity in adjusting the bank's money position is entirely up to the individual bank. Not infrequently, however, such choice reflects the overall reliance of bank policy upon either phase of management—asset or liability.

Proper money position management calls for the weighting of two factors in determining which of the alternatives it will invoke: the duration for which the additional reserve funds are needed, and the cost involved in choosing one alternative over another. It may, for example, be found more costly to sell securities than to borrow from another bank, particularly if the market price of securities has declined or if the additional funds needed to correct the bank's reserve position are needed only for a very short time. Again, it may be found more desirable to borrow funds the bank needs than to call outstanding loans, or to reduce the size of loans the bank is asked to make. Public relations may loom larger in such instances than will correction of the bank's reserve position at the expense of the local or the national economy. The methods more generally used by bank management for short-run adjustments are federal funds purchases and resort to various types of borrowing; but to effect long-run adjustments in the reserve position, the bank is more likely to liquidate some of its assets.

Although money position management is primarily directed at the optimal pattern of meeting a deficiency in the reserve position through asset or liability management, a large bank can usually work both sides of the balance sheet for income—referred to as balance sheet management. Indeed, the justification for carrying both short-term liabilities and short-term assets on the books at the same time would rest primarily on a favorable earnings spread. For example, federal funds bought can be arbitrated against loans. Such opportunities are usually seized when feasible.*

It follows then that banks need to maintain adequate primary reserves. Clearly it is not possible to lay down fixed rules regarding the size of a bank's primary reserve account. What would be desirable for one bank might not be for another. Moreover, what would be desirable under one set of circumstances may not be for another. Obviously then, individual bank requirements should determine the size of the primary reserves. Primary reserves must be sufficiently large to meet legal reserve requirements. Moreover, banks must carry additional funds, working reserves, which must be sufficient enough to meet day-to-day operational needs. The size of working reserves would thus depend primarily upon the bank's operational requirements.

Primary reserves, as determined by legal and operational requirements, must be managed as efficiently as possible. Banks are a profit-seeking enterprise and maximum utilization of their resources is naturally desirable. Carrying sizable amounts of primary reserves means in fact sacrificing income for liquidity. Indeed, with the potential need for liquidity on the probable side, a bank would obviously forego income unnecessarily by holding large primary reserves. Banks, therefore, should keep these nonearning assets to a minimum. The maintenance of minimum primary reserves is generally thought of as a test of good management. A skilled management shifts the burden in meeting all possible demands for funds to the secondary reserve account, "which in reality is the wellspring of liquidity."[5]

---

*Banks outside New York City, and especially those located in regional federal funds centers such as Boston, Philadelphia, Cleveland, Chicago, or San Francisco, usually lend to government security dealers under repurchase agreements, using funds they in turn have borrowed locally. Clearly the amount that these banks lend depends upon money market conditions in their areas.

SECONDARY RESERVES

Like primary reserves, as a term, secondary reserves represent an economic rather than an accounting concept, and hence secondary reserves, too, do not appear in commercial bank balance sheets as a separate category. However, this item constitutes a key part of a bank's functional balance sheet that stresses the uses of the bank's resources.* The assets that make up these reserves are found in the investment and, to a certain extent, in the loan portfolio of a bank. As stated earlier in this chapter, there is no hard and fast line of demarcation between a bank's secondary reserves and its investments and loans. What differentiates these reserves from a bank's other income producing assets is that they are held primarily to meet a bank's liquidity needs. More specifically, a secondary reserve is a reserve that may be drawn upon to replenish the primary reserve whenever the latter becomes depleted.[7] Withdrawals of deposit first encroach upon the primary reserves, but a bank cannot afford to allow its primary reserves to be drawn down and remain below a desirable operating level. Withdrawal demands, therefore, require rapid replenishment of the primary reserves, and for this purpose the secondary reserves are used. Consequently, secondary reserves constitute essentially the real source of bank liquidity in meeting deposit and loan demands for funds.

As stated above, secondary reserves are held by banks to provide primary reserves whenever necessary. Two general situations may give rise to primary reserve depletion: seasonal deposit and loan demands, and cyclical and/or unforeseen demands. Banks are subject to seasonal losses of primary reserves because of seasonal lending and withdrawal of deposits. Some seasonality in loan and deposit demands is found in nearly every geographic compartment of a country's economy.† Since both of these movements tend to occur during

---

*The term "secondary reserves" is traced back to the late 1920s. It was then that, for the first time, bankers and prominent students of banking began to realize the significance of the subject and to discuss it in meetings, conventions, and bank magazines.[6]

†Though no local economy is completely independent of the national economy, there are some economic features of communities that may exert important influence upon local bank loan and deposit trends. Agricultural communities, for instance, are characterized by recurring seasonal patterns of loan and deposit demands that are markedly different from those of industrial or suburban communities. Differences in seasonal trends may even be found between communities of the same type. As expected, these differences would stem basically from the varied economic strength of each individual community. Thus, the pattern of seasonal loan and deposit demands in any two agricultural communities would be affected, for example, by the crop(s) cultivated and the existence of any livestock enterprises; in industrial communities, by such factors as the type and number of industries located in the area; and in suburban communities, by whether, for example, such communities are growing or old and declining.

specific times of the year, secondary reserves may be arranged to meet these needs. That is, with the pattern of these fluctuations generally predictable, it is possible for commercial banks to maintain sufficient liquidity to meet seasonal deposit drains and loan demands. In addition, banks must be in a position to cope with potential demands that are remote but nevertheless possible. Such demands may be predictable but they may also be a product of unforeseen or extraordinary developments. A bank must, therefore, be in a position to meet withdrawal demands arising, for example, from fluctuations in the business cycle, runs, and local depressions in sensitive industries. The charting or analysis of loan and deposit trends over a number of years in the past, and a knowledge of the current makeup of the bank's loan and deposit positions, as analyzed in Chapter 2, should greatly help management in determining the bank's aggregate liquidity requirements at any particular time and therefore facilitate the effective employment of bank funds.

The situations discussed above make it clear that the employment of funds within the secondary reserve category follows different patterns. Liquidity of the seasonal type can be provided by assets that possess certain important attributes, namely, prime quality (minimum of default risk), less than a year's maturity (minimum of interest rate risk), and in general a high degree of marketability (rapid and certain salability). Short-term, high quality, but non-marketable assets can also be considered in this class, with liquidity in this case based upon a flow of funds at maturity. In other words, the liquidity of these assets, and hence bank liquidity, would inevitably rely upon the flow of funds at a given maturity date rather than upon their flexibility as marketable instruments. Management should reduce the participation of these assets in the secondary reserves. Instead, it should place excessive reliance upon readily marketable assets so that even if the demand for funds came earlier than anticipated, the bank would not have to resort to substantial borrowing.

Obviously, considered eligible as secondary reserves of the seasonal type are those money market instruments that have the characteristics mentioned above. Among the most widely accepted instruments in this category of secondary reserves are the bankers' acceptances (a bill of exchange [international], or a draft [domestic] with a definite maturity drawn on and accepted by a bank, where once accepted, it may be sold or discounted in the market by the holder so that he may obtain his funds immediately from the transaction); short-term obligations of the U.S. Treasury (Treasury bills and Treasury certificates of indebtedness); and in general any obligations of the Treasury or the federal agencies that are coming up for redemption in less than a year's time. Loans do not generally qualify, for they do not possess the aforementioned characteristics. In the first place, bank loans are not marketable. It is true that eligible open market commercial paper may be rediscounted at the Federal Reserve Bank, yet this is not a sale in the true sense. As noted earlier, this constitutes bank borrowing, and as such it is not a right but a privilege, which is limited to short periods of time. However self-liquidating a loan may be, it takes a relatively short period of time for a good loan to become a poor one and, therefore, to lose much of its liquidity value for the bank. This holds especially true during a period of adversity, when even short-term commercial loans may run into difficulties and require many renewals or extensions before final payment is made. Another reason for excluding loans from secondary reserves is that they do not possess any diversity, being concentrated geographically in the area or community that the bank serves. About the only loans that could be considered as eligible, other than the open market commercial paper that can be rediscounted at the Federal Reserve Bank, would be those loans that are of a very short term nature, such as, the sale of federal funds (which are one- or two-day loans to other banks), and the call loans (which may be terminated at any time on very short notice, and are usually made to security brokers and dealers for the purpose of purchasing or carrying highly marketable securities).

Secondary reserves of the nonseasonal or cyclical type are designed to supplement the secondary reserves of the seasonal type and facilitate the making of adjustments against cyclical or unforeseen demands; that is, they are designed to provide for a bank's protective and loan liquidity requirements that are of a cyclical or unforeseen nature. To provide cyclical liquidity, management must be generally aware of the way in which the business cycle affects the local economy or market served. This holds especially true during the contraction phase of the business cycle when deposit and loan declines are accentuated. During such periods, commercial bank activities are favorably affected by fiscal policy. The expansion of federal debt to finance deficit spending, which characterizes these periods, makes it possible for banks to partly offset declining loan outlets by placing idle funds into government securities. This acquisition of securities also offsets partly the declining deposits since it results in an overall deposit expansion for the banking system. Of course, the individual bank is not the banking system, and adequate liquidity provisions must still be made against cyclical demands. Here, again, management's past experience coupled with knowledge of the bank's current deposit and loan makeup would be important determinants of the degree of cyclical liquidity needed.

The liquidity characteristics of the assets that may be included in this category fall short of the strict requirements placed upon the secondary reserve holdings of the seasonal type, but still exceed those of the assets included in the "bond portfolio," the latter term used hereafter to refer to that portion of the investment portfolio outside of both the seasonal and nonseasonal classes of the secondary reserve category. In other words, with the potential need for liquidity further removed, a bank can accept somewhat greater interest rate risk for income purposes. It follows then that secondary reserves of the nonseasonal type represent allocation of funds to high-grade investments of a marketable nature, possessing a maturity of short-intermediate term (a maturity that ranges from one year, where the secondary reserves of the seasonal type leave off, to five years). Thus secondary reserves of the nonseasonal type may be selected from the promises to pay of the federal, state, and local governments, and of corporations (that is, public utilities). In practice, many banks prefer to employ the bulk of the funds available in this category in Treasury obligations maturing in from one to five years because of the high degree of marketability of these securities.*

Each of the two distinct types of secondary reserves is designed, then, primarily to fulfill one function: to provide, respectively, short-range and longer-range liquidity. The basic asset characteristics of each of these two classes of secondary reserves, as discussed above, should, therefore, be inviolate for all intents and purposes. There is, however, some ability to shift emphasis within their frameworks, and this pertains to the maturity pattern of the assets held in each class. Specifically, there is some latitude for adjusting the maturity pattern of the assets held in each class of secondary reserves in accordance with the prevailing market climate (level of interest rates) and the monetary policy pursued. Potential market vulnerability and income considerations are the basic factors behind adjustments in the maturity pattern of secondary reserves. The latitude for such adjustments is somewhat greater for nonseasonal secondary reserves than for seasonal.

During periods of monetary ease, which coincide with economic contraction, interest rates are low and market prices of bonds high. During such periods, secondary reserves in general should be as short as possible. What this means is that as new or maturing funds become available for employment in the secondary reserve category, there should be an increasing emphasis on the shorter-end maturity pattern of this account. This shift in emphasis from the longer to the shorter end of the maturity pattern of the secondary reserve account would have as a result the temporary ballooning of the shorter-term secondary reserves. This move would allow management to take advantage of the subsequent increase in business activity, which would entail higher interest rates and lower bond prices along with expanding loan demands. Conversely, during periods of tight money, which coincide with boom periods, interest rates are generally high and market prices of bonds low. In such periods, secondary reserves should gradually shift in the direction of the longer-end maturity pattern of this account—the five-year term. This move acts as a hedge

---

*Some writers, when discussing the nonseasonal type of reserves, prefer to do so independently of the secondary reserve category. In other words, they present this type of reserves as a third category of bank reserves lying between the secondary reserves and the bank's bond portfolio. The term they use in identifying this tertiary reserve category is "investment reserves."[8]

against having to refund during the ensuing phase of the business cycle (recession) and consequently accepting lower-interest-rate instruments. As might be expected, this lengthening of maturities is possible only for secondary reserves of the nonseasonal type, the maximum maturity of which may normally extend to the five-year range. Secondary reserves of the seasonal type offer no latitude for maturity adjustments. Indeed, with these reserves generally geared toward a certain pattern of liquidity requirements, maturity lengthening would occur only for any excess or unassignable protective and loan liquidity, and then, perhaps, for not more than the two-year limit. It follows, therefore, that nonseasonal secondary reserves may be drawn down below desirable size provided that the offset is found in the seasonal secondary reserves. The latter reserves, however, should never be drawn down below desirable size; for, with banks generally striving to keep no excess cash in their primary reserve account, the shorter-term secondary reserves constitute in essence the first line of a bank's defense.[9]

Because of the very importance of secondary reserves in meeting a bank's liquidity needs, tests have been developed to measure the degree of commercial bank liquidity. The two ratio tests most commonly referred to in this respect are that of liquid assets to total assets, and of liquid assets to total deposits. Liquid assets may, of course, be interpreted in broad or narrow terms. In the former instance, for example, liquid assets would be considered a bank's cash assets and secondary reserves of both seasonal and nonseasonal nature; in the latter case, liquid assets would be considered a bank's cash assets minus required reserves plus seasonal secondary reserves. This latter definition of liquid assets appears to be conceptually preferable in measuring the degree of bank liquidity. In this context, then, the ratio of liquid assets to total assets would be reflective of the relative importance of a bank's liquid assets among its total assets. In other words, this ratio reveals the liquidity quotient of a bank's asset account. The ratio of liquid assets to total deposits portrays what percentage of a bank's deposits is held in liquid form. Both ratios are significant because they reflect the ability of a bank (or of the banking system) to honor depositors' withdrawal demands and to grant loans.

ALTERNATIVE USES OF LIQUID ASSETS

It follows from the above discussion that secondary reserves constitute a bank's real liquidity reserves of both short- and long-term nature. Traditionally they must meet all of a bank's liquidity requirements and, when the needs for which they were provided arise, must be readily converted into cash with little or no loss.

Beyond this essential function, secondary reserve assets offer the bank a number of other important uses. The securities that make up a bank's secondary reserve account, and more importantly the U.S. government securities, can be used, for example, in obtaining funds from the Federal Reserve Bank. Other than discounting eligible paper, a bank can obtain funds from the Federal Reserve Bank in the form of advances on the strength of the collateral afforded. A highly qualified collateral in this respect has been the U.S. government securities. Advances secured by U.S. government securities have grown to be a very common means of borrowing from the Federal Reserve. Much of this rise in advances has been due to bank reluctance to discount customers' notes because of fear as to the possible implications this would entail for its image. More importantly, however, it has been due to the very strength of U.S. government obligations as collateral and its contribution in simplifying and expediting the process of such borrowing.

Securities of the liquidity account may also constitute the subject of a repurchase agreement. Most often the security underlying the agreement is a U.S. Treasury obligation. The substantial growth of the federal debt and the development of a highly organized U.S. government securities market have accounted for the frequent use of Treasury securities in repurchase agreements. These securities may be lent directly to dealers whose trading desks have made short sales and are hence in need of making deliveries. For such lending arrangements banks charge a fee and require dealers to provide adequate collateral.

Another use of U.S. government securities is in meeting the pledging requirement on public deposits. More specifically, commercial banks that accept federal government deposits are required to secure such deposits by pledging U.S. government securities against them. These securities, whether from the bank's liquidity account or the bond portfolio, are typically pledged with the bank's trust department to insure the safety of these deposits in the event of insolvency. Their replacement by other types of collateral is possible, although the secretary of the treasury reserves the right of requiring amounts in excess of 100 percent of the value of the deposit if the collateral is deemed of great potential risk.

This pledging requirement extends also to state and local government deposits, with U.S. government securities, and sometimes the securities of state and local government, usually pledged to insure the safety of these deposits. Although this requirement is an important matter, the extent to which it is enforced by local governments is more a matter of local custom than careful consideration of the potential hazards involved.

All business decisions normally are accompanied by constraints as to the range over which action can be taken. The alternative use of liquid assets described above constitutes one such dimension of decision making for a bank. Money market instruments and more generally investment securities used in any of the above capacities cannot be readily sold to provide liquidity. The efficiency of these investments as liquidity media is thereby lessened.

SUMMARY

To achieve a balance between liquidity, solvency, and profitability, a bank employs its funds in four ways: to maintain primary reserves, to provide secondary reserves, to meet customer credit demands, and to purchase investment securities for income.

Primary reserves, also known as cash assets, constitute a functional category not appearing in a bank's statement of condition. Nevertheless, it is an important banking concept and relates to those assets that are used to meet legal and day-to-day operational requirements. This helps explain their breakdown into required reserves, which are legally stipulated reserves against deposit liabilities; and working reserves, which include cash in vault (coins and currency), correspondent bank balances (deposits), cash items in process of collection, and balances at the Federal Reserve Bank over and above the legally required reserves (excess reserves).

From this makeup of primary reserves, it follows that to a large measure they are not part of the liquidity position. In the case of deposit withdrawals, primary reserves would provide only a fraction of the outflows, for as deposits decline, corresponding releases from the required reserves would provide only a small part of the requisite liquidity. As for meeting the liquidity needs arising from loan demands, primary reserves are of no help whatsoever. Thus, primary reserves do not constitute true liquidity reserves.

Secondary reserves, like primary reserves, refer to an economic concept rather than an accounting one and do not, therefore, appear in a bank's statement of condition. The size of the secondary reserves is determined indirectly by those factors that influence the variability of deposits and loans. Secondary reserves must therefore at all times provide the reserve liquidity necessary to meet seasonal and nonseasonal (or cyclical) demands for funds. Qualifying as reserves for this purpose are the gilt-edged short- and intermediate-term securities of the bank's investment account, which thus ensures that under all foreseeable circumstances they can be converted into cash with little or no loss when the needs for which they were provided arise. Bank liquidity requirements will thus be covered at all times with a minimum degree of risk. Thus, secondary reserves represent a bank's basic liquidity reserves.

Aside from the fact that they can be sold to provide liquidity, the securities that comprise the secondary reserves offer a number of other important uses to a bank. These securities, and especially the obligations of the U.S. government, may be used as collateral against Federal Reserve advances, can be the subject of repurchase agreements with security dealers, and can be pledged against public deposits in compliance with such requirements.

NOTES

1. Roland I. Robinson, *The Management of Bank Funds,* 2d ed. (New York: McGraw-Hill Book Co., 1962), pp. 13–18.

2. Ibid., p. 15.

3. *Federal Reserve Bulletin* (October 1976): A7.

4. Robinson, op. cit., p. 71.

5. Edward W. Reed, *Commercial Bank Management* (New York: Harper & Row, 1963), p. 131.

6. Paul M. Atkins, *Bank Secondary Reserve and Investment Policies* (New York: Bankers Publishing Co., 1930), p. i.

7. Ibid., pp. 39–40.

8. See Robert G. Rodkey, *Sound Policies for Bank Management* (New York: Ronald Press, 1944), pp. 30–33. This approach is also followed in Roger A. Lyon, *Investment Portfolio Management in the Commercial Bank* (New Brusnwick, N.J.: Rutgers University Press, 1960), pp. 26 ff., 135 ff.

9. Lyon, op. cit., p. 148.

4

THE LOAN
ACCOUNT—
POLICY CONSIDERATIONS

The core function of commercial banks is the granting of credit. While banks offer a wide spectrum of financial services, direct lending is their main function, the one in which they have a natural advantage by tradition and organization. Bank credit has been responsible for the development and growth of many small and moderate-sized businesses that would have otherwise withered and died. By providing productive credit, banks have contributed in the growth of their respective communities and in the advance of local economic well-being.

Aside from its public service character, bank lending is a quite profitable activity. In fact, it is the most profitable activity of commercial banking and hence the greatest contributor to bank profits. Income from the loan account has contributed annually from 60 to 70 percent of total operating income. The remaining 30 to 40 percent is contributed by the many other activities of commercial banks.

The loan function is important on other grounds too. Lending is instrumental in creating and maintaining good deposit relationships, which are potentially essential for the furthering of bank lending. The close and continuing contact established with the borrower is also instrumental in broadening the market for other bank services.

The above helps explain the prominent place of loans among bank assets and, more specifically, vis-a-vis investments, a bank's second major category of earning assets. There are distinctive differences between the acquisition of each of these assets. As noted earlier, investments constitute open market purchases of securities some of which, as we have seen, serve as secondary reserves, while loans constitute direct customer demand for funds. Specifically, investments are evidences of interest-bearing debt offered for sale in the open market, and the acquiring bank does not anticipate establishing a continuous or permanent relationship with the issuing company. In other words, the acquisition of securities is generally conducted impersonally and is influenced by objective criteria such as relative interest rate, quality of the issue (rating), maturity, and marketability. Banks purchase these securities either at the time they are issued or later on by acquiring them from other investors in the open market. A loan, on the other hand, is arranged through direct face-to-face negotiation between the borrower and the lending bank, and is, hence, of personal nature. Bank lending is thus influenced significantly by subjective criteria, as occurs, for example, in evaluating the borrower's character, the type and length of his relationship with the bank, and the new business he may potentially generate for the bank.*

These differences between loans and investments make apparent the need for well-formulated loan policies and practices. Sound lending policies and practices reflect themselves in the quality of the loan account and, hence, in bank solvency. Indeed throughout most of the history of commercial banking the quality of the loan portfolios has been closely linked with banks' solvency. This traditional link between the quality of loans and banks' solvency exists today because banks' loan portfolios contain the bulk of their assets. This chapter will discuss the basic considerations that determine the loan policies of commercial banks. The subject is introduced with a historical overview of the evolution of loan portfolios; this is thought essential since it ties past experiences with the present and focuses upon the factors that have influenced and shaped loan portfolios then and today.

EVOLUTION OF COMMERCIAL BANK LOAN PORTFOLIOS

The leading earning asset of commercial banks in the United States until at least the 1920s was the so-called commercial loan. As implied by its name, this type of loan was granted to finance the commercial credit needs of businesses. Its prominence in commercial bank portfolios reflected the traditional view of commercial banking that all banks' earning assets should consist principally of such loans. By holding these short-term assets, the banks, it was held, would possess the most liquid earning assets and would, therefore, be able

---

*The line of distinction between loans and investments is often only a fine one. Thus, we may find hybrid types that defy watertight classification in one or the other category. Examples of such hybrid types are the loans made by a group of banks (syndicated loans) to a single borrower, and the private placement of corporate bonds among financial institutions.

to meet their demand deposit liabilities when called upon to do so. Those who advocated this theory argued, moreover, that if banks were to limit their lending to advances for short-term commercial purposes, the supply of money would have the desirable elasticity. It was reasoned that if trade increased, this would presumably give rise to a larger volume of bills of exchange. As these bills are discounted at banks, demand deposits will increase, and so will the quantity of the circulating medium. Control over the quality of credit was hence sufficient to ensure that the proper quantity of money would follow. The expansion of the circulating medium was expected to be in proportion to the growth in the volume of business activity. Similarly, if business is declining, fewer bills will be drawn as older ones mature and are paid off, and consequently the total of discounted loans in bank portfolios will diminish and with it the total of demand deposits. A contraction of the circulating medium was therefore expected to accompany a decline in business activity.

Consequently, the traditional theory of commercial banking—which is also referred to as the "commercial loan theory of credit" or the "real bills doctrine"[1]—emphasizes the direct relationship between the quantity of money and the needs of business. More specifically, the banking process is held to be firmly rooted in business activity. Indeed, by creating deposits against good self-liquidating commercial notes, banks were expected to provide a system that would be automatic, sound, and adjusted to the needs of trade. The role of commercial banks was therefore presumed to be passive—banks accompanied and facilitated changes in business but did nothing to induce them.

The commercial loan theory of credit dates back to the eighteenth century and is of English origin. "Given its most elegant statement in all its history by Adam Smith in the *Wealth of Nations,*"[2] this theory served as the cornerstone of central banking policy until World War I. The outbreak of the war brought a sizable expansion of public debt, and commercial banks—which until then held some securities in violation of the prevailing principles of banking theory if not of practice—were now generally encouraged to invest in some of these securities. Moreover, a new theory of bank liquidity gained momentum. Emphasis was gradually shifted from the desirability of self-liquidating commercial loans to the concept of liquidity achieved by "shiftability."[3] A shiftable asset was considered to be any asset that could be shifted (sold) to others when a need for money arises. With securities considered as more readily shiftable (salable) than loans, banks were thus drawn gradually into the investment markets.

In the years that followed the war, increasing amounts of securities came to be included in commercial bank portfolios. As the outcome of an ever increasing private initiative as well as a growing role of government in everyday economic life, investment securities constituted important outlets for bank funds. With the passage of time, the investment holdings of commercial banks grew into sizable proportions. This rise in the relative importance of investments in commercial bank assets may be attributed to two major events—the depression of the 1930s and the Second World War. In the 1930s, the depression brought in most countries both a sharp decline in the private demand for loans and a substantial increase in government borrowing to finance budgetary deficits. Then, again, throughout the Second World War, commercial banks bought substantial amounts of government securities, as a result of both a huge increase in government borrowing and a contraction in the demand for loans by private borrowers. Commercial banks thus became important holders of government securities, these having by far outstripped the volume of bank loans. The paramount position of the Treasury among commercial bank borrowers is reflected in the relevant data of the era. Thus in 1945, Federal Reserve member bank holdings of U.S. government securities reached an unprecedented height; they accounted for 73 percent of the earning assets of all member banks. If all other securities held by these banks are also taken into consideration, investments constituted 79 percent of these banks' earning assets, and loans, but 21 percent. The change in the composition of commercial bank earning asset portfolios during this period is shown in Figure 11.

Since the end of World War II, commercial bank earning assets have been generally dominated by loans, reflecting the spectacular postwar rise in loan demand. The efforts of commercial bank managements to satisfy demands for loans for creditworthy borrowers led banks into making loans that are of longer maturity, cover a much wider variety of borrowers, and extend to many more purposes than originally envisaged. More importantly, however, this move reflected the ongoing changes in banking attitudes. The sharp decline in the demand for loans in the 1930s had generated substantial pressures upon banks to seek and consider new outlets for their funds. These pressures, accentuated by the banks' dwindling proportion of savings flowing into nonbank financial institutions, forced important changes in bank attitudes toward extending maturities in their loan portfolios. Moreover, bank management had acquired more experience in meeting deposit withdrawals and had gained more confidence in its ability to design portfolios that were only partly composed of short-term or highly liquid assets. In other words, they had found that through prudent asset management, a mixture of very liquid and not so liquid assets could achieve the desired degree of overall liquidity.

Thus, the loan portfolios of commercial banks in the postwar years have included such items as intermediate- and long-term loans to consumers, homeowners, and business firms that would not qualify as liquid assets under the traditional theory of bank liquidity and would qualify only in part, if at all, under the shiftability theory. However, commercial bank loans of this type do qualify under the "anticipated-income theory" of liquidity developed in 1949.[4] This theory gives primary emphasis to the borrower's ability to repay loans as they mature. Thus, in making loans of the type cited above, banks generally rely on the debtors' income and its coverage of debt service requirements. This

FIGURE 11

Pattern of Loans and Investments in Total Earning Assets of Commercial Banks, 1834–1975
(in percent)

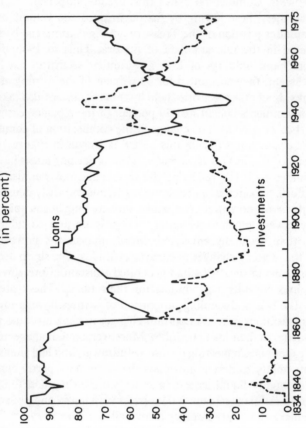

Note: Data are based upon all commercial banks except for the period 1865–95, when national bank statistics were used.

Sources: U.S. Department of Treasury, *Annual Report of the Comptroller of the Currency,* 2 vols. (Washington, D.C.: U.S. Government Printing Office, 1897); U.S. Department of Commerce, Bureau of the Census, *Historical Statistics of the United States: Colonial Times to 1970,* 2 parts (Washington, D.C.: U. S. Government Printing Office, 1975); Board of Governors of the Federal Reserve System, *All-Bank Statistics: United States, 1896–1955* (Washington, D.C.: Federal Reserve System, 1959); and *Federal Reserve Bulletin,* various issues.

coverage is determined on the basis of inclusive cash flow projections, which ordinarily provide a reliable indication of the quality of the loans being financed. Hence, the future cash flow of the borrower, rather than the nature of particular transactions being financed, assures the self-liquidating character of a loan because it will determine a borrower's overall ability to meet interest and principal payments as they fall due on a continuing basis. If the debtors' anticipated income is estimated correctly, the bank will have a flow of funds that can be used to meet depositors' claims and/or other loan demands. During normal times bank lending of this type would function in about the same way as bank lending based on the commercial loan theory of liquidity.

Since the early 1960s, the loan portfolios of commercial banks have been affected by the emergence of a new theory, which became known as the "liabilities management theory."[5] As stated earlier, liability management banking was originated by large metropolitan banks under strong pressures at the time: growing demand for loans, as the economy experienced recovery from the 1960–61 recession, plus an inadequate growth of deposits at these banks. According to this new doctrine, it is no longer necessary for a bank to observe traditional standards with respect to self-liquidating loans and liquidity reserve assets, since such funds can be acquired in the money market whenever a bank experiences a need for liquidity. In other words, a bank can meet its liquidity needs by creating additional liabilities. There are a number of possible sources from which the individual bank may draw to meet liquidity needs during the last phase of periods of cyclical expansion. These involve, for example, issuing CDs, purchasing federal funds, borrowing at the Federal Reserve, issuing short-term notes, raising capital funds from the sale of capital notes, preferred stock, or common stock, and using the Eurodollar market. The importance of these sources and the impact of Federal Reserve regulation upon their effectiveness have been discussed in Chapter 1.

Liability management has been viewed as a major banking innovation and, as such, it has influenced significantly the outlook of bankers. Indeed, it is a far cry from traditional banking and the need for short-term self-liquidating commercial loans. Bank lending is symptomatic of new banking attitudes that are becoming increasingly general in the banking industry. There is no longer such a thing as a standard bank loan or borrower. Although some classes of borrowers and loan arrangements are more characteristic than others, bank lending has been evolving in response to new opportunities. For the most part, opportunity has been the mother of innovation, to paraphrase an old saying. The fact that banks have been so alert to opportunities and so resourceful in exploiting them is a plus factor in any assessment of our financial system.

One of the innovations in bank lending has been the lease financing that began in the early 1960s and involves today a sizable number of banks. Finance leasing of equipment ranges from small items of office equipment to commercial aircraft and oceangoing tankers. The bank purchases the asset at the request of the lessee, who assumes virtually all responsibilities of ownership, including maintenance and payment of insurance and taxes. The profitability of leasing derives from the bank's ability to depreciate the leased chattel for tax purposes.

Two other highly publicized innovations are the various check credit plans and bank credit cards, both of which involve the extension of credit basically in the form of installment credit. Check credit plans take a variety of forms, but all have one characteristic in common—check credit customers are extended a prearranged line of credit that can be activated at their discretion. The plans all combine some of the characteristics of cashier's checks, traveler's checks, check guarantee, and overdraft banking. Bank credit cards, on the other hand, are not linked to a checking account and involve a three-party arrangement—among the cardholder, the bank, and the merchant. These cards involve the extension of bank credit to consumers, with the merchant serving, in effect, as a go-between. This innovation has increased substantially consumer credit, and it seems that in the years ahead it will involve the gradual substituting of consumer credit for trade credit. As customers increasingly "charge it" with their bank instead of with the merchant, the latter needs less financing to carry his receivables.

Electronic recording, transmission, and manipulation of data will add further momentum to the growth of consumer credit. In the years ahead, the electronic funds transfer system is expected to affect consumer credit by introducing a process that would work as follows. An electronic identifier, possibly in the form of a credit card, would provide positive identification of a card holder on the basis of his voiceprint, fingerprint, or photograph on such card. With merchants and banks in the area in an on-line computer terminal, a consumer wishing to make purchases would insert his identification in the retailer's remote terminal. The merchant would be credited instantly and the customer charged accordingly. A sufficient balance in the customer's account would make a green light flash on the terminal while an insufficient balance would allow the individual to borrow against a preauthorized credit arrangement (line of credit). In the event that purchases exceed the line of credit, a yellow-light flash at the terminal would inform the individual that he has the choice of either asking the bank for more credit or the merchant concerned for the extension of such credit. Electronic transfers of funds thus promise to substantially simplify consumer credit processes and therefore play a primary role in the further growth of this type of credit.

Having discussed past and present trends in commercial bank loan portfolios, we may now consider the factors that influence loan policy at the level of the individual bank.

ESTABLISHING LOAN POLICY

To provide the framework within which bank lending takes place, banks must establish a lending policy. This policy determines the direction and use of a bank's funds, controls the composition and size of the loan account, and describes the conditions under which a loan may be made.

As is true for all other aspects of banking activity, the responsibility for determining the loan policies of a bank rests with its board of directors. The board of directors must provide answers to such loan policy questions as the overall size of the loan portfolio, its composition by maturities and by major loan types, and the terms of lending (contract rate of interest, collateral, repayment schedule, and so on). Moreover, it must provide the administrative framework for the carrying out of the lending function. To properly discharge its responsibility, the board should see that loan policy is expressed in writing and is subject to periodic reviews in the light of changing economic conditions.

Since lending is important to the bank and the community it serves, loan policy formulation requires the exercise of sound judgment and an acute awareness of conditions and expectations in the market. The starting point, therefore, in the loan policy formulation is the accurate assessment of the credit needs of the community or market a bank serves or intends to serve. It has long been recognized that the basic responsibility of a bank lies in the serving of the credit needs of its community. There is no greater service that a bank can perform for the community it serves than to provide the loans needed by creditworthy businesses and individuals.

In small communities this need for credit can be assessed by the actual demand for loans. In such communities, bank officers and directors are usually in a position to have an intimate knowledge of most of the economic activity of the area and the developments that may be shaping up. In large communities, however, such knowledge can be obtained by means of a formal market survey. Indeed, in such communities a formal market survey, if nothing else, provides a periodic check for management. But in whatever type of community a bank may operate, its management must know the credit needs of its present and potential customers, both for the short and long run, as a basis not only for establishing loan policies but also for determining the bank's liquidity needs and investment policy.

When bank management has a fairly clear concept of what volume and character of loan demands the bank will be called upon to meet, it must appraise its own willingness and ability to meet those demands. In some communities local demand for loans is strong and practically insatiable, while in other more developed and stable communities bank management may have to seek out opportunities for sound loans. In either case, the controlling principle should be the community's credit needs and the bank's capability for meeting those needs.

Once liquidity provisions have been made (primary and secondary reserves) and there is adequate capital for absorbing loan losses, a bank should be in a position to make all the sound loans it can. In other words, given adequate liquidity and capital protection, a bank's ability to expand its loans is limited only by its resources. If a bank's resources are inadequate for meeting the full volume of loan demands requested of it, management may proceed to fill them indirectly. More specifically, bank management may provide for the financing of specific loan demands by participating in or negotiating placement of the requested loans with correspondent banks or other financial institutions, itself retaining, however, the servicing of such loans as a means of effecting continuous relationships with its own customers. A bank's ability and willingness to accomodate directly or indirectly local loan demands is the most important factor in creating and maintaining depositor relationships. In addition, such ability and willingness to lend contributes to the economic well-being of the community and thereby broadens the market for bank services, so that the bank shares in the prosperity it has helped to bring about.

Management has over the years developed certain criteria that assess the overall loan commitments of a bank in terms of its capacity to lend. These criteria are various key balance sheet relationships expressed in the form of ratios. Foremost among these are the loans-to-deposits ratio and the loans-to-capital ratio. As implied, these ratios aim to portray the relationship of a bank's loans to its deposits and to its capital accounts. Of these two ratios, the most widely used is the loans-to-deposits ratio. Because it is readily computed and compared, this ratio is in general use as a yardstick for asset management. Specifically, it is used to demonstrate the extent to which available resources have already been used in accommodating the credit needs of customers. The presumption is that the higher the ratio of loans to deposits, the less able a bank will be to make additional loans.*

Commercial bank managements have come, at various times, to accept a certain percentage of loans to deposits as being an acceptable determinant for the size of the loan portfolio desired. As might be expected, this ratio experienced considerable variation over the years, reflecting the prevailing economic conditions and more specifically the credit demand of these years. Since 1914, for example, the average loans-to-deposits ratio for all commercial banks in the United States has varied from a high of 80 percent loans in 1920 to a low of 17 percent in 1944.

---

*This ratio is frequently used by management as a liquidity indicator because, by portraying the relationship of a bank's loans to its deposits, it also reveals the amount of funds still readily available to a bank for liquidity purposes.

The loans-to-capital ratio measures the extent to which a bank's loan losses may be safely absorbed by its capital account without jeopardizing the bank's continuing viability. Here, too, management has come to accept maximum desirable ratios of loans to capital, that is, the loans of a bank should not exceed by more than seven times the capital funds of that bank.

These ratios have become critical guides for commercial bank managements. Indeed, not infrequently, a bank's management may feel uncomfortable when its ratios get too far out of line with those of other banks regarded as comparable in size and character. Apart from the questions that may be raised by the top management's conflicting assessments of the uncertain future, there are likely to be pressures generated by the inquiries of large corporate depositors and other individuals whose good opinion is important to the welfare of the individual bank. Bankers do not permit the judgment of such influential outsiders to substitute for their own, but they are forced to concede it some weight, or risk adverse action such as transfer of important deposit accounts to competitors. The attitude has thus developed that whenever these ratios approach what is considered as the maximum acceptable ratio for all banks or for banks of a certain size and character, management should try to become more cautious and selective in its lending policies.

However important the ratios may be concerning limits to overall lending capacity, they must not be taken to imply that they are in any sense magic numbers. True enough, some element of tradition clings to particular values for these ratios; such tradition, however, must be flexibly interpreted in the light of the current situation. What is meant by this is that these ratios become especially meaningful if interpreted in the light of such relevant magnitudes as the composition of the loan portfolio (by maturities and by major loan types), the size and composition of the bond portfolio, business expectations, management philosophy, and respectability in comparison with all commercial banks or with other banks of the same size and character.

As stated earlier, loan portfolio composition is customarily examined by maturities and by major loan types. Maturitywise, a bank's loan portfolio may be classified into short-term, intermediate, and long-term loans. Short-term loans are usually defined as those with a maturity of one year or less, intermediate loans are from one to five years, and long-term loans are in excess of five years.

The traditional form of commercial bank credit has been the short-term business loan. Bank preference for such loans has been justified on the grounds that the shorter the term of a loan, the smaller the risk involved, and, hence, the higher the degree of its liquidity. Short-term loans are customarily employed to finance the working capital needs of businesses in such forms as inventories (of raw, semifinished, or finished materials), to meet payrolls, to finance goods in transit, and for other similar purposes. Repayment of the loan is made with the proceeds of the current sales of the firm, and is hence self-liquidating only to the degree that the current operations prove successful. Lacking funds at maturity, some borrowers may either borrow from a second bank to repay the first, or secure renewals of their loans, in whole or in part. Some advantage results from the first alternative—the borrower is forced to submit to credit analysis by the second bank. The second alternative has led to the wide use of intermediate credit in the form of term loans.

Intermediate bank loans, by definition, are those with a maturity ranging from the short-term to the long-term loan categories—that is, from one to five years. It is not uncommon, however, to have loans made for a period of ten years and still consider them as intermediate loans. A type of loan most often considered as intermediate loan is the term loan. A term loan is usually defined as a loan to a business firm with an original maturity of more than one year. In the early and experimental period of term lending, maturities tended to be short—from one to five years. As banks, however, became more confident of their ability to safely provide such credit, term loan maturities were extended to ten years, though not infrequently they may even exceed this limit.

Functionally, a term loan is one that, regardless of its maturity rate, will be amortized by installments paid out of the net cash income of the business over the life of the loan. Term loans are thus easily adapted to financing the credit needs of a business whose ability to repay is related to its anticipated earning power. Term loans have been sought by and made to businesses that are either too small to raise money in the capital market by the sale of bonds and stocks, or have access to such markets but find term borrowing more advantageous for price reasons. To borrowers, therefore, it is the availability and cost of such lending that makes it more attractive than other kinds of intermediate-term capital. Looked at from the side of the bank, the term loans replace intermediate-and long-term corporation bonds, which a bank would otherwise be buying and carrying in its bond portfolio, and have the added advantage of protective provisions in the loan agreement that permit the bank to exercise more control over the debtor and its activities than would be true if it carried bonds. Term loans are usually made to businesses for the purpose of financing working capital increases and the purchasing or improvement of fixed assets plant, equipment, and machinery). Term loans represent one of the few means available for the financing of fixed capital by small and medium-sized firms.

Loans with a maturity of five years or more when contracted are characterized as long term. The most common type of such loans is the real estate loan. Originally, lending on the security of real estate was considered unduly illiquid and hence inappropriate for commercial banks, whose liabilities were so largely payable on demand. The growth of time deposits and inactive demand deposits over the years, however, changed these attitudes. Thus commercial banks, to match their time deposit liabilities, undertook gradually somewhat less liquid but high-class real estate loans. Real estate loans have grown since to be one of the chief outlets for time deposit funds in commercial banks. Real estate loans range from 10 to 30 years in maturity and are amortized in monthly payments. Real estate credit takes the form of loans to individuals and businesses to finance the purchase of land, the construction of holdings, or other improvements on land, and is secured by a mortgage on the property (residential mortgage lending, commercial mortgage lending, construction mortgage financing). Real estate loans are also made to farmers for the purchase of farm land. This type of real estate credit, however, is relatively insignificant.

Loan maturity distribution in the portfolio would reflect a bank's maturity policy. Such policy must be flexible, permitting adjustments in the portfolio that reflect changing economic conditions. Blind adherence to a given maturity structure would benefit neither the bank, its depositors, nor its stockholders. The cyclical nature of the economy and its impact upon the monetary system would require the change or shift of emphasis in bank maturity policy to give recognition to changes in the strength of loan demand. During periods of slackened loan demand, which normally coincide with business recession and monetary ease, banks should engage primarily in short-maturity loans. Conversely, during periods of peak loan demand, which normally coincide with high business activity and monetary restraint, banks should emphasize term lending. This shift in loan maturity policy to reflect changes in the market conditions and the demand for loans, would enable a bank to substantially improve its long-range rate of income. Indeed, by refusing to make loans other than those of short term in periods when loan demand and (consequently) interest rates are low, banks are in a position to make rather large term loans at the height of loan demand and command unquestionably higher rates of interest. By following this pattern of loan maturity policy, banks provide themselves with portfolios that stretch out over succeeding periods of lesser loan demand and income.*

Statistics on the composition of commercial bank loan portfolios are customarily presented by major loan types. These loan types are determined by the borrower or the purpose for which the funds are to be used. Table 5 presents information regarding the loans of all insured commercial banks in

---

*Banks, by and large, have been pursuing a reversed pattern of loan maturity policy. In other words, during periods of slackened business activity and loan demand they have been willing to extend term loans, while in periods of high business activity and loan demand they have tended to reduce term loans and to engage primarily in short-term lending. Clearly this pattern of maturity policy is not as profitable over the long run. Its use, however, is understandable because short-term lending presumably adds to a bank's flexibility and ability to accommodate a larger number of customers, and permits bank adherence to custom and tradition.[6]

TABLE 5

Loans of All Insured Commercial Banks, December 31, 1975
(millions of dollars)

Type of Loan	Amount	Percent of Total
Real estate		
Residential	82,609	15.4
Other	52,571	9.8
Commercial and industrial	174,906	32.6
Agricultural	20,135	3.8
For purchasing or carrying securities	10,880	2.0
Consumer		
To purchase automobiles	33,307	6.2
For credit cards	12,363	2.3
Other loans to individuals	60,870	11.3
All other	89,385	16.6
Total	537,026	100.0

Source: Federal Deposit Insurance Corp., *Bank Operating Statistics* (Washington, D.C.: Federal Deposit Insurance Corp., 1975).

1975. At the end of December 1975, loans outstanding totaled $537 billion as compared to a mere $38 billion in 1947. The various types of loans and their relative importance as depicted in Table 5 reflect basically the current pattern of customer credit demands. As shown in this table, an important kind of bank loan is the real estate or mortgage loan. Real estate loans are those made to finance the purchase of real property, including both farms and urban real estate. This category of loans is popular with banks because of their high yield, but they are less liquid than other types of loans. Commercial banks constitute an important source of funds in the mortgage market along with other non-banking financial institutions (insurance companies, savings and loan associations, mutual savings banks). As of 1975, real estate loans accounted for 25 percent of the total loans made by insured banks, ranking second in importance to business loans.

About one-third of all loans granted in 1975, according to Table 5, were commercial and industrial, or business, loans, which include seasonal loans, working capital loans, term loans, and open market paper. Such loans are usually much more important both relatively and absolutely for metropolitan banks than for middle-size and small banks. Part of the rise in metropolitan bank lending came from foreign business borrowing. These loans involved the financing of plant expansion or working capital needs of businesses located in less developed countries where credit has regularly been in short supply and hence relatively expensive.

Loans made by banks for the purpose of purchasing and carrying securities compose another category of bank loans. These loans are made to investment banking houses for the flotation of new security issues; to security brokers and dealers for their own accounts or for the accounts of their customers; and directly to individuals who wish to borrow part of the purchase price of securities. Banks customarily make these loans on a secured basis. This category of loans is of little or no importance to the smaller banks but increases in importance with the size of banks. As might be expected, the majority of such loans are made by the large metropolitan banks.

Agricultural loans are those made to farmers for short-term, intermediate-term, and long-term needs other than the purchase of real estate. The most common types of farm loans made by commercial banks are to finance seasonal expenses (for crop and livestock production) and intermediate-term investments (farm machinery and equipment). Commercial banks are not the primary source of funds for farm credit and are exceeded in importance by other institutions both private and public, the latter specializing in farm credit. Agricultural loans generally tend to increase in importance with the decrease in size of banks.

Consumer loans consist chiefly of loans for purchasing installment paper from retailers and finance companies; direct cash loans that are payable in a lump sum or in installments; and repair and modernization loans for homes. Consumer loans have grown considerably in importance over the years. After the mid-1960s, bank credit card plans became the most dynamic growth component of total consumer credit offered by commercial banks. The high yield of these loans has made them popular and relatively more important to middle-size banks and those larger ones that initiated credit card plans. In the aggregate, consumer loans rank third in importance among the different categories of commercial bank loans.

The last category of commercial bank loans, "all other" loans, is the catchall classification that includes such bank loans as those to domestic and foreign banks, nonbank financial institutions, charitable and educational organizations, hospitals, churches, and all others that are not included by the FDIC classification in any of the other categories.

However characteristic the above picture may be of the composition of the loan portfolios of commercial banks, it is in no way reflective of the loan breakdown in the portfolio of each individual bank. Indeed, the types and proportions of loans carried in the portfolio vary greatly from bank to bank. Three key elements are responsible for such variation in loan portfolio composition: the economic character of the area in which a bank is located, or the market served, the background and evolution of a particular bank, and the preferences of management within the framework of current opportunities and pressures.

The economic character of the area in which a bank is located largely determines the fields of lending in which it will specialize. Banks located in areas where the economy is predominantly agricultural, inevitably find themselves engaged primarily in agricultural and real estate loans. In consequence, banks in these areas have far greater proportions of these types of loans in their loan portfolios than banks located in large urban centers. Indeed, the latter banks, oriented toward providing bank services to both firms and individuals located in large urban centers, build a loan portfolio predominantly with commercial and industrial loans, consumer loans, and mortgage loans. And if one of these centers functions as the national money market, then the larger banks of this center could reasonably be considered as money market banks —a fact that would account both for the great proportion of loans for the purchasing of securities found in their loan portfolios and for the importance of correspondent bank accounts among their deposit balances.

The influence of the economic environment on the composition of a loan portfolio under a unit banking system is, of course, somewhat different from the influence on a loan portfolio under a branch banking system. Under the latter system, banking is generally conducted by a few large metropolitan banks with branches on a statewide scale. This very characteristic of branch banking contributes to a highly diversified commercial bank loan portfolio with risks spread over different companies, industries, occupations, individuals, and geographical areas. At the same time, however, branch banking renders loan portfolios impersonal, that is to say, less representative of the specific needs of local communities and groups of individuals. In any case, whether the area served by a bank is local, regional, or statewide is, of course, a matter of legal prescription, which governs the structure of commercial banks.*

Given the economic characteristics of its market, a particular bank's opportunities to make loans depends on the established patterns of business contacts and loan practice that its management has developed over the years. These patterns—which may have been the result of special talents or tastes of the bank's leading loan or executive officers, or of incidentally useful connections or conditions—also have the tendency of developing institutional roots in highly trained and specialized lending officers, special reputations, and the like, which bestow upon the individual bank a particular character as portrayed in the type of business it does and as expressed in its loan portfolio composition.

This helps explain how some banks have become known as, for example, textile, electronics, or oil banks. Specialization of this type can be profitable for a bank, particularly where a degree of expert knowledge not common in

---

*There is a wide disparity in the law as to the size of the area a bank can serve. This disparity stems from differences in the degree to which state authorities permit branch banking. Statewide branching is prevalent in 21 states and the District of Columbia, limited area branching is prevalent in 14 states, and unit banking in 15.[7]

the banking industry prevents other banks from effectively competing. It does, however, open the bank to a potential peril. Clearly, substantial loan concentration in the portfolios of such banks would be unavoidable. Such concentration, however, can be partly offset by seeking credit outlets in contrasting industries or in industries not subject to the same cyclical influences. This move, coupled with a good income investment policy, geographically and/or industrially diversified, can hold the risks of loan concentration within tolerable margins.

The foregoing influences set the framework of possibilities within which bank management makes current policy decisions pertaining to the composition of the loan portfolio. Not only is there ample choice within this framework, but the framework itself is not unalterable and may be changed gradually and within limits by the additions to established patterns fostered by current policy. The preferences of management with respect to loan portfolio composition, as these are affected by such considerations as yield, risk of loss, and liquidity (average rate of loan payoff), have a strong effect upon the actual composition at any time. This is especially true during a period of monetary restraint. During such a period, the general demand for credit is so strong that banks are confronted with more loan requests in practically every category than they can possibly accommodate. Then, indeed, more than in any other phase of the business cycle, management exerts a decisive influence upon the types and volume of loans to be made.

Management's preferences for proper balance in the portfolio among the various loan types is expressed in the form of limits upon various loan categories. These limits, except were provided by law,* are not firmly fixed for all times but are flexibly adjusted or altogether eliminated in line with changing conditions. Limits on specific categories take the form of absolute magnitudes or of percentage relationships that broaden loan categories, or of relationships to time (including savings) deposits or to capital accounts. These limits become especially important when the initial phases of a restrictive credit policy set in. For it is during this time that management adopts a more cautious and selective approach in the extension of loan funds. The implementation of such an approach affects all loan categories and all borrowers. However, there are significant differences in the degree of this effect and in the manner of its transmission both for major loan categories and for the individual borrower.

---

*Such limits are imposed, for example, on real estate loans, construction loans, and the financing of international trade transactions. The total volume of real estate loans a national bank can make is limited to 100 percent of its time (including savings) deposits or 100 percent of its capital and surplus, whichever amount is the greater. In the case of construction loans, these cannot exceed 100 percent of the bank's capital structure. As for banker's acceptances to finance international transactions, these cannot exceed 50 percent of the bank's capital structure.[8]

The categories that would be the first to feel the impact of credit restraint vary depending on the character of the loan market in which the bank finds itself. A restrictive lending policy would affect primarily the bank's major lending categories—that is to say, the categories that constitute the overwhelming bulk of the loan portfolio. Regulation of such categories is both an effective and necessary instrument of general loan policy.

The loan categories that usually feel more the impact of credit restraint are real estate loans, consumer loans, and loans to brokers and dealers. By contrast, commercial and industrial loans, unless they constitute the overwhelming bulk in the loan portfolio, tend to feel less the effects of a restrictive policy. This must not be taken to imply that commercial and industrial loan applicants will not be required to meet the higher standards that are progressively imposed as credit tightens, or that these applicants will receive priority over others seeking loans. The great diversity among borrowers within loan categories does not permit such a generalization to hold. But it does imply that such commercial and industrial borrowers who can meet the higher standards will be the last to be turned down as a bank's lending limit is approached. The explanation behind this privileged position of commercial and industrial borrowers is that management considers their proper accommodation as essential in maintaining the bank's lending base in the form of commercial deposits. It is basically the compensatory deposit balances associated with commercial and industrial loans that places them first in management preference vis-a-vis the loans in the other categories during a period of credit stringency.[9]

Management's preferences must be broken down not only by broad categories of loans but also by individual borrowers within these broad categories. In assessing the desirability of individual loan requests, management employs certain criteria that serve as a basis for a bank's lending policy. Because these selection criteria constitute qualification criteria from the borrower's point of view, they can serve as screening devices to control loan volume. These criteria include the compensatory balances of the borrower; the credit rating of the borrower and—for secured loans—the type and marketability of the security pledged as collateral; the contractual rate of interest; the purpose of the loan; the liquidity of the loan as determined by the payout schedule; and the existence or prospect of a continuing relationship with the borrower. Bank loan policy does not differentiate between the importance of these criteria, though in practice they are applied with varying degrees of emphasis.[10]

Compensatory balance is viewed by management as a criterion of primary importance in assessing the desirability of individual loan requests. Compensatory balance is associated with borrowing on an unsecured basis. As might be expected, the requirement for such balances varies among banks and is influenced by prevailing money market conditions. Generally, however, it runs from 10 to 20 percent of the amount borrowed or the maximum amount of the line of credit established by the bank. The way this requirement is applied varies with banks. In some banks it is applied rigidly—borrowers' balances are expected to be maintained at the minimum or not fall below it throughout their indebtedness to the bank. In other banks, borrowers are given more latitude —the deposit balance must equal the specified minimum on the average or over the course of the year. Clearly, the former rule is much more burdensome to the borrower than the latter.

Banks place more emphasis on compensatory balances as qualification for loan accommodation in a period of credit stringency. During such times, a borrower's legitimate claim on a bank for loans is expected to be a multiple of his average balances, which is gradually reduced (thus increasing the compensatory balance requirement) as the bank's credit-granting capacity approaches its maximum. Management emphasis on compensatory balances has been frequently interpreted as a device for increasing the effective rate of interest on the specific loan. However important this may be, it does not constitute the full explanation for management's concern. The deeper significance of the compensatory balance lies in the relationship of a bank's lending capacity to its deposit base. In order for a bank to be able to lend it must have deposit funds, and borrowers must be so disciplined as to contribute their part in giving the bank lending power. Finally, the compensatory balance constitutes a protective device for the bank in dealing with borrowers whose credit is not above reproach. Thus, if a borrower's default appears imminent, the bank can apply the balance on deposit against the loan, thereby offsetting a portion of it. This legal practice (right of offset) enables a bank to obtain a slightly better settlement than would otherwise be possible; that is, it enables the bank to become a general creditor for the remainder of the loan rather than being just a general creditor of the bankrupt customer.

Another important selection criterion is the credit rating of the borrower and, if the loan is to be secured, the type and marketability of the security pledged. This criterion is intended to evaluate the safety of the loan outlets; that is to say, to judge the risk that the borrower will not fulfill the terms of the loan agreement and the recourse available to the bank in the event of default. The safety of a loan, and hence the risk of default, depends upon both the willingness and the ability of the borrower, be it individual or business, to meet loan obligations as they fall due. The willingness of the borrower to honor contractual obligations is essentially a matter of character, sensitivity to social pressures, and consciousness of the consequences of voluntary default; character refers to the personal integrity of the prospective borrowers—their intention to meet their obligations to the bank without default of any kind. If the social standard is one of honoring financial obligations rather than willfully and conspicuously evading them, the pressure for meeting such obligations will be further strengthened. Also, awareness of the consequences of voluntary default for the future further adds to a borrower's intentions (and even, one might say, his anxiety) in meeting debt obligations. Though the moral foundation of credit is important, the safety of the loan will depend, in the final analysis, upon the ability of the borrower to perform—that is, to pay his debts.

Judgment of the ability to pay generally depends upon the credit applicant's stock of wealth and its marketability or liquidity, his protective income during the life of the debt, and the existence of any claims—current or prospective—against his wealth and income. The stock of wealth, less any debts outstanding, represents the financial worth and strength of the potential borrower. This net worth serves to assure the confidence of the creditor that the borrower will be able to honor his obligations as they come due. A potential debtor's future net income is the source for dept repayment. Earning capacity therefore constitutes a basic element of both creditworthiness and lender confidence. The advance of accountancy has enabled the development of a variety of tools (budgeting, ratio analysis, cash flow estimates, and pro forma statements) that focus on these aspects of a loan applicant's record and prospects; together they make up the credit or financial statement analysis.

In arriving at a decision of creditworthiness, a bank's credit department must give consideration to each of the factors noted above, namely, character, capital, and capacity. These factors make up what writers in banking frequently refer to as the three c's of credit. If these criteria fail to justify the creditworthiness of a would-be borrower, a fourth element is taken into consideration, the security pledged. Security is provided in most instances to support the weakness found in one or more of the credit factors, and hence to render attractive a weak credit situation. The security pledged for collateral must be readily converted into cash, and its market value must be greater than the value of the loan that it secures. The security provided may take the form of a direct pledge of property (that is, stocks, bonds, inventory, receivables, equipment, and real property); guaranties (that is, cosignatures and endorsements); or protective covenants in the loan agreement on the future financial conduct of the borrower (that is, to maintain certain minimum balance sheet ratios, not to pledge certain assets as long as the loan is outstanding, to limit dividend payments).

By using standard and dependable yardsticks of credit analysis to determine a loan applicant's credit rating, and by requiring security when complete creditworthiness is questioned, management in essence aims to control the quality of the loans in the portfolio and hence, virtually, the performance characteristics of the major loan categories and the entire loan account with respect to the risk of default. The risk of default is, of course, gauged in monetary outcomes just as it is with yield. In an uncertain world these are matters of judgment rather than knowledge. Both risk and yield are thus essential elements of probable outcomes of a specific loan. Management does not ignore the interrelationship of these two elements with other criteria, to be mentioned below.

The importance of the remaining selection criteria to be mentioned here depends upon their effect on the risk-yield spectrum of potential earnings. The contractual rate of interest establishes the ceiling on anticipations pertaining to potential payments by the borrower.[11] Management's concern over the purpose of a loan may be guided by risk-assessing considerations or such broader considerations as loan volume control. The relationship into which a bank enters with a typical customer, especially a business firm, has many aspects. Customer relationship includes the deposit itself, an assumed obligation by the bank to extend credit to the customer on terms and amounts to be determined by prevailing conditions, and the rendering of different other financial services (such as payroll and account collection services, registrarships and trusteeships). Management's concern for a long-term customer relationship depends on bank deposits and credit-granting capacity or on the customer's record of weathering previous difficulties as an index to his future performance and the degree of risk involved.* The payout schedule is important in various respects: namely, in relation to the element of yield, since it affects a bank's ability to accommodate—with given lending capacity—a maximum number of deposit customers; in relation to the element of risk, since loan repayment is geared to the nature of the transaction financed and hence to the risk involved in the individual loan; and in relation to the liquidity of the loan itself.

The structure of interest rates set by banks for the various loan categories reflects the aforementioned selection criteria as weighted by management. Clearly, the relative importance of these criteria varies with loan categories. The fact that a bank makes loans of various categories or loans of the same category to various borrowers at different rates of interest indicates a degree of substitutability among loan characteristics. This, of course, is to be expected as a result of variations in the multiple criteria considered from borrower to borrower. Indeed, bank judgment concerning uncertainties is as liable to error as the market for bank loans is susceptible to imperfections.

Of the selection criteria discussed above, some are included among the formal terms of the loan agreement—rate of interest, repayment schedules (maturities), and specific collateral—while others are administered informally

---

*Management concern over customer relationships holds especially true for large established customers. These customers are usually the most mobile in the credit markets, which means that if a bank refuses to accommodate them, another bank will most likely not refuse them, because of their impressive credentials. Refusing such a customer would inevitably cause the loss of his business in the future. Turning down, however, small borrowers will have only marginal consequences or none at all, upon potential bank profits, since such borrowers are generally immobile or locked in to one source of credit, that is, the bank with which they do business.[12]

—credit rating, compensatory balances, customer relationship, and purpose of the loan. Of these criteria, some are more important than others in making management's preferences effective in practice. In the case of commercial and industrial loans, for example, the requirement for compensatory balances serves as an automatic device for acceptance or rejection of loan requests and hence for controlling loan volume in this category. In other cases, as in real estate loans and loans to dealers in government securities, variations in interest rates are used to control loan volume. In still others, as in direct installment loans to consumers, alteration of down payment and maturity requirements are used as weeding-out devices. The effects of these various control devices upon loan categories are both qualitative and quantitative. They are qualitative because by reducing risk they in fact increase the effective yield of the loans within a category. This effect, however, falls short of altering the average characteristics of the loans within the category. It follows, therefore, that use of these devices basically controls volume without altering essentially the average characteristics of such loans. Clearly, when the average characteristics of a loan category are altered, the relative importance of the entire category in the total loan portfolio will be changed. Such a change would be reflected in the bank's overall portfolio.

Use of the control devices suggested above depends to a large extent upon the competitive climate. Indeed, the competitive situation in which a bank finds itself establishes limitations as to the use of some of the control devices mentioned above—specifically, the devices that are incorporated in the formal terms of the loan agreement, such as interest rates and maturities. Given the competitive climate, it seems unlikely that a bank would take individual action and change its lending terms for any loan category without precipitating a loss or gain of loan customers, depending upon what the case may be. In other words, with changes in formal terms readily spread among borrowers, no bank can risk singly setting noncompetitive terms for any major loan category without affecting gravely its loan position. It follows, therefore, that given a competitive situation, banks should make use primarily of the informally administered devices—that is, credit rating and compensatory balances—because they can be discretionally and inconspicuously employed in particular instances. Unless, of course, anticipations of change in the general economic conditions, and hence in the credit situation, are widely shared, in which case an individual bank may alter the formal lending terms—interest rate and maturities—of its longer-duration loans, that is, the term and real estate loans. Clearly, expectations of rising general demand for credit (optimistic expectations) would affect both the interest rate and acceptable maturities of longer-term loans by raising the former and shortening the latter, while expectations of slackening credit demand (pessimistic expectations) would have a reversed effect.

It follows that in making loan policy decisions, the primary task of management is to make adjustments to changing conditions as these are manifested by tendencies and conditioned by expectations. The management that fails to make such adjustments and bases its decisions solely on current developments cannot be considered as exercising management powers. Thus, the principal responsibility of management lies in making decisions guided by the competitive situation, the bank-borrower relationships, and the anticipations pertaining to the performance of significant magnitudes in the general economic framework.

The composite attitudes and actions of commercial bankers in making policy decisions concerning their loan portfolios would exert important influence upon the general level of economic activity. The type of economic activity supported by the extension of bank credit affects the distribution of capital among industries and among firms within industries, thereby exerting important influence upon what is produced, how much of each product is produced, as well as where the products are turned out. The effect of bank loans upon investment spending will, of course, be maximized if bank funds flow where their productivity is highest and if competitive conditions generally prevail in business markets. The resulting higher productivity would promote specialization and foster economic development and growth with positive effects upon economic welfare.

ADMINISTRATION OF THE LOAN POLICY

The administrative framework for the carrying out of the lending function is an integral part of loan policy. In other words, loan policy making extends to the establishment of an effective lending organization and the adoption of the necessary procedures for the proper execution of the lending function. Specifically, the directors must also determine the organizational structure of the lending function, delegate authority to loan officers, and set procedures for the review of loan applications.

The lending organization varies considerably from one bank to another, reflecting, among other things, differences in the size of the bank, the types of loans made, the quality of management, and the attitude of the board of directors toward the delegation of authority. Generally speaking, the legal responsibility for bank lending rests with the entire board of directors. It is customary, however, to assign responsibility for supervising the lending function to a senior management member or to a loan committee that would ensure that loans are made in accordance with the law and the bank's own policies. In small unit banks, for example, this responsibility is assigned to the chief executive officer. Thus, the president of such banks is at the same time the principal lending officer and, therefore, handles all types of loan requests, whether for consumer, business, or real estate purposes. Other officers may be charged to perform limited lending functions along with their other activities. Under no circumstances, however, should the directors themselves be actively involved in the granting of loans. Such involvement is a poor loan policy not only because of their lack of technical or specialized knowledge but also because of their community affiliations with political, social, and business interests.

In large-size unit banks, there is usually more delegation of authority and lending specialization. In such banks it is customary for the board of directors to assign to a loan committee the responsibility for supervising the lending function. This committee may be composed of a specific number of directors (directors' loan committee) or of loan officers (officers' loan committee). The latter holds especially true for larger banks, which, in response to specialized loan demand, have the lending function usually carried out by such specialized departments as consumer, real estate, agricultural, and business or commercial. In such cases the officers' loan committee may be composed of officers of the same loan department (intradepartmental committee). With an organization of that kind, obviously very few, if any, loan requests would be referred to the board of directors for action.

The delegation of authority in large banks extends beyond the establishment of the loan committee. Lending officers are customarily assigned maximum dollar lending limits, both for secured and unsecured loans, which gives them the authority to decide independently of the committee, on loan requests within their assigned limits. These limits are usually higher for lending officers in large banks than for those in smaller banks. Such authority is given by the board of directors and is subject to periodic review.

Just as with unit banks, the lending organization of branch banks exhibits important variation. It is not uncommon, however, for branch officers and managers to have a limited loan authority. In such instances loan requests above these limits must be referred to the head office for consideration by the branch's regional supervisor. In the event that the specific request is higher than the supervisor's limit, it would be referred to the bank's loan committee. Clearly, a high degree of centralization in lending authority is undesirable because of the detrimental effects it involves. Such centralization results in significant delays, reduces drastically the element of personal contact, which is so important in credit evaluation, and gives rise to poor customer relations.

In deciding upon loan requests, lending officers must have the benefit of all relative information about the applicant. While in small banks the credit officer himself must gather and analyze this information, in larger banks this task is performed by credit departments. The functions of the credit department are basically the same in all banks: it assembles, records and analyzes credit information with the objective of ascertaining the degree of risk associated with each loan request and determining the amount of credit that the bank can prudently extend in each case. In some banks the credit department may make recommendations on a credit request, in others it may not. In any case the final decision is left to the lending officer and/or the loan committee.

In arriving at a judgment of the character, capacity, and capital of a loan applicant, the credit department of a bank draws upon several sources of information. These include borrowers themselves and credit-reporting agencies. Current information about borrowers is essential in making bank loans and must come from the borrowers directly or indirectly. This necessitates a close relationship between the borrower and his bank, with the former providing the bank with pertinent financial data and submitting to specific and general questioning on related matters. The bank can verify the disclosures with some outside checking. In the case of a business loan it can proceed to make not only trade checks (that is, checking with various suppliers and customers of the firm), but also checks on other banks with which the borrower was previously related.

Although most banks prefer to undertake their own checking, they often, in addition, subscribe to the services of credit-reporting agencies, whose function is to compile data on the creditworthiness of individuals and businesses. In doing its own checking, a bank may, for example, use the services of retail credit bureaus, which provide reports on individuals upon request and also publish regularly bulletins containing consumer information. In using credit-reporting agencies, a bank has access to a number of sources. One such source, and one of the best known, is Dun & Bradstreet, whose service extends to over 125 types of business activity. But there are several other credit agencies that are classified as special mercantile or trade agencies. These agencies specialize in compiling important information on a particular trade or industry (that is, the food industry, the leather industry, and the jewelry industry) or on a limited number of allied trades or industries. An example of the latter is the Lyon Furniture Mercantile Agency, which specializes in such fields as home appliances, furniture, and department and general stores.

Other sources of information that may be tapped by bank credit departments in determining the creditworthiness of applicants—if such applicants are large businesses—are public records, where reference is made, for example, to pending lawsuits, bankruptcy proceedings, and transfers of property; trade journals, which report developments and trends in the particular industries in which bank customers are engaged; public accounting firms; and newspapers, magazines, circulars, bulletins, and directories.

Once adequate information has been collected, the credit department would proceed to analyze it in determining the applicant's record and prospects. If the applicant is a business concern, financial analysis will rely upon several tools developed in the financial domain (that is, ratio analysis, budgeting, cash flow estimates, and pro forma statements), the technical description of which goes beyond the purview of the present discussion. What is important, however, is that credit analysis would contribute significantly in determining the creditworthiness of the loan applicant.

The credit information and analysis of the pertinent data, whether of businesses or consumers, constitute a bank's written record of its investigation. Because of the present and potential importance of such information for the bank itself and other banks, the effort is made to preserve it in an orderly fashion—in an individual folder or file readily available for the use of the loan officer, loan committee, and even the board of directors. The credit department must keep these files up-to-date as new information comes to its attention. By providing a factual picture of the creditworthiness of the borrower, credit files are thus at the heart of the lending function and are essential prerequisites for the effective operation of a commercial bank.

As stated earlier, credit analysis does not involve decision making but at best a recommendation to loan officers and/or the loan committee, which will review the credit information and decide as to the action to be taken. As is implied, in arriving at such decisions, loan officers are always expected to consider what is good for the bank. After all, the purpose of the lending policy is not to serve as an end within itself but to promote the objectives of the lending function.

A necessary part of the lending officer's responsibility is to keep abreast of the loans outstanding. That is to say, once a loan has been made, the lending officer is usually responsible for supervising such a loan. Loan supervision implies keeping in close contact with the borrower and monitoring his financial activities. This may include plant visits, securing the borrower's periodic financial statements, and reviewing requests for renewal or additional funds. An in the event of difficulty with the loan, the lending officer will exert every effort to collect the amount outstanding.

An essential corollary of active and aggressive lending is an effective collection system. Successful bank lending implies making goods loans and keeping them current through a vigorous collection policy. Such policy would thus allow the bank to keep loan losses within tolerable limits.

The first explicit sign that a bank receives from a loan in distress is usually an indication from the borrower as to his inability to comply with original repayment terms. Not infrequently a bank may even see this difficulty approaching through its process of loan supervision. Whatever the case may be, with the first indication of customer delinquency, a bank should take appropriate measures. These measures may range, for example, from the revision of a borrower's payment schedule to meet new circumstances, to the implementation of strong-arm tactics. Prompt action may sometimes make the difference between the success or failure of an active lending policy.

When delinquencies arise they should be brought promptly to the attention of the loan committee or the board of directors. Detailed reporting is especially warranted when delinquent loans are large (as is the case in many commercial loans), with such reporting containing information as to the cause of the delinquency and the subsequent measures instituted by the lending officers. On the other hand, small loans (that is, consumer loans) may be referred to in the delinquency reports in a more generalized manner—that is, in terms of aggregate amounts per type or class of loan.

Comparative data on delinquency rates, especially for consumer loans, are made available regularly through the publications of local credit bureaus, state bankers' associations, and the American Bankers Association. The direct comparison of these data with individual bank figures should provide a reasonable index of the soundness of a bank's lending and collection policies.

While the overall lending practices of banks are considered satisfactory, frequent criticism has been voiced about the loan administration of some banks. Such criticism has focused upon bank emphasis on collateral instead of on borrowers' ability to repay out of earnings (capacity); the failure to use information available; the use of inefficient, lenient, and tardy collection procedures; the tendency to equate loan size with borrowers' integrity and overall creditworthiness; the extension of too many loans on the basis of character references and outdated information; the giving of extensions and permitting of pyramiding of loans by marginal loan customers; and the extension of loans that do not contain adequate legal provisions to protect the bank in case of collection difficulties.[13]

SUMMARY

Lending constitutes the third priority in the employment of bank funds. After a bank has taken care of its primary and secondary reserve needs, it can devote itself to the business for which it is best fitted—making loans. Lending is the core activity of commercial banks, and in this area they profess experience, expertise, and flexibility, which give them a clear competitive advantage over all other financial institutions. This explains the prominence of loans among commercial bank assets and their prime contribution to bank profits.

Throughout most of the commercial banking history of this country loans have been the most important asset held by banks. The traditional view of commercial banking, dating back to the eighteenth and nineteenth centuries in Europe, is that bank assets should consist principally of short-term loans arising from the financing of commerce, or commercial loans. By holding these short-term assets, the banks, it was argued, would possess the most liquid earning assets and would, therefore, be able to meet their demand deposit liabilities when called upon to do so. With the outbreak of World War I and the ensuing expansion of public debt, commercial banks were encouraged to invest in securities. From then on there was a gradual rise in commercial bank holdings of investment securities to a position of prominence among bank assets. This trend reached unprecedented heights first during the depression of the 1930s and then during World War II. Outcome of the sharp increases in bank investments in this 20-year period was a pronounced change in the asset composition for commercial banks and, more specifically, in the relative importance of investments vis-a-vis loans in bank earning asset portfolios. Drastic as it has been, however, this shift in bank earning asset portfolios, it was but a deviation from a historic asset distribution pattern in commercial banking. Indeed, throughout banking history loans have exceeded investments usually by a wide margin. This normal asset pattern also characterizes the post-World War II period. Specifically, the vigorous demand for credit from the private sector in the postwar years provided commercial banks with strong incentives to expand their loan portfolios, and hence to increase bank earnings. The almost exclusive reliance, however, of Federal Reserve policy throughout this period on bank credit restraint to promote a sustainable rate of economic growth and to counter inflationary pressures, led commercial banks to monetize part of their holdings of government securities to meet the postwar demand for loans.

Not only has the proportion of bank loans to total or earning assets increased in the postwar period, but also the very character of bank loans has undergone important changes during this period. The changes in the character of bank loans reflected the competitive pressures from within and without the industry and were in direct response to the basic shifts that occurred in the private credit demand of the postwar years. Serving, as they do, every sector of the economy, commercial banks of necessity mirrored in their portfolios the shifts that took place in the postwar spending patterns of borrowers. Thus, there has been a phenomenal expansion of consumer, mortgage, and business loans, and a marked lengthening of average maturities in the loan portfolios of commercial banks.

However important current trends in commercial bank loan portfolios may be, they do not necessarily reflect the trends in the portfolio of each individual bank. Indeed, there is substantial variation from one bank to another as to the types and proportions of loans carried in their loan account. Given a certain size of local credit demand, three key elements are generally responsible for variations in loan portfolio composition: the economic characteristics of the area or market served, which has a profound effect as to the field of lending a bank will enter; the background and traditional business contacts of a particular bank, which helps explain the development of industry-specialized banks; and management preferences, which exert a decisive influence upon the type and volume of loans in the portfolio at any specific time. Management preferences, according to Federal Reserve surveys, are expressed through certain lending criteria, which act as screening devices in controlling loan volume. These criteria include, for example, a particular loan's contract rate of interest, the borrower's compensatory balances, the repayment schedule, the prospect of a long-term customer relationship, and the purpose for which the loan is requested (whether for seasonal needs, working capital needs, or speculative purposes).

The board of directors must constantly review loan portfolio policy and adjust it in the light of changing conditions. Such actions would render loan policy flexible and adjust the maturity characteristics of the portfolio to the cyclical nature of the economy. Stated differently, such action would allow the maturity characteristics of the loan portfolio to coincide with the proper phase of the business cycle and add significantly to the profitability of the loan portfolio. The stress should be on short-maturity loans during periods of slackened loan demand (which coincide with business recession and monetary ease), and on long-maturity loans during periods of peak loan demand (which coincide with high business activity and monetary restraint). The effectiveness of such policy would depend to a large extent upon the soundness of the relative data and the application of informed judgment.

NOTES

1. Lloyd W. Mints, *A History of Banking Theory* (Chicago: University of Chicago Press, 1945), p. 9; also see pp. 27–29.

2. Ibid., p. 9.

3. On the "shiftability" theory of liquidity see H. G. Moulton, "Commercial Banking and Capital Formation, III," *The Journal of Political Economy* 26, no. 7 (July 1918): 723; Waldo F. Mitchell, *The Uses of Bank Funds* (Chicago: University of Chicago Press, 1925), pp. 15–17, 19ff; Rollin G. Thomas, *Modern Banking* (New York: Prentice-Hall, 1937), pp. 161–69.

4. Herbert V. Prochnow, *Terms Loans and Theories of Bank Liquidity* (New York: Prentice-Hall, 1949).

5. G. W. Woodworth, "Theories of Cyclical Liquidity Management of Commercial Banks," in *Banking Markets and Financial Institutions,* ed. Thomas G. Gies and Vincent P. Apilado (Homewood, Ill.: Richard D. Irwin, 1971), p. 158ff.

6. Roland I. Robinson, *The Management of Banks Funds,* 2d ed. (New York: McGraw-Hill Book Co., 1962), p. 248.

7. Federal Deposit Insurance Corp., *Annual Report* (Washington, D.C.: Federal Deposit Insurance Corp., 1975).

8. *United States Code Service,* Title 12 (Indianapolis: Bobbs-Merrill Co., 1974), Sections 371 and 373.

9. For empirical data on sampled management preferences among loan categories, see Donald R. Hodgman, *Commercial Bank Loan and Investment Policy* (Champaign: University of Illinois, Bureau of Economic and Business Research, 1963), Chapter 3.

10. Duane C. Harris, "Rationing Credit to Businesses: More Than Interest Rates," *Business Review,* Federal Reserve Bank of Philadelphia (August 1970): 3–14.

11. Robinson, op. cit., p. 208.

12. Harris, op. cit., p. 8.

13. "The Quality of Credit is Strained," *Business Week*. (June 26, 1971): 70–74.

5

THE INVESTMENT
ACCOUNT—POLICY
CONSIDERATIONS

With lending lying between the second and fourth priorities in the management of bank funds, investment operations—the fourth priority—may be said to straddle the lending operations of commercial banks. On the one side, they provide the necessary degree of bank liquidity in the form of short-maturity money market instruments (secondary reserves). On the other side, they employ whatever funds cannot be loaned to provide income for the bank in the form of long-maturity capital market instruments (bond account). Liquidity, in the first instance, and income, in the latter, thus constitute the determining factors in the acquisition and holding of securities. This dual role of investment securities is not, however, identifiable in a bank's balance sheet, where reference to investment holdings is made only according to issuer.

The basic considerations that underlie the liquidity aspect of a bank's investment policy have already been considered in discussing a bank's secondary reserves. A notable part of investment operations, however, is still to be discussed, and this pertains to the other aspect of a bank's investment policy, the residual or income maximizing portion of investments—the bond account. Clearly, this dual aspect of investment policy results from the differing functional roles of various investment operations, which play an important part in the framing of a bank's general investment policy.

As we did in discussing lending, here, too, we shall attempt to focus upon the factors that underlie a bank's investment policy making and, specifically, upon bond portfolio policy considerations.

ESTABLISHING INVESTMENT POLICY

Every commercial bank is involved in investment operations. The framework of these operations, whether for liquidity or income, must be well defined.

Experience has shown that this can be attained only by reducing into writing (in detail or in broad general terms) the guidelines for such operations. However, to guard against the inflexibility of such operations over a period of time, it is imperative for investment policy to be periodically reviewed in the light of changing economic conditions.

Formulating a bank's investment policy generally implies the setting up of standards and the establishment of procedures for the management of a bank's investment portfolio. Developing an investment policy offers a bank's board of directors a wider framework than can be said for loans. Unlike the loan portfolio, the distributional character of which reflects local conditions and can therefore be controlled only within limits, a bank's investment portfolio can be planned in advance and consequently be tailored to bank wishes. Investment policy, therefore, has this unique element: it can be designed around the types of investment instruments that are available in the open market.

The degree of detailed planning by which the board of directors sets investment policy would vary from bank to bank, and would be indicative of the margin of latitude for maneuvering in the application of such policy. However detailed such planning may be, the basic aspects of bank investment policy will cover the quality of the securities that banks should buy, the type of diversification desired, marketability guidelines, the maturity policy to be pursued, and the internal organization for the carrying out of the investment function. We shall now turn to each of these general considerations and attempt to trace their effect upon bond portfolio policy.

The first specific is to identify the bond portfolio itself. In contrast with protective investment, which was discussed earlier and pertains to secondary reserves, income investment refers to a bank's bond account—that sector of the investment portfolio outside the secondary reserve categories. As such, it includes securities with maturities generally longer than five years, and represents the core of a bank's residual loanable funds. The bond portfolio may therefore be said to constitute the residual asset category, upon which falls the burden of final adjustments in a bank's asset position. With no specific liquidity requirement to fulfill, and with local loan demands met or the bank's lending limit reached, the chief function of these funds is to generate income for the bank.[1]

Although employment of these funds in the open market is geared toward the generating of income for the bank, aggressive pursuit of it could undermine the bank's continued existence. No security investment should be bought simply because it offers a high yield or because it seems to afford the opportunity of a capital gain. There is much more involved than simply the yield or the prospect of capital gain. What must also be considered in appraising the available investment instruments are the risks inherent in them. This risk appraisal is the combination of a credit factor (risk of default) and a market factor (interest rate risk), as discussed earlier. The issue, therefore, is one of taking into consideration the risks being accepted in the execution of the bond portfolio policy.

A bank's main source of income, as well as of risk exposure, is its loan account.[2] Since the funds employed in the bond account are residual in character, it follows that, as far as risk taking is concerned, the bond portfolio should be approached from the standpoint of a residual income producer. This means that with the bond portfolio generating supplementary income, risk taking must be kept within certain limits. The framework for risk taking is, to a great extent, determined by the amount of capital available for application against the portfolio. Acceptance of risks beyond portfolio ability to absorb them (in the form of capital adequacy), should be avoided, as lying outside the framework of a realistic and productive investment policy. Within the confines of this basic policy consideration, efforts must be directed toward the realization of adequate income.

Banking cannot point with pride to its past experience in investment operations. An authority describes this experience in the following manner:

> The bank failures of the depression brought to light many horrible examples of the mismanagement of investment accounts, but the period exemplifies an even further situation. The experience of commercial banks was worse than it needed to be and much worse than that of the insurance companies and the mutual savings banks both of which had had longer experience in investment operations.[3]

As the above discussion indicates, banks should seek as the end result of their bond account that amount of income which is consistent with safety of principal. Indeed, with the funds invested in the portfolio ordinarily turning over less rapidly than loans and liquid assets, safety of principal must always be of paramount consideration. What this means is that in building their bond portfolio, banks must seek to buy securities of high quality. Sacrifice of quality for income is justified only within acceptable limits:

> Since it is not normal, in the sense that it represents average experience, for the security behind any given issue to improve, any realistic investment program will take cognizance of the historical fact that bonds as a whole tend to deteriorate in quality.[4]

Quality must not be regarded as static or absolute, but as changing and relative:

It is axiomatic that no bond is good enough to buy and then forget. A positive policy of quality improvement is therefore necessary not only to strengthen the protection represented by any given investment portfolio, but in order to do nothing more than maintain its status quo.[5]

Accepting lower-quality bonds in the portfolio is of questionable merit. Such a move exposes a bank to the possibility of notable quality, and therefore market, deterioration during a period of depressed economic conditions. In fact, such investments could become so downgraded that examining authorities could require they be, partially or totally, priced down, according to current market. It follows that the quality of the securities bought must necessarily be high to discount any price deterioration in bad times.

Concern over the 1929–31 investment experiences of commercial banks led Congress to intervene soon after and legislate on banks' investments, in an apparent effort to establish quality guidelines for banks to follow. With the element of quality, however, changing and evolving over time, regulatory authorities were faced with the difficulty of defining and regulating a relative concept. This led them to emphasize marketability, which has since been viewed as a criterion for quality.

Marketability is obviously a criterion of quality, for if an obligation possesses quality, investors will be eager to purchase it, and vice versa. This approach raises the question of defining marketability. Though there are differing degrees of marketability, in general a marketable instrument is one that can be readily sold, and hence converted into cash, through the securities market mechanism, at a minimum, or no, price concession. A more refined approach would be to consider the difference between the bid and asked quotations for a security. Financial experts suggest that a margin of one point or more between such quotations is an indication of limited marketability.[6]

Banks have every reason to emphasize marketability or shiftability in their portfolios. With deposits providing the overwhelming portion of loanable and investible funds, marketable securities would at any time ensure promptness in the disposition of a block of a given issue of securities, without any significant adverse effect upon price quotations. For banks that pursue an aggressive investment policy (that is, geared to the cyclical nature of the economy), marketability considerations are of major importance. Such banks must be able to adjust, through sale, most of their portfolio when they desire to do so. In these instances marketability can be ensured by holding nationally known issues that are capable of attracting buyers under any market conditions.

Though marketability must be maintained throughout the investment portfolio, there will be instances in which management may be forced to deviate from this principle. This occurs when the community or municipality served resorts to a local issue to take care of its needs. In such a case, banks, for reasons outside investment portfolio operations, may have to, in whole or in part, load up with the local issue. It is generally the rule rather than the exception that such local credits are of limited marketability. By form, of course, these credits constitute investment of funds; in essence, however, they have all the characteristics of a local loan. It is only realistic, therefore, that such local credits be viewed as additions to the loan portfolio, in the form of term loans, rather than to the investment portfolio. For obvious reasons, such credits should not be part of the fundamental considerations influencing bond portfolio management.

Of the various securities available in the market, obligations of the U.S. government enjoy the highest marketability of any type of security. The riskless character of these securities and the highly organized market available* enable the holder to convert them into cash with minimal loss. These attributes of U.S. government securities have rendered them the most common and convenient type of security desired.

Of significant marketability also are the obligations of U.S. government agencies, and sponsored corporations which are traded in the same market as the direct obligations of the federal government. Agency securities have grown rapidly since the 1960s as the number of agencies authorized to issue their own securities has increased.† Though agency securities do not constitute direct obligations of the federal government, they are nevertheless regarded by the investment community as having credit quality similar to that of U.S. government securities. For it is the general belief that the federal government would not allow the default of any one of these obligations. Agency issues have thus been treated as nonrisk assets and are frequently reported in bank statements separately from other risk assets.

Unlike the issues of the federal government and its agencies, the obligations of the various states and their political subdivisions (that is, cities, counties, towns, and so on), usually referred to as municipal obligations, exhibit wide variations in terms of creditworthiness, just as do the obligations of the

---

*Not all U.S. government securities are marketable. The familiar series E savings bonds comprise the bulk of the nonmarketable government debt.

†Among the most important, and in fact the major issuing agencies, are the Federal Land Banks, Federal Intermediate Credit Banks, Banks for Cooperatives, Federal Home Loan Banks, and Federal National Mortgage Association.

In early 1975, the securities of these agencies totalled $76.5 billion which accounted for 87 percent of the total securities outstanding of U.S. government agencies and sponsored corporations. Their importance in federal agency financing has earned them the reputation of the "big five" agencies. These agencies have been actively borrowing on both a short- and a long-term basis.[7]

private sector. True, many of these municipal obligations enjoy a high credit rating—certainly a higher one than that of some of the bank's local loan recipients. Few banks, however, would venture to invest in these issues, as well as in those of corporate obligors, without their making some use of outside investment advice. This service is supplied by private investment advisory agencies that rate the credit standing of all those municipal and corporate obligors whose securities are actively traded in the market.*

Because of the many shadings in the credit standing of municipal and corporate obligors and the relatively limited number of rating categories, the placing of bonds in the same classification, and hence giving them the same rating, must not be taken to imply that they are of absolutely equal quality. It implies rather that they are basically of the same expected investment performance. Then, too, there may be rating variations among agencies as to the security of a certain obligor. Though such variations cannot be avoided, the rating standards are generally known and compatible.

Clearly, these ratings are not of full and absolute value as they tend to trail behind the conditions that cause them to change; that is, such ratings tend to trail the market, not be abreast of it. Despite the inherent limitations, these ratings have provided important institutional and individual investment guidance. The ratings of private agencies received wide attention with what amounted to their official recognition by the comptroller of the currency. In the regulations promulgated by the Office of the Comptroller of the Currency governing bank investment practices, ratings are referred to as presumptive evidence of investment quality and are considered a fair yardstick of quality differences among securities. Specifically, in "Investment Securities Regulation," first issued in 1936, the comptroller of the currency, in defining the investment securities eligible for purchase by Federal Reserve member banks, describes them, from the standpoint of quality, as securities that are not "predominantly speculative in nature."[9] Banks are thus referred to the published opinions of rating agencies to identify the rating classification assigned to specific securities. Considered eligible for a bank's portfolio are the general

---

*Two of the most widely known rating agencies are Moody's Investors Service and Standard & Poor's Corporation. Each of these agencies uses a system of letters to differentiate between the various grades of bonds. In each system the three highest-grade classifications are considered to be the least-risk ones and are identified by a capital letter A followed by letters to distinguish the three grades; the Moody's system uses a lowercase a to distinguish among the three highest grades (that is, Aaa, Aa, and A for the three grades in that order), while Standard & Poor's expresses the same grades with all capital designations (AAA, AA, A). In the same manner the two agencies differentiate three grades of the B class and three grades of the C class for bonds containing higher degrees of risk. Standard & Poor's goes further by having a D class with three classifications for bonds in default.[8]

market obligations that are readily marketable and are rated within the top four classes by leading agencies in their investment-rating manuals.*

But bank investments are not limited to bonds included in the rating manuals and reports. Unrated securities (that is, securities of small face value or of small localities) also are recognized as eligible for purchase by member banks, even though they enjoy limited marketability. The responsibility for their quality rests, of course, with the bank's top management. The emphasis is thus placed by the Comptroller's Office upon the safety and soundness of these issues rather than their marketability.[10]

As banks do not differentiate in their published statements between secondary reserves and bond account, no statistical reference can be made as to the type of eligible securities found in the bond account. Any discussion, therefore, as to the type of securities held by banks must be limited to the aggregate level—that is, the investment portfolio of commercial banks. Of the various securities that are eligible for a bank's portfolio, direct obligations of the U.S. government—which include bills, certificates, notes, and bonds—have enjoyed great popularity. Their attractiveness to commercial banks is based primarily on the superior quality and marketability that these securities possess. In addition, these securities are generally free from involuntary redemption prior to a set maturity date, are most commonly and conveniently used as collateral (that is, for public deposits, for loans from the Federal Reserve banks), require less supervision, and are available in almost any desired maturity consonant with bank investment policies.† These attributes made U.S. government obligations the most important feature of bank investment portfolios for the three-and-a-half decades ending in the late 1960s.

The preponderance of U.S. government obligations in bank portfolios, as shown in Figure 12, started in the early 1930s. With the loan demand generally low and the pressure on commercial banks to augment income rising significantly, banks became active buyers of investment securities. The sizable losses

---

*In his definition of quality, the comptroller of the currency does not make direct reference to the security-rating services. Though explicit mention is no longer made of the rating classes recommended, his regulations still give recognition to the investment stature of the obligations rated in the first four brackets of rating manuals. This has been taken to imply that listing in the top four grades—down through Baa, or BBB—confirmed by two services, makes a security eligible for a bank's investment portfolio.

†Treasury bills, the most liquid of all Treasury issues, are discount obligations with initial maturities of from three months to one year; certificates of indebtedness are limited to a one-year maturity, Treasury notes have initial maturities ranging from one to seven years, and Treasury bonds usually have maturities in excess of ten years at the time of issue. The first three types of Treasury securities (bills, certificates, and notes) have maturities consonant with a bank's secondary reserve policies (of seasonal and nonseasonal nature), and the last type (bonds), with bond portfolio policies.

FIGURE 12

Investment Holdings of Commercial Banks, by Type of Security
(billions of dollars)

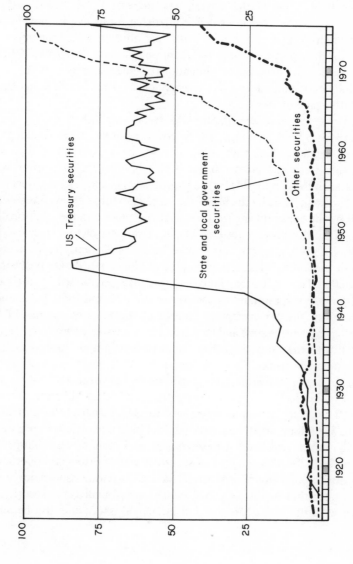

Source: Board of Governors of the Federal Reserve System, *Historical Chart Book* (Washington, D.C.: Federal Reserve System, 1974).

131

they had sustained, however, during the years 1929–31, had led to a shift in emphasis among alternative investment instruments and a more conservative approach to investment portfolios. This shift in emphasis favored the securities of the federal as well as of the state and local governments, though more markedly so those of the federal. The increase in the federal debt, which resulted from the Treasury's deficit financing (designed, in part, to stimulate the economy), gave commercial banks and other investors the opportunity to build up their portfolios of government obligations. Thus from 1932 to 1935, bank holdings of government obligations doubled, and by 1934 the investment portfolio of commercial banks exceeded loans—a relationship that lasted until the latter part of 1955.

The war years accentuated the trend established during the prewar decade, with bank holdings of U.S. government securities reaching unprecedented heights. Thus, from 1941 to 1945, bank holdings of such securities increased from $22 billion to nearly $91 billion. This expansion was made possible on the supply side by the huge deficits of the federal government, and on the demand side by the use of the large amount of excess reserves accumulated by the banks during the decade of the 1930s and the additional reserves created by the Federal Reserve banks in support of the Treasury's requirements. In postwar years, commercial banks have greatly reduced their holdings of Treasury obligations, prompted by the extraordinary postwar demand for loans. This reduction, however, was also occasioned by their desire to invest more substantially the securities of state and local governments and profit from the tax-exemption feature of these issues. In the 1970s, bank holdings of tax-free state and local government issues have grown very rapidly; so much so that nowadays they are of primary importance in the portfolios of commercial banks. Thus, by March 31, 1976, state and local government obligations in commercial bank portfolios amounted to $100 billion as against $85.4 billion in U.S. Treasury obligations and $38.4 billion in "other securities." The latter category includes, basically, federal agency obligations amounting to $33 billion, with the remaining $5.4 billion made up of corporate bonds, foreign issues, and Federal Reserve bank and other stock holdings.* Prior to the early 1930s, this category of securities was of principal importance in the investment portfolios of commercial banks. Corporate issues enjoyed a preponderant position in this category as well as over all other security holdings because of the limited federal and municipal issues and also because of the

---

*Banking regulations prohibit banks from purchasing or acquiring stocks except to protect themselves against losses on debts owed the bank, or as permitted by law in special cases. These special situations allow stock ownership provided that it does not exceed the bank's capital stock and surplus or a specified percentage of it.

emphasis placed upon income. By the end of 1930, this category of securities amounted to $7.4 billion, and accounted for over 50 percent of all investments of commercial banks as compared to 17 percent in 1976.[11] If allowance is made for the federal agency obligations included in this category, all remaining issues would amount to a mere 2.4 percent of all security holdings.

A bank's investment portfolio, then, is usually some combination of obligations of the U.S. government and federal agencies, obligations of states and their political subdivisions, and obligations of the private sector. Because obligations of the U.S. government and federal agencies are of superior quality, no statutory limitation exists as to their proportion in a bank's investment portfolio. In other words, the amount of these obligations that a bank may choose to hold at any time is a matter of individual bank judgment. But there are limitations on bank holding of all other types of obligations, namely, of the states and their political subdivisions and of the private sector. In the case of obligations of the states and their political subdivisions, these limitations are partial, applying only on holding of specific issues, that is, revenue bonds;* whereas for obligations of the private sector these limitations refer to the entire class. A bank's investment in the above obligations is limited by banking regulation to an amount equal to 10 percent of the bank's capital and surplus. This regulation, which is also applicable to bank loans to any single borrower, is commonly referred to as the 10 percent rule and was enacted to insure diversification of bank investments in those obligations that are considered to be risk assets.[†]

The yield that a bank obtains on the acquisition of a bond varies with the type and quality of the bond. This is amply illustrated in Figure 13, which depicts the postwar evolution of the yields of U.S. government bonds, of state and local government bonds, and of obligations of the private sector, and the relationship of these yields to one another.

---

*Revenue bonds are those that are not backed by the taxing power of the issuing body but by the special receipts of the projects being financed. Examples of revenue bonds are the obligations issued to finance toll roads, toll bridges, parking lots, stadiums, and other utilities. Unlike revenue bonds, however, general obligations of states and their political subdivisions—also known as full-faith and credit obligations—have the full taxing power of the issuing body behind them, which renders them the best and hence most sought-after municipals. Their creditworthiness is also recognized by regulating authorities, which, in fact, allow banks to hold unlimited amounts of such securities.[12]

†In the comptroller's "Investment Securities Regulation," the obligations of the U.S. government and federal agencies, as well as the general obligations of states and their political subdivisions are classified as a type 1 security; in other words, as "a security which a bank may deal in, underwrite, purchase and sell for its own account without limitation." Obligations of international financial institutions and revenue bonds of states and their political subdivisions are classified as type 2 securities, and all other obligations, as type 3.[13]

FIGURE 13

Bond Yields
(in percent)

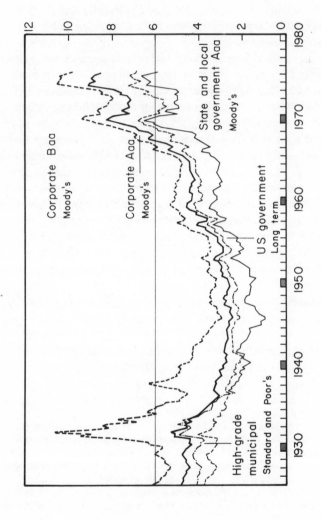

Source: Board of Governors of the Federal Reserve System, *Historical Chart Book* (Washington, D.C.: Federal Reserve System, 1976).

As is known, security prices and yields have an inseparable relationship of an inverse nature; that is, when bond prices increase, yields decrease and, conversely, when bond prices decrease, yields increase. Thus, the value that the open market places at any one time on the quality of an obligation, or the creditworthiness of an obligor, is reflected in the yield of the obligation. Figure 13, therefore, may be said to also reflect the importance that institutional and individual investors have attributed, over the years, to the types of securities illustrated in this graph. By June 30, 1976, second-grade (Baa) corporate bonds yielded 9.72 percent and high-grade (Aaa) corporates yielded 8.62 percent, whereas U.S. government obligations yielded 6.92 percent and high-grade (Aaa) municipals yielded 5.85 percent. The lower yield in the market has been that of municipal bonds, because of the interest-exemption feature of these securities in federal taxation. Tax-exempt securities tend to carry a lower nominal yield than securities with a comparable face value; yet their actual after-tax yield is generally higher than that of comparable but taxable securities. The tax-exempt quality of these securities has rendered them a highly attractive investment, especially for commercial banks and other investors— institutional and individual—who are in a high income tax bracket. For such banks one can make an approximate comparison between the yield of tax-exempt municipals and the yield of taxable bonds by doubling the quoted yield of municipals. For example, a 4 percent yield on a tax-exempt municipal would be roughly equivalent to an 8 percent yield on a fully taxable obligation of the federal government. For smaller banks, which are subject to a lower marginal tax rate, the benefit of tax-exempt municipals is reduced.*

The tax-exempt quality of municipals and their consequent attractiveness to large investors are reflected in the market, where such securities command higher prices and yield lower returns, as seen in Figure 13. The higher price, however, rarely reflects the whole tax benefit; the extent to which it does will depend upon market conditions. As a general rule, tax-exempt obligations will provide yields ranging from 22 percent to 48 percent lower than the yields from fully taxable obligations of comparable quality and maturity in the bank investment portfolio.

---

*The federal income tax on banks and corporations with income of $25,000 or less is 22 percent, which is the normal tax rate. For incomes in excess of that amount, however, there is also a surtax of 26 percent, which makes the total tax levied equal to 48 percent. A bank in the 22 percent income bracket would, therefore, keep 78 percent of its taxable income while a bank in the 48 percent bracket would keep 52 percent of such income. Thus, a tax-exempt security, when compared to a taxable obligation yielding 4 percent, will be worth 5.13 percent to a bank in the 22 percent income tax bracket [4.00/(1.00-.22)], and 7.69 percent to a bank in the 48 percent bracket [4.00/(1.00-.48)]. Clearly, the actual after-tax yield of these securities is generally higher than that of comparable but taxable securities.[14]

Apart from tax considerations, Figure 13 also depicts the premium paid by investors for the undisputed credit of the U.S. government, as compared with the highest-grade corporate obligations. Similarly, the yield differential between high- and medium-grade corporates portrays the value that investors attribute to quality or creditworthiness.

Closely related to quality considerations in the management of the bond account is the principle of diversification. Diversification is one of the fundamental and most significant rules of investment policy whether it pertains to banks or any other institutional and individual investors. Diversification is a generally accepted method of reducing risk in the investment account to manageable proportions. It may be defined as a process of spreading risk, prompted by the need to minimize the effect of poor judgment and the impact of economic conditions on the investment portfolio. Diversification is effected through the purchasing or holding of investment issues that spread over a wide enough spectrum. The holding of an assortment of securities in the portfolio, rather than a limited number of issues bunched at one time or in one place, would tend to reduce losses by averaging them out over the long run.

Proper diversification can be ensured by providing in the investment policy of a bank that a certain percentage of the investment portfolio be invested in particular types of securities or by establishing a ceiling on the funds that may be placed in specific types of securities. Clearly, the types of securities specified reflect the kind of diversification desired. Diversification may take various forms, such as by industry, geographical area, type of security, and management. Of these, two forms stand out in banking practice—diversification by industry and by geographical area, with the latter constituting the principal form of risk spreading in the portfolio.

Diversification by industry has, of course, significance only with respect to holdings of corporate securities. The traditional grouping of corporate securities has been into industrials, railroads, public utilities, and miscellaneous securities.[15] Each of these groupings traditionally has been further divided into subgroupings. Thus, industrial securities may be further subclassified, for example, into securities of heavy or capital goods industries and of consumer goods industries. Similarly, railroad obligations, once the aristocrats among bonds and a one-time bank favorite,* used to be distinguished, depending upon the principal type of service rendered, into such classes as passenger and agricultural lines. Public-utility holdings, too, may be further classified into such categories as gas, light, and telephone. Clearly, the degree of detail in the classification of corporate securities would depend to a large extent upon

---

*In the late 1890s and the early years of the present century, railroad bonds were almost the only ones listed on the New York Stock Exchange.[16]

the size of such holdings and the feasibility of such classification. As holdings of corporate securities, however, generally constitute only a minor portion of bank portfolios (as pointed out earlier), the traditional three-way classification would seem to be rather adequate.

Diversification of corporate obligations by industry does not, of course, exclude the possibility of a geographic distribution of these securities within each of the groupings and/or subgroupings referred to above. In such a case, risk spreading in corporates would be by industry and geographic area. Because of the minor amounts of corporate securities in the investment portfolios of commercial banks, diversification in corporates may be said to be of limited significance. By contrast, the leading application of the principle of diversification may be said to be in state and local government securities, with risk spreading done on a geographic basis. Indeed, with municipal obligations constituting the largest holdings of investment securities in commercial bank portfolios, diversification becomes of special importance here. As stated earlier, municipal securities represent debt of the various states and their political subdivisions. This debt has grown considerably over the postwar years, reflecting the increasing use of debt financing by state and local governments. Because of the large number of issuers and issues, there is a wide variation in the types of securities available. This variation is, of course, to be expected since each issuer has a different economic base not only vis-a-vis other issuing governments, state or local, but also over time. Some states or localities are agriculturally oriented, some industrially, some commercially, while others are fairly well diversified. In some the pace of economic change is slow, and in others faster. Some issuing governments are heavily indebted, others are less so. Differing portions of this debt are in the form of revenue obligations, supported by the earnings of some business venture, and in the form of general obligations, with the full taxing power of the issuing body pledged to assure repayment.

Clearly, of paramount importance in the geographic diversification of risk is the location of the credit—that is, of the issuing governmental body or obligor. What this means is that in building up its portfolio of state and local government securities, a bank should seek to purchase—over and beyond such local issues as are required for reasons of good customer and community relations—securities that are dependent upon areas of the country beyond the local community. In doing so, a bank minimizes exposure of its bond account to the economic conditions of the local economy and hence to the effects of area blight. Investing, therefore, in the municipal issues of other areas provides adequate hedging against local risk and safeguards the shiftability of the bond account. Inclusion of nonlocal, general market, tax-exempt municipals in the bond account is advocated in view of the fact that a bank's loan account is itself, and by necessity, made up of local credits. Indeed, with the loan portfolio consisting basically of local credits, a large position in local municipals in the bond portfolio would only accentuate the concentration in assets subject to adverse developments in the local economy. Local concentration in lending, and hence in the loan account, is not only inevitable but normal and to be anticipated. Indeed, it is difficult for all but the very largest banks—under a unit banking system—to make loans throughout the country and therefore to effect real diversification in their loan portfolios. Management may not be able to diversify the bank's loan account as much as it would like to, but the bond account offers an opportunity to do so. The investment portfolio offers management the opportunity to hedge against local risks by qualifying for it securities that have a different geographic, and hence economic, base for their strength. In planning, therefore, investment operations, management may offset concentration in the loan account by following a policy of not duplicating it.[17] In other words, the bond account must be viewed as complementary to a bank's loan account. This type of relationship constitutes an important test of diversification. "One of the tests of diversification of investments is to find out the extent to which the investment portfolio, *combined with* the loan account, gives a reasonable over-all balance" in a bank's earning assets.[18]

The bond account, therefore, offers management the only opportunity to achieve the diversification of a bank's earning assets. Hedging against local risks has long been regarded a sound banking practice. A word of caution must be advanced here, however, if management is to reap the full benefits of diversification. Diversifying against local risks in the portfolio means that a bank should avoid purchasing local or nearby open market securities in favor of securities from issuers located in other areas. By doing so, however, management foregoes investing in quality securities with which it may be thoroughly familiar from its lending activities, and must rely instead upon outside investment advice and other data for its knowledge of specific credits issued by remote localities. This drawback makes it imperative for management to restrict its nonlocal investments to securities of unquestioned credit standing. Such a step should suffice to protect the portfolio from any fast-deteriorating situation and meet a prudent standard for geographic diversification.

Too much diversification is as undesirable as too little or none. Indeed, the policy of diversification must not be carried too far. Diversification must not be taken to imply the purchase of small amounts of securities from every eligible issue that comes along to round out the portfolio. Such interpretation would tend to render the portfolio position too difficult to manage, give rise to higher bookkeeping expenses, and reduce the marketability of individual holdings since these would consist of small or odd lots. Too much diversification, therefore, can become cumbersome and is apt to reduce the effectiveness of the portfolio.

An important supplement to quality and diversification considerations in the management of the bond account is the investment factor of maturity. Maturity considerations, as these pertain to residual investments, include some critical issues for bank policy makers. Specifically, maturities raise two important questions for bond portfolio policy: setting a maximum maturity limit for investment securities, and determining the maturity composition of the bond portfolio. In the first instance, management is called upon to establish a maximum limit as to the maturity of the investment securities, if such limit setting is deemed sound policy, and in the latter instance, to determine the maturity distribution of the bonds in the portfolio after due appraisal of the prevailing economic climate. The scheduling of maturities within the portfolio and their rescheduling, whenever warranted, also bring the portfolio manager into the area of taking profits and losses, which have their own special tax connotations. These aspects of the maturity issue are all interrelated but can perhaps be understood more readily if they are examined separately.

In the employment of funds in the bond portfolio, bank management is faced with the problem of determining the maximum maturity of the securities to be acquired. If the intention is to hold these securities until final maturity, a bank actually commits itself to receiving for a fixed period of time a stated income. This, after all, is the essence of a true investment. The longer that period of time is, however, the greater the uncertainty will be over conditions not only at the time when the obligation falls due and the funds are available for reinvestment, but also throughout the interval that the security is held. This uncertainty is comprised of two factors—a credit factor and an interest rate (or income) factor.

With respect to investments involving credit risks, there is always the possibility that the credit standing of the obligor will vary over time. The longer the time, the greater will be the possibility of change. Since banks usually acquire the securities of obligors with high credit standing, the possibility of deterioration is greater than the chance of improvement. The magnitude of the risk involved can be amply demonstrated by reference to the attitude of investors at the turn of the century who used to view favorably the purchase of railroad bonds with maturities of 100 years.[19] Later market developments made apparent the danger involved in such long commitments.

Even though a bond may be free of credit risk, it is still subject to interest rate risk—the risk that its market price will fall because of a rise in the market level of rates. As stated in Chapter 2, this phenomenon is a result of the contractual rate of interest that bonds carry when issued, and of the changes in the general level of rates that occur in the market at any given time between the demand for and supply of funds. Banks could, of course, minimize their exposure to interest rate risk by acquiring securities when bond prices are low and interest rates high, and selling them when the opposite conditions prevail. However, it is usually when interest rates are high that banks have the least funds available for investments, because of the strong demand for loans. By contrast, when interest rates are low and the demand for loans is weak, banks usually have surplus funds for employment in the bond portfolio. Consequently, when banks enter the market to buy bonds, these bonds, reflecting the prevailing interest rate trends, carry a low contractual rate of interest. Banks that purchase bonds when interest rates are low face the risk of a depreciation in the bond account when subsequently interest rates increase. For such an increase will affect adversely the market value of these bonds. Banks cannot, of course, afford to dispose of their bonds at such times, as they will sustain capital losses. They will try instead to hold them until maturity or until bond prices increase again, as a result of a reversal in interest rate trends, and reach a level that will permit banks to sell without realizing substantial losses. If, however, in response to unusual withdrawals or intense customer loan demands, banks are forced to sell a portion of their bond portfolio at low prices, they will clearly sustain sizable losses.

There is, therefore, always the uncertainty over the prospective level of interest rates both at the time when the obligation falls due and the funds are available for reinvestment, and more so throughout the period that the security is held. The longer the maturity, the greater the possibility that market value (and income) over the long run will be (favorably or unfavorably) affected by changes in the level of rates. An investment, for example, in a 32-year bond at 3.5 percent is tantamount to accepting that the average return on one-year funds will not exceed 3.5 percent over the next 32 years.* Management, therefore, needs to be constantly aware of the fact that security prices rise when interest rates fall, and decline when rates rise, and that the price swings resulting from any given change in rate will widen as maturity is extended.

It is apparent that the longer the term of maturity, the greater the potential for quality deterioration and market vulnerability acceptance, which, if carried to an extreme, is inconsistent in part with the philosophy that the bond account is the core of the residual loanable funds. The question, therefore, that bank management is faced with is how far the maturities should be extended.

As depicted in Figure 14, it was not until the end of World War II that the general movement in interest rates turned upward. Based on the rising trend in interest rates that the market has known since, it is easy to conclude that there should be some fairly short-term limit to the maturities of commercial bank investments. Bank experience with longer term bonds has not been favorable; a number of banks found themselves with substantial depreciation on holdings of such bonds acquired 15 to 20 years ago. If a bank is purchasing securities for income to maturity it should also be prepared to accept receiving over a period of years the stated income. If it cannot live with it, then it should

---

*Such was the case for instance in February 1958 when the U.S. Treasury refunded five issues amounting in total to $16.8 billion, by offering holders in exchange three new issues, one of which was a 32-year bond maturing in 1990 and yielding 3.5 percent per annum.[20]

FIGURE 14

Long- and Short-Term Interest Rates
(percent per annum)

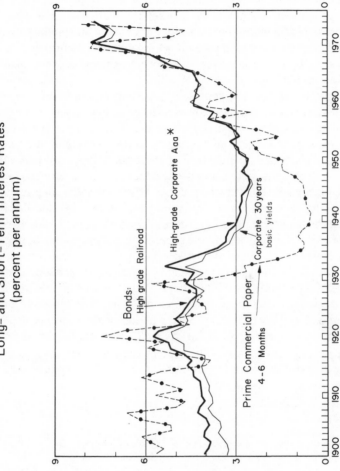

*New series from 1932 on.
Source: Board of Governors of the Federal Reserve System, *Historical Chart Book* (Washington, D.C.: Federal Reserve System, 1974).

141

never buy it.[21] Obviously, forecasting the state of the market and the demand for bank loans in the decade ahead, in planning for bond-portfolio maturities, is a hard task. In the light of the uncertainties involved in a rapidly changing world, management might well limit portfolio commitments to no longer than maybe 10 or 15 years, even though this too may be considered a long time.

Yield curves can be very instrumental in this respect. A yield curve represents the pattern of yields in the market at a particular time. This curve can be constructed by plotting graphically the yields of outstanding securities of comparable quality (or credit standing) for different maturities.* A yield curve can thus be constructed for U.S. government obligations, municipal bonds, or corporate bonds.†

As might be expected, the slope, steepness, and contour of the yield curves for securities have varied substantially over the years in response to the general currents in the economy. Generally, there are three distinct types of yield curves: increasing, or upsweeping; decreasing, or downsweeping; and constant, or horizontal. Examples of the shape of these three types are presented in Figure 15. A decreasing yield curve is one where the short-term rates exceed the longer-term rates; an increasing curve exists when the long-term rates exceed the short-term rates; and a constant yield curve, when the short-term rates match the long-term rates. The shape of the yield curve is closely related to the state of the economy and to the countercyclical operations of monetary and fiscal policy. When business activity is high, short-term interest rates advance upwards reflecting on the one hand the growing demand for credit and on the other the probable restraint on commercial bank credit creation by the Federal Reserve System. Longer-term rates, reflecting expectations of a return to more normal market conditions over a period of time, do not ordinarily increase as fast or to as great an extent. As, in the process of rising, short-term rates approach long-term rates, the shape of the curve will tend to become flat.‡ Once they rise above the long-term rates, as they have done on occasions in the past, the curve will be descending.**

---

*A yield curve is simple to construct. The vertical axis of the graph represents the yield in percent, and the horizontal scale the number of years to maturity. The yield curve itself can be constructed from the information presented on a daily bond quotation sheet. The yield and corresponding maturity of the issues to be included in the curve are plotted on the chart and a curve is drawn to connect them. If there are several variations, a curve can be drawn to connect at the greatest concentration of points.

†A yield curve for the U.S. government obligations is published regularly in the *Treasury Bulletin,* a monthly publication of the U.S. Department of the Treasury.

‡This was, for example, the case in the latter part of 1957 and again in most of 1959. Both of these periods were characterized by credit tightening and advancing short-term interest rates.

**This kind of yield pattern was encountered in late 1957 and again in late 1959 as a result of the credit tightening process.

FIGURE 15

Hypothetical Market Yield Curves

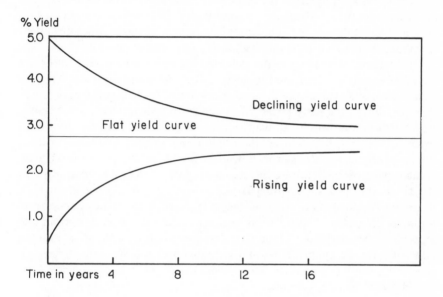

Source: Compiled by the author.

When business conditions are slack and the demand for money low, monetary policy is customarily geared toward creating easy money conditions; that is, toward channeling funds into the commercial banking system to increase credit availability. The general abundance of funds depresses sharply short-term rates, while the decline in longer-term rates lags behind. It is during such recessionary periods that the yield curve is usually ascending.*

The slope of the yield curve, also referred to as the term structure of interest rates, has been the subject of much theoretical debate. Outcome of this debate was the emergence of three theories that attempt to explain the prevailing term structure at any one time. These are known as the market segmentation, expectations, and liquidity preference theories.[22]

---

*Yield curves of this type were prevailing in 1954 and again in 1958 as a result of the recessions of 1953–54 and 1957–58.

The first theory holds that the behavior of the yield curve at any one time is mainly due to market segmentation; that is, particular classes of borrowers and lenders largely stick to particular maturities because of legal requirements, managerial policies, or traditional practices. This has led to the compartmentalization or segmentation of the market for debt instruments on the basis of the maturity of these instruments. Maturity yield differentials between the two segments would thus reflect imbalances between the maturity structure of debt demanded and that of debt supplied at any one time in these markets.

Coincident movements in the yields of securities with different maturities are possible and are attributed to general changes in the economic environment, which influence supply-demand relationships in all maturity ranges. For example, during the early phase of economic expansion, commercial banks, responding to a growing loan demand, would liquidate relatively short-term securities, causing the yield on these maturities to rise. At the same time, similar pressures upon longer-term lenders would lead them to sell off some of their longer-term securities, thereby causing the yield of these maturities to rise. Thus, the yields on Treasury issues, for example, would rise throughout the maturity distribution. Another factor responsible for coincidental movements in the yields of securities is arbitrage—the shift of lenders from one segment of the market to the other (intersegment movement) in an effort to take advantage of opportunities and maximize yields. This tends to keep all rates in line with one another. The possibilities of this sort of movement are considered to be rather limited.

Opposed to this type of explanation is the expectations hypothesis. The expectations theory holds that the long-term rates are an average of a series of expected short-term rates. Consequently, the yield curve would normally be flat because the holder of a longer-term debt instrument will earn, on an average basis over a specified period of time, the same amount as a holder of a series of short-term debt instruments. Over the course of the business cycle the relationship between the long-term and short-term interest rates will change and hence a shift will occur in the level of the yield curve. At a cyclical trough, the yield curve will be ascending (positively sloped), reflecting investors' expectations that interest rates will be rising in the near future. Thus, they will be unwilling to buy long-term securities at the present prices, but will be inclined to buy short-term securities so that later on they can be in a position to acquire long-term securities carrying higher yields. Thus a premium is paid for short-term maturity outlets in the form of lower yields, while sellers and issuers of long-term securities are forced to offer more favorable yields to attract buyers. The reverse is true during a cyclical peak. In other words, as business expansion approaches a peak, the expectations theory predicts a downward sloping (negatively sloped) yield curve. This implies that investors expect interest rates to be lower in the near future and hence they will be more inclined to favor long-term securities to maintain the current yield. Investing in short-term securities, even at present high rates, will only entail opportunity losses later since at maturity they will have to reinvest the funds at the going lower rates. Prices for bonds will most likely be driven up and yields will consequently fall, while in the money market the opposite trends will prevail.

The liquidity preference theory holds that the risks of holding long-term maturities are greater than those of holding short-term maturities and that the investment community prefers to avoid risk; therefore, the yield curve normally would be ascending (positively sloped) with long-term rates higher than the short-term rates. Over the course of the business cycle, the slope of the yield curve will be the same (positively sloped), reflecting the risks inherent in holding long-term securities.

These three approaches are dramatically opposed only in the hands of their most fervid apostles. It is possible to combine elements of these theories into a broader picture of the determination of the term structure of interest rates. Most empirical work in this area supports this approach.[23] Investor expectations appear highly significant in the process. Yet, the fact that the yield curve is frequently positively sloped suggests the existence of liquidity preference on the part of the investors; that is, of the need for some inducement to take the risk of holding longer-term securities than they would actually prefer. These preferences of investors and issuers—in some instances for short-term securities and in others for long-term ones—bring about a degree of market segmentation raising the possibility that differences, at any one time, in the relative supplies of securities in various maturities could modify the slope of the yield curve at least marginally.

Examples of yield curves are presented in Figures 16–18. Figure 16 illustrates an upward sloping yield curve for U.S. government securities as of March 31, 1960. One of the significant facts presented in this curve is the steepness of the curve, which reveals the relationship of intermediate interest rates to other rates prevailing in the market.* In the 1960 curve, the rates started at about 3.00 percent and rose approximately to 4.10 percent before going back down to 4.05 percent. Banks, therefore, in March 1960 would have in general concentrated their purchases in intermediate maturities; that is, in securities maturing in 1965.† This would hold true of course provided that the banks' secondary reserve needs did not dictate otherwise.

---

*This bend, known as "shoulder," is a reflection of the relationship of intermediate interest rates to the two extremes, that is, the short and long ends of the curve. If intermediate yields are evenly spaced between the short and the long ends of the curve, there is very little shoulder (as, for example, in Figure 17); when intermediate-term interest rates are closer to long-term rates, then there is quite a bit of shoulder.

†For the yield curve on callable issues, maturities of 1966 would have been generally desirable.

FIGURE 16

Yields of Treasury Securities, March 31, 1960
(based on closing bid quotations)

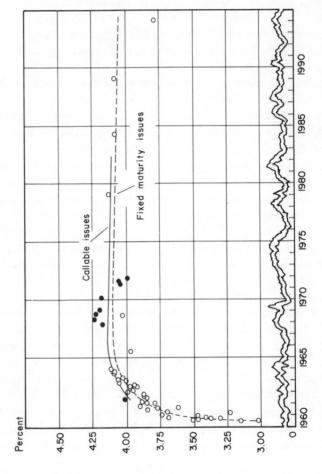

Explanation: The points represent yields to call when prices are above par, and to maturity date when prices are at or below. The smooth curves for the two classes of points are fitted by eye.

Source: U.S. Department of the Treasury, *Treasury Bulletin,* May 1960.

FIGURE 17

Yields of Treasury Securities, March 31, 1975
(based on closing bid quotations)

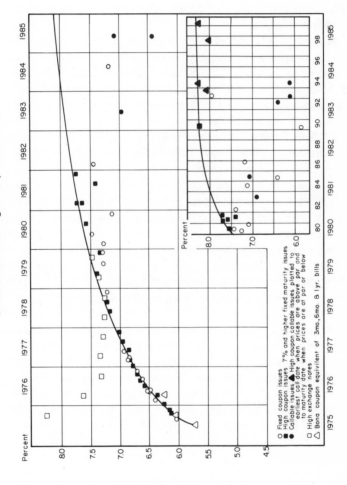

Source: U.S. Department of the Treasury, *Treasury Bulletin*, April 1975.

Figure 17 illustrates an upward sloping curve for U.S. government securities as of March 31, 1975. This curve differed somewhat from that of 1960. For one thing the spread in rates was greater than in 1960. In the 1975 curve the rates started at about 5.70 and rose approximately to 8.25—a difference of 2.55 percent—while the 1960 curve had a spread to maturity of 1.05 percent. These spreads made long maturities comparatively more attractive in 1975 than in 1960. Banks in March 1975 would have in general concentrated their purchases in maturities of 1988, for after that maturity date the yield curve gradually leveled out.

Although yield curves in most periods display smooth rising or falling patterns, exceptions occasionally occur. Such exceptions have occurred in the postwar period in 1957, 1959–60, and 1966 when economic activity was high and the demand for funds exceeded the available supply. As seen in Figure 18, the yield curve of June 30, 1966 portrays a peak that lies between the very short end and the long end of the curve, and is hence called a humpbacked yield curve.* Banks, and other interested investors, could clearly have concentrated their purchases in maturities of 1969, as the yields on intermediate-term securities were above all other yields.

Yield curves, consequently, are a very valuable tool for management in determining what specific issues to buy and in selecting the most attractive maturity point. Banks look for the bend in the yield curve. It is in this section of the curve that purchases usually concentrate as it is the most profitable for the commercial banks. With income the primary consideration in the bond portfolio, a bank must aim to earn as much of it as is consistent with the interest rate risk involved. A steep yield curve tells the bank that it is being compensated for the additional maturity. Finally, however, a point is reached where additional compensation for the additional maturity diminishes or may even be nil. If the bank is to realize little compensation for the acceptance of additional market risks, clearly there is not much point to the further extension of funds. It is not generally thought to be to a bank's best interest to have its portfolio maturities exceed the 15-year maturity range: "As a rule, there is little to be gained from the standpoint of income by moving into maturities beyond the fifteen-year range, and the bulk of a bank's investment portfolio might well be kept within this range."[24]

---

*When banks are faced with a growing reserve pressure from the Federal Reserve System or by a continued demand for loans, they are forced to liquidate some of their governmental securities. To minimize their capital losses in the face of rising yields and falling prices, they concentrate in the selling of securities with relatively short maturities. To the extent they hold large amounts of intermediate-term maturities as they enter this phase of the business cycle, their sale of these intermediate securities creates a hump in the yield curve.

FIGURE 18

Yields of Treasury Securities, June 30, 1966
(based on closing bid quotations)

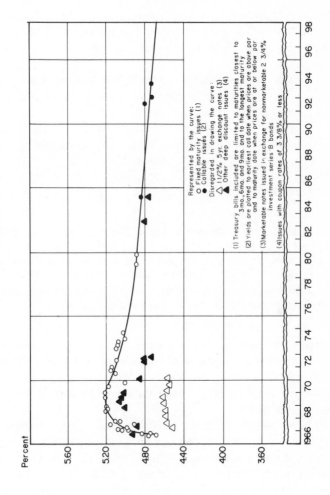

Source: U.S. Department of the Treasury, *Treasury Bulletin,* July 1966.

149

This rule, though of great importance in determining maximum portfolio maturities, should not be adhered to dogmatically; management should leave open the possibility of making exceptions to this rule when warranted by circumstances. There have been, for instance, periods in which the trend of interest rates was downward.* Should management be convinced that this phase of history is in process of repeating itself, there would be ample justification to stretch maturities beyond the 15-year mark. On the other hand, if indications point toward continuation of the loan demand at the level of the 1970s, or that it will grow stronger, management may shorten maximum maturities in the portfolio in view of a possible need to expand the loan portfolio.

The other major issue that management is confronted with in the shaping of a bond portfolio policy is determining the maturity distribution of the securities in the portfolio. Banks have frequently solved this problem by resorting to a device known as spaced maturities, which in fact is but another facet of diversification. This device allows banks to space maturities in the portfolio more or less evenly within the maximum maturity range established. This can be attained by setting, for example, percentage limits or absolute dollar limits for the various maturities in the portfolio:

> Once an account has been put on a spaced basis and as long as there are neither additions nor withdrawals from this investment account, the proceeds from the securities which mature each year can be reinvested in securities of the longest maturity admitted to the account. Since time itself tends to shorten the maturity of the account, this reinvestment tends to keep the average maturity of the account constant.[26]

In this way, the bank will assure itself of an average portfolio maturity of half the maximum and an income of at least average yields, or slightly better. And if the economy is booming, reinvestment of the proceeds of maturing securities at the longest end of the maturity schedule should assure the bank of maximum income on the portfolio.

A large number of banks today are still using the spaced maturities principle in their portfolio operations. Of these, some apply this treatment only to a sector of their investment portfolio, such as the secondary reserves, while others apply it to the entire investment portfolio. In the former instance, of course, a bank has little choice to act differently. However, to apply this

---

*This was, for example, the case in the United States throughout the 1930s and early 1940s. In fact it was not until the end of the Second World War that the general interest rate movement turned upward; see Figure 14.[25]

scheme to the entire investment account is to settle for average results. For bank directors who are not sufficiently versed in a more flexible portfolio policy or just do not wish, for one reason or another, to introduce and frame such a policy, the average results of maturity spacing are doubtless better than those of intuitive judgment. Maturity spacing is probably an acceptable portfolio approach for small banks. But for the banks that are willing to replace a static rule with an analytical procedure and informed judgment, it will certainly make no sense, for instance, to reinvest the funds derived from maturing securities at the longest end of the maturity schedule when the economy is sluggish and monetary authorities pursue a policy of active ease. For if they do, they will find themselves with sizable book losses in their portfolio when the economy eventually recovers and interest rates start rising.

For management to adhere to the spaced maturities method rigidly and in all kinds of economic weather would be to close its eyes and ignore the opportunities that exist today for portfolio improvement and added long-run income for the bank:

> It is my conviction that the best interests of neither the bank's depositors nor stockholders are well served by flatly denying the patent reality of market opportunities as they occur. For me the most attractive aspect of today's seesawing, dynamic money market is the relative frequency with which such opportunities recur.[27]

Much more realistic than the spaced maturities approach to portfolio operations would be the introduction of a flexible bond portfolio policy to cope with a volatile money and capital market. Clearly such a policy entails a more difficult and exacting task for portfolio management. For rather than reviewing established objectives periodically, and occasionally adapting them to changed conditions, as is true of other bank activities, here management must constantly review market outlook and decide on the most appropriate placement of funds as these become available for reinvestment or as opportunities present themselves for improving the portfolio's maturity or yield position.

The ideal portfolio practice, then, should be to shorten maturities when interest rates are expected to rise, and to lengthen maturities when rates are likely to fall. This is tantamount to saying that it is advisable to hold short-term securities when business activity starts picking up slowly and the credit demand is expected to grow, and to lengthen maturities when the first indications of an approaching recession start setting in and the credit demand is expected to fall.

The major difference between this approach to portfolio management and the spaced maturity method is primarily the formal incorporation of expectations within its analytical framework, in the form of forecasting certain variables regarded as relevant to portfolio decisions.

An investment policy formulated around soundly based data and logically reasoned conclusions should always produce better than average results in the bond portfolio:

> A sound portfolio manager may not make any spectacular moves. . . . However he will take advantage of every important opportunity that is presented to improve earnings and he *will never make the big mistake* of being trapped in either an excessively short position when interest rates drop sharply or in a top-heavy long term position when an "unexpected" major rise in rates takes place.[28]

Management's forecast function is greatly facilitated today not only by the volume of available data but also by following closely the activities of the monetary and fiscal authorities charged with the responsibility of alleviating or counteracting the business cycles. Close observation of the Federal Reserve monetary policy and its countercyclical measures provides portfolio management with important clues as to the direction of the bond market.[29]

The business cycle, a phenomenon as old as the economic history of this country, is characterized by alternate periods of high-level business activity and lulls or recessions. Taken individually, no two periods of high business activity or of comparative recession have been, or are likely to be, exactly identical. Yet all expansions or all contractions in economic activity have had the same basic characteristics. Thus all periods of brisk economic activity have been characterized by high levels of employment, rising prices, a growing demand for bank credit, increasing interest rates, and commercial banks borrowing from the Federal Reserve banks to maintain their required reserve position. As these developments take place, the Federal Reserve, which is committed to a policy of anticyclical credit action, intervenes to gradually restrain the expansion of credit before the general business conditions get out of hand.

Periods of recession have been characterized by increasing unemployment, relative price stability, a weak loan demand, falling interest rates, and excess bank reserves. During such periods, the Federal Reserve pursues an easy money policy by channeling funds directly into the commercial banking system, through the open market operations, to revitalize business activity. It should not take much for an alert management to identify these signals in general terms and adjust portfolio policies.[30] In the boom phase of the business cycle, management should shape portfolio policy toward the lengthening of maturities as monetary policy becomes more and more aggressive. This move serves as a hedge against the possibility of having to refund or reemploy these funds at the succeeding phase of the business cycle and consequently to accept lower interest rates. This move will also ensure a market appreciation, when interest rates fall, for those bonds purchased at higher interest rates, and make it possible for the bank to realize capital gains in a period of market ease. By contrast in the recession phase, the bank should gear its investment policy toward employment of the new and maturing funds in the short-term sector of the portfolio. A low level of initial income at this phase of the business cycle allows the bank to take advantage of a subsequent rise in business activity as it unfolds itself and affects portfolio values.*

The real issue at stake, however, is not that portfolio management will fail to identify the specific phase of monetary policy. Rather, it is that in its ambition to increase portfolio income, it may try to hold out to the last point, and may miss the market altogether:

> The tendency to gamble unnecessarily has usually been responsible for the somewhat less than favorable results which some bankers have encountered in the management of their bond portfolios over the years. . . . This speculation on the future has no place in portfolio management if consistently good results are to be achieved.[32]

The pattern of investment policy suggested above—stay short when money rates are low, and lengthen out when economic activity is brisk and interest rates high—pertains to all funds available for employment or reemployment in the bond portfolio; that is, all new funds (new deposits) and maturing funds (proceeds of maturing portfolio assets). This adjustment in portfolio securities, also known as "portfolio switching,"[33] need not wait until these funds are made available nor limit itself to these funds. Whenever the opportunity occurs to adjust maturities to current economic conditions, management may also include in its maturity adjustment operations (barring an unforeseen need to increase secondary reserves) issues that will mature within the next year or two. By selling issues a year or two in advance of their maturities, that is to say, by refunding in advance, the bank will sustain losses. These losses, however, are usually more than offset by subsequent gains.

In periods of boom, when emphasis is placed on the lengthening of the portfolio in anticipation of the next business recession, the losses sustained through advance refunding are more than offset by the higher yields obtainable

---

*Despite the importance of staying short at this phase of the business cycle, there is frequently a strong bank "temptation to meet the immediate problem of earnings by reaching out for longer maturities because of the relatively higher yields, even though prices are high. At such times it is not always recognized adequately that any investor assumes a risk when he buys the longer bond. It is the possibility that yields may go higher with a consequent loss of capital value. Even a relatively small change in yield will mean a relatively large change in the market value of a long-term bond. Although an investor is more likely to remember this when the time for liquidation comes, it is more profitable to remember it when the initial investment decision is made."[31]

on new investments or, more significantly, by the tax benefits involved.* Indeed, there should be no difficulty in reemploying the proceeds of the advance refunded securities in the market, during a period of tight money conditions and rising interest rates, and in acquiring longer-term higher-yielding securities; that is, securities of comparable or higher coupon rate of interest but of somewhat longer maturities selling at a price below par (at a discount). On the other hand, however, the losses sustained through advance refunding would moderate the bank's tax exposure on the income realized from the higher level of loans and interest rates during the current (boom) period. Refunding in advance thus combines loss taking with maturity lengthening while at the same time producing increased income for the portfolio and guaranteeing a capital gain at least by maturity.

When the economy is in a state of recession and easy money conditions prevail, portfolio management is in a position to realize capital gains. Indeed, with interest rates generally low, portfolio holdings acquired in the preceding phase of the business cycle and carrying a higher coupon rate, will experience a market appreciation. These security holdings will now sell at a premium. Profit taking in this phase of the cycle would help offset the bank's income reduction sustained from both the negligent loan demand and the lower interest rate pattern of the short-term sector, in which are employed all funds available for investment in a period of market ease.

Consequently, two general rules may be formulated to guide management's switching of maturities in the portfolio. Depending upon whether the economy is booming or receding, management must lengthen maturities when taking losses or shorten maturities when taking profits.[35] To do otherwise would only increase market vulnerability of the portfolio with consequent effects upon its overall performance.

It has been a growing practice among banks to earmark a reserve account for the profits and losses resulting from investment operations, which is known as a bond valuation reserve account. This account can be established in a number of ways. One method is by transferring all bond capital gains, after income tax charges, to the reserve account; another approach is to create it by appropriating earnings out of the undivided profits account in periods of high returns. Once the account has been established, it is a bank practice to place all net bond profits, as these occur, in the reserve account and to charge all losses, after taxes, against the same account; in other words, all net security

---

*Tax law permits banks, like other taxpayers, to deduct from the current income losses on securities sold, provided that there are no offsetting profits in the same year. On the other hand, banks are allowed to treat profits on securities sold (if held for more than six months and not offset by losses in the same year) as capital gains subject to a tax of only 30 percent rather than the 52 percent federal income tax rate.[34]

losses are charged against the after-tax profits taken in the course of the business cycle.

Use of this reserve account represents conservative accounting procedure since it isolates the effect of bond portfolio transactions from the operating results of the year. For if the losses were to be charged against the undivided profits account and the capital gains added to it, bond portfolio transactions would have an undue effect upon the bank's current operating income and hence its actual profitability. The existence of a separate reserve account thus leaves unaffected the undivided profits position of the bank and makes it possible for management to continue its dividend policy or its annual transfer of profits to the surplus account regardless of the portfolio action taken in effecting investment policy.

Accounting rules also provide for a distinction between this security reserve account and a security trading account. While the former reflects portfolio adjustment in relation to broad changes in economic conditions and interest rates, the latter reflects the outcome of a bank's day-to-day trading activity. The practical implication of this difference between switching and trading lies in the way that these transactions are shown in bank statements. Profits and losses from trading are taken into consideration in determining a bank's operating income, while gains and losses from switching are not, being considered as unusual transactions. Once operating income is established, portfolio gains and losses are considered in arriving at net profit.

Having reviewed the factors and considerations that enter into the shaping of a sound and flexible portfolio policy, it is only appropriate to discuss briefly the execution of portfolio policy.

ORGANIZATION OF THE INVESTMENT FUNCTION

A bank's investment policy should also provide for the internal organization to carry out the investment function. The size and form of such organization exhibits significant variation from one bank to another, reflecting, among other things, differences in the size of the bank, the type of securities purchased and held, involvement in underwriting activities, and the latitude of the authority delegated by the board of directors.

As with lending, the legal responsibility for bank investing rests with the entire board of directors. Here, too, however, it is customary for the board to assign the responsibility for supervising the investment function to a senior management member or to an investment committee, which would ensure that investments are made in accordance with legal prescription and the bank's own policies.

In small banks where the relative importance of the investment portfolio is limited, the investment function is likely to be of a part-time nature. In such instances, this function is usually delegated to the leading full-time executive officer, the president, who may also be the principal lending officer. In such banks, a number of alternative approaches may be used to overcome the lack of proficiency in investment portfolio management. One approach would be to concentrate on risk-free securities, that is, invest in and hold U.S. government securities. On many occasions, such holdings may be combined with local municipals. Another approach would be to include also nongovernment securities, on the basis of the information available by rating agencies. Obviously, the availability of such information substitutes for the lack of individual knowledge and judgment. Such reliance can be detrimental since ratings only trail market developments and are not abreast of them, cannot claim to be faultless, and do not include very small issues that may otherwise be of high quality. A final, and in all respects better, approach would be to use the services of the large city correspondent, which ordinarily has the specialized staff to effectuate its investment policy. Reliance upon correspondent expertise would complete transactions at opportune times and generally provide important guidance in the management of the portfolio.

In large banks there is usually more delegation of authority. As with lending, here, too, it is customary for the board to assign responsibility for effecting the investment policies of the bank to an investment committee. In the larger of these banks, the investment committee would serve as the liaison between the board of directors and the bank's investment or bond department, which carries out the investment function. In such banks, the investment department gathers, records, and analyzes data with the objective of determining the degree of risk (credit and interest rate risk) among alternative investment opportunities and evaluating the bank's ability to assume such risk. This information is made available to investment officers who are customarily authorized to trade in securities. Just as with loan officers, investment officers, too, are assigned maximum dollar trading limits that give them the authority to purchase or sell securities up to a certain amount independently of the investment committee. However, they are required to report periodically to this committee about the bank's investment position.

Once securities are bought and become part of the bank's investment portfolio, the investment department is expected to assess these securities on a continual basis. This aspect of the investment function, along with the research and analysis aspects mentioned above, are carried out by a group of individuals specializing in the various phases of the investment program. The investment department staff, however, is small compared with the staff of the credit department. This is to be expected since a bank's investments are the obligations of a few, while loans are made to thousands of individuals, business firms, and others. Furthermore, bank investments, and especially national bank investments, are generally limited by legal prescription to specified classes of issues, of which default-free federal government obligations have been a long-time favorite and convenient holding.

Whatever the form of organization of the investment function, the execution of portfolio policy should not be overburdened with constraints and limitations. Excessiveness in either of these, whether it pertains to quality, maturity, or income, can end up negating the benefits of a flexible policy. Flexibility in investment policy, therefore, must be understood to extend also to the working aspects of a portfolio policy and not just to its broader perspectives. Failure to realize this may render the portfolio manager a passive spectator of market developments as these shape up and influence the financial world around him.

SUMMARY

The present chapter has dealt with the fourth and last priority in the employment of bank funds—investment for income. Residual loanable funds can be employed in the form of long-maturity capital market instruments to provide the bank with maximum income. Income maximizing investments, which make up a bank's bond portfolio, cover the long end of the investment account, as against secondary reserves, which, as we saw earlier, emphasize liquidity and cover the short and intermediate end of the investment account.

Maximizing income must not be taken to imply purchasing instruments that offer the highest yields. Rather, it means that the aim of the bank's portfolio policy should be to obtain the maximum income with the minimum exposure to risk. Thus, in framing bond portfolio policy, the board of directors must take into account a number of basic considerations: the quality of the securities to be bought, diversification, tax considerations, the general level of interest rates at the time that securities are being purchased, and maturities in the portfolio.

The quality of the securities that may be purchased is generally regulated by supervisory authorities in an effort to minimize the risk of default inherent in most investment obligations. Banking regulation is very specific with regard to the securities that are eligible for a bank's investment portfolio. Because of the general acceptance of ratings as an indication of quality, highly rated securities are generally qualified for purchase on the part of banks. As a matter of policy, commercial banks should take investment portfolio risks that complement the risks taken in their loan portfolio. Loans constitute the principal source of bank income as well as risk exposure. Thus, high-risk exposure in the loan portfolio would justify a high-quality and lower-income investment portfolio, and vice versa, depending upon the growth or stability of the local economy.

Closely related to quality considerations is the principle of diversification of risk both geographically and by industry. With the general decline of corporate securities in investment portfolios, geographic distribution of security holdings constitutes the main form of diversification of risk. Its leading application is in state and local government securities, or municipals, and is generally encouraged in view of the localized nature of the loan account.

Tax considerations are of vital importance in investment portfolio management especially for large banks. Indeed, for banks in the 48 percent income tax bracket the purchase of tax exempts or municipals ensures substantial tax reduction. This helps explain the spectacular rise in municipal securities in bank portfolios in the postwar period. In fact, they have even surpassed, in importance, U.S. government security holdings and have become the leading component of commercial bank investment portfolios.

Another basic consideration in portfolio management is the prevailing level of interest rates at the time that securities are being purchased. The importance of this factor lies in the fact that a subsequent change in the level of interest rates would affect inversely the market value of the securities held, causing the bank to sustain sizable losses or capital gains upon liquidation of these securities. Clearly the magnitude of these effects would be different for securities of different maturities.

Because of the interest rate effect upon bank investment portfolios, investment policy, once established, must be constantly reviewed and adjusted in the light of changing conditions. Flexibility, therefore, must characterize the investment policy of commercial banks. This flexibility of policy, geared to the cyclical nature of the economy, stresses that the maturity characteristics of the investment portfolio be similar to coincide with the proper phase of the business cycle. The stress is on the short-term area of the investment portfolio during periods of business recession and monetary ease, and on the long-term area of the portfolio during periods of high business activity and monetary restraint. Guidelines for the pursuit of a flexible investment policy will provide the trend of monetary policy. More specifically, the net reserve position of the banking system may be considered as a basic guideline for the direction of monetary policy and hence for the appropriate portfolio course of action. A flexible portfolio policy formulated around soundly based data and logically reasoned conclusions should produce the best results possible in the dynamic environment that surrounds the present-day banker.

NOTES

1. Robert G. Rodkey makes a case for a permanent bond account prior to bank lending, in *Sound Policies for Bank Management* (New York: Ronald Press, 1944), pp. 53–70.

2. Roland I. Robinson, *The Management of Bank Funds,* 2d ed. (New York: McGraw-Hill Book Co., 1962), p. 338.

3. Ibid., original ed. (1951), p. 283.

4. James W. Wooster, Jr., *Bankers' Handbook of Bond Investment* (New York: Harper & Brothers, 1939), p. 149.

5. Ibid.

6. Edward W. Reed, et al., *Commercial Banking* (Englewood Cliffs, N.J.: Prentice-Hall, 1976), p. 332.

7. See *Federal Reserve Bulletin,* A37.

8. Harry Sauvain, *Investment Management,* 3d ed. rev. (Englewood Cliffs, N.J.: Prentice-Hall, 1967), pp. 132–34.

9. U.S. Department of the Treasury, Office of the Comptroller of the Currency, *Comptroller's Manual for National Banks* (Washington, D.C.: U.S. Government Printing Office, 1971), Part 1, Section 1.3(b), p. 2–1.

10. U.S. Department of the Treasury, op. cit., Section 1.4, pp. 2–2, 2–3.

11. *Federal Reserve Bulletin,* op. cit., p. A16; investment data for March 1976 are adjusted to reflect the older classification of security holdings (that is, government agency issues have been included in the "other securities" category in line with prior years' reporting practice).

12. Sauvain, op. cit., pp. 64–65.

13. U.S. Department of the Treasury, op. cit., Sections 1.3, 1.7, pp. 2–1, 2–2, 2–3.

14. Roger A. Lyon, *Investment Portfolio Management in the Commercial Bank* (New Brunswick, N.J.: Rutgers University Press, 1960), pp. 81–85. He further elaborates on this point and cites examples of the differential effect of tax-exempt and taxable securities on banks of different sizes and under varying market conditions. His approach is based on the previously held tax rates of 30 and 52 percent, respectively.

15. Paul M. Atkins, *Bank Bond Investment and Secondary Reserve Management* (Boston: Bankers Publishing Co., 1940), pp. 283, 285–87.

16. Ibid., p. 286.

17. Robinson, in op. cit., p. 341, states: "Probably the leading principle of diversification that a bank needs to follow is that of not duplicating its loan account."

18. Ibid., p. 342.

19. Sidney Homer, *A History of Interest Rates* (New Brunswick, N.J.: Rutgers University Press, 1963), pp. 326, 331.

20. Robert Bernerd Anderson, *Treasury-Federal Reserve Study of the Government Securities Market,* 3 parts (Washington, D.C.: Board of Governors of the Federal Reserve System, 1959–60), Part 2, p. 12.

21. George H. Hempel, "Basic Ingredients of Commercial Banks' Investment Policies," *The Bankers Magazine* 155 (Autumn 1972), p. 54.

22. David Meiselman, *The Term Structure of Interest Rates* (Englewood Cliffs, N.J.: Prentice Hall, 1962); Phillip Cagan, *Changes In the Cyclical Behavior of Interest Rates* (New York: National Bureau of Economic Research, 1966); B. G. Malkiel, *The Term Structure of Interest Rates: Expectations and Behavior Patterns* (Princeton: N.J.: Princeton University Press, 1966); Robert H. Scott, "Liquidity and the Term Structure of Interest Rates," *Quarterly Journal of Economics* 79 (February 1965): 135–45; Frederick M. Struble, "Current Debate on the Term Structure of Interest Rates." *Monthly Review,* Federal Reserve Bank of Kansas City (January-February 1966): 10–16.

23. Two useful summaries of work in this area are Burton G. Malkiel, *The Term Structure of Interest Rates: Theory, Empirical Evidence, and Applications* (New York: McCaleb-Seiler Publishing Co., 1970); and James C. VanHorne, *The Function and Analysis of Capital Market Rates* (Englewood Cliffs, N.J.: Prentice-Hall, 1970), Chapter 4.

24. Lyon, op. cit., pp. 143–44.

25. On the historical pattern of the interest rate movement in the United States from the beginning of the last century on, see Homer, op. cit., p. 337.

26. Robinson, op. cit., p. 370.

27. Daniel M. Kelly, "Bank Investments in a Dynamic Money Market," *Bankers Monthly* (November 1957): 24.

28. Harry W. Lussey, "Portfolio Policy Now," *Bankers Monthly* (February 1960): p. 17.

29. Karl R. Bopp, "A Flexible Monetary Policy," *Business Review,* Federal Reserve Bank of Philadelphia (March 1958): 5.

30. Lyon, in op. cit., pp. 148, 154, quantifies those signals for portfolio management by suggesting that the best indicator of the specific phase of monetary policy would be the reserve position of the banking system. Thus, excess reserves of over $200–300 million would imply an easy monetary policy phase while a net "borrowed" reserves figure in excess of this amount would indicate a tight monetary policy.

31. Karl R. Bopp, "Borrowing from the Federal Reserve Bank—Some Basic Principles," *Business Review,* Federal Reserve Bank of Philadelphia (June 1958): 4.

32. Lussey, op. cit., p. 17.

33. Hempel, op. cit., p. 57.

34. *Internal Revenue Code* (Chicago: Commerce Clearing House, 1975), Section 1201 a, p. 4343ff. These tax provisions create at first glance a seemingly inconsistent situation in which commercial banks can at times make profits by taking prior losses. For an elaborate discussion of the tax technicalities involved see Lussey, op. cit., p. 38ff. His approach is based on a 25 percent capital gains tax rate, which was valid until December 31, 1974.

35. Hempel, op. cit., p. 58.

6

CONCLUSION:
OPTIMIZING PORTFOLIO
MANAGEMENT

The emphasis in this book has been on the management of bank funds through the formulation and implementation of sound and flexible policies. Though these policies are the same for all banks, it is necessary that each individual bank's directors and management put their own variety of flesh and blood on the bare bones of the policies outlined in this discussion. Once this is done, the finer details of finished policy will evolve. Blind adherence to a banking practice, or to any policy shaped abstractly, serves neither the bank, its depositors, nor its stockholders. Ignoring the need for continuous adjustments in banking policies that reflect changing economic conditions would be courting trouble, frequently in the form of significant losses. The function of portfolio management, therefore, must be to relate internal banking requirements to the external, and ever-changing, economic conditions via the medium of portfolio policy.

Beyond the adoption of some minimum but perhaps essential requirements, which may themselves be altered as the basic underlying conditions change, few absolute and arbitrary limitations should be placed upon bank operations. While in a given period certain criteria may be laid down as guidelines to bank activity, the cyclical nature of the economy and the results of its impact upon the monetary system and financial markets may frequently require not only shifts of emphasis in bank policy but also a close and continuing supervision of existing guidelines in recognition of changing relationships.

The book has postulated that a commercial bank has access to three sources of funds; it acquires funds from invested and senior capital, from deposits, and from institutional borrowing. Banks rely heavily on debt to finance the acquisition of bank assets. The most important form of such debt is deposit liabilities—demand deposits, and time and savings deposits, competitively attracted. Stated differently, banks rely heavily on debt sources to finance the acquisition of bank assets, the vast majority of which constitute in fact the debts of others. This situation has earned banks the reputation of being dealers in debt. This very origin and nature of bank funds has rendered their management a critical aspect of bank efficiency. Efficient management of funds is crucial for the efficient performance of the banking functions. Efficient funds management implies the most effective use of all sources of bank funds in attaining optimum portfolio balance between liquidity, solvency, and profitability, consistent with the constraints imposed by law, regulation, and interests of the community. These portfolio objectives suggest a certain order of priority in the employment of bank funds.

In the employment of bank funds, and hence in the formulation of bank policies, four priorities must be observed: maintaining primary reserves, providing secondary reserves, meeting customer credit demands, and investing for income.

Primary reserves are generally maintained in the form of cash and hence constitute the most liquid assets of commercial banks. The bulk of the primary reserves consist of the legally required reserves held as deposit balances at the Federal Reserve or as vault cash, plus balances in correspondent banks. Because these are cash assets, banks, for obvious reasons, try to maintain, beyond their required reserves, only what is necessary to assure efficient day-to-day operations and compensate correspondent banks for their services.

Secondary reserves, or protective investments, perform precisely the role suggested by their name: they are basically designed to provide liquidity. Bank acceptance of funds repayable upon demand or within a given period of time, and the necessity to meet legitimate loan demands, focus upon the need for liquidity, rendering it of primary importance. Because of this need, probable liquidity requirements cannot be made subservient to other considerations. The investment portfolio, constituting the main source of liquidity, must be so arranged that such requirements will be met at all times with the least possible risk.

There are, of course, various levels of potential liquidity needs—levels of high, medium, and low probability. Because investments entail only two major categories of risk—the credit or default risk, and the market or interest rate risk—those investments creating liquidity against the probable needs must be of the highest quality and shortest maturity. As the degree of probability declines, standards can be broadened somewhat to include possibly slightly greater default and interest rate risks. The secondary reserves, long a byword in banking circles, are usually considered that portion of the portfolio providing a broad liquidity base. It has become increasingly useful to see this as a two-part base containing secondary reserves of seasonal type and of nonseasonal or cyclical type. The former should include those investments aimed at covering the probable needs, and the latter, those portfolio assets aimed at covering the less probable liquidity needs. Such a division of investment or liquidity accounting provides the banker with a more accurate picture of his needs and his investment position, and may result in a more economical use of investment funds.

As a rule, seasonal-type secondary reserves should never be allowed to fall below a minimum desirable level based upon probable liquidity requirements. If a shortage should occur, steps should be taken to rebuild the liquidity base as rapidly as possible. On the other hand, nonseasonal or cyclical-type secondary reserves are more flexible but should generally be allowed to decline below a desirable level only in the event of a concurrent increase in excess funds in the seasonal-type secondary reserves. This might well be the case when flexible portfolio policy considerations suggest that investment emphasis fall upon the short-term portion of the portfolio.

Once a bank has made itself liquid and safe, it should devote itself to the business for which it is best qualified, the granting of loans. Loans are the leading earning asset of commercial banks. Until at least the 1920s, the leading type of loan in the United States was the commercial loan. Since it was short term and self-liquidating (that is, it generated the wherewithal for its own repayment), the commercial loan was considered the appropriate earning asset for banks, in view of the fact that banks had most of their obligations in the form of deposits or (earlier) bank notes, redeemable on demand. Little by little, however, it was elbowed out of its place of prominence by other types of loans, that is, first by consumer loans, mortgage loans, securities loans, term loans, and, later, by the appearance and spread of bank credit card lending, and even the beginnings of bank leasing to business (which amounts to lending productive assets rather than money per se). Thus, although nowadays some classes of borrowers and loan arrangements are more characteristic than others in bank lending, there is no such thing as a standard bank loan or borrower.

This evolution in bank lending was an outcome of several factors. First, there has been considerable change in the thinking and attitudes of bankers and regulatory authorities concerning liquidity as applied to earning assets. It became apparent, for example, that it was not so much the maturity of the assets that affected a bank's liquidity position as it was the quality of the assets themselves, their marketability, or shiftability, and the bank's own ability to issue acceptable liabilities to provide liquidity when needed. Second, as banks obtained more experience in meeting their liquidity needs, they gained more confidence in their ability to design portfolios with an asset mix that offered the greatest utility to the bank. This led to substantial improvements and refinements in the techniques of funds management. The third development, which in a sense was a cause of the other two, stemmed from the strong economic pressures for new outlets and improved earnings performance. Commercial banks were under strong economic pressures for new sources of bank earnings especially after the depression and the sharp decline in the demand for commercial loans. In addition to this internal pressure for earnings, which forced banks to extend the maturities of their assets, the banking industry in the twentieth century has witnessed the development of another kind of competitive pressure: Nonbank financial institutions, which grew rapidly in size and number, began to perform functions similar to some of those performed by commercial banks. Commercial banks found that if they were to keep attracting funds, they would have to offer interest rates on savings deposits that were competitive with those offered by these financial institutions (that is, savings and loan associations, and mutual savings banks). The payment of higher interest rates in turn required higher returns on bank portfolios if earning levels were to be maintained. Though both of the pressures described above, internal and external, were important, it was especially the last one that pushed banks more vigorously into consumer loans, real estate loans, and term loans, and subsequently—in the World War II years—into the market for government securities, both federal as well as state and local.

In the postwar years, a new factor arose to cause the process of change in commercial bank operations to gain new momentum. This time, a phenomenal expansion in private loan demand exerted important pressures toward changes in the asset structure of commercial banks. Sustained by the postwar growth of the U.S. economy, this credit demand created new opportunities, which banks have been very resourceful in exploiting. Thus the postwar period has been characteristic of shifts between and within categories of commercial bank earning assets. At the same time new uses of bank loans appear to proliferate.

The pattern of commercial bank operations has thus been changing in response to changes in the tastes of customers, improvements in the techniques of funds management, and to the extent that banks are permitted by laws and regulations to respond to the changing needs of the economy. Despite ever-expanding bank activities, lending continues to be the core of the commercial banking function. Formulation and implementation of sound and flexible lending policies are among the major concerns of bank directors and managers. Well-planned lending policies and carefully established lending practices are crucial if a bank is to perform its credit-creating role effectively and develop and grow in response to community needs. The soundness of these policies will be reflected in the effectiveness with which a bank meets the credit needs of the community or markets involved. Policy decisions must be established as regards the type and volume of bank loans, the maturity distribution of these loans, and the overall size of the loan portfolio. Policy decisions must also determine to whom the bank will lend and what the loan terms will be.

Loanable funds in excess of local loan demand are employed in the investment market. This constitutes the fourth and last priority in the use of commercial bank funds. Specifically, residual loanable funds can be employed in the longer end of the investment portfolio, under certain conditions, with income rather than liquidity as the primary factor. The use of the secondary reserves, under a flexible policy, assists the portfolio manager in controlling his longer-term bond portfolio. The effect of time on such a portfolio position is often overlooked; should too large a portion of longer-term funds shift into the short-intermediate or intermediate-term range, it will become evident in reviewing the position of the nonseasonal reserves. Steps can then be taken to remedy the problem.

The secondary reserve and bond account, therefore, provide a context for a flexible investment policy, with such a policy centered on the considerations that determine the basic employment of funds in these given areas. The flexibility of policy is geared to respond to the cyclical nature of the economy, changes in monetary policy, and probable fluctuations in the financial markets. The essential aim is, on the one hand, to emphasize the short-term area of the portfolio in employing new funds, maturing funds, and proceeds from profit realization transactions, during periods of low yields and high bond prices (which normally coincide with business recession and monetary ease under conditions of a flexible monetary policy), and, on the other hand, to emphasize longer maturities in employing new funds, maturing funds, and proceeds of loss transactions, designed to reconstruct the portfolio balance during periods of higher yields and lower bond prices (which normally coincide with business improvement and monetary restraint). The liquidity sector of the investment portfolio, however, serves as a limiting factor when policy determines that emphasis be placed upon longer maturities, thus protecting the basic requirements of the investment portfolio from an overly aggressive policy of maturity extension.

Equally flexible must be a bank's loan policy. Taking cognizance of the business cycle is equally important in the development of a flexible loan policy. It is essential to emphasize the short-term area of the loan portfolio during periods of slackened loan demand, which usually coincide with business recession and monetary ease. Conversely, one must emphasize longer loan maturities (that is, term lending) during periods of peak loan demand, which normally coincide with high business activity and monetary restraint. Such a pattern of loan maturity policy allows a bank to substantially improve its long-range rate of income.

Flexibility, therefore, must characterize both the loan and investment policies of commercial banks. This flexibility of policy, geared to the cyclical nature of the economy, stresses that the maturity characteristics for both loan and investment portfolios be synchronized with the phases of the business cycle. The stress is on the short-term area of the loan and investment portfolios during periods of business recession and monetary ease, and on the long-term area of the portfolios during periods of high business activity and monetary restraint. Guidelines for the pursuit of a flexible loan and investment policy are provided by the trends of monetary policy. More specifically, the net reserve position of the banking system may be considered as a basic guideline for the direction of monetary policy and, hence, for the appropriate development of the portfolio.

The practice of a flexible loan and investment policy, as described, raises portfolio operation out of the "average" category and thus should produce the best possible results, for it enhances the effectiveness of portfolio management. While flexibility as to maturity represents the essential part of a flexible policy, successful portfolio management also demands that flexibility exist also in the use of the various types of loan and investment outlets. Yield differentials must guide the placement of funds in particular sectors of the market, and as these differentials change, portfolio policy should be sufficiently liberal to allow for response to more attractive opportunities as they develop. To maximize portfolio benefits from many market opportunities demands flexibility in all respects rather than dogmatic adherence to one type of outlet.

Over the years various efforts have been made to assist bankers in the management of their portfolios by means of quantitative analysis (see the Appendix). Important models have thus been developed that concentrate on the allocating of funds among various alternatives, with the purpose of securing the highest expected earnings consistent with the degree of risk the bank is willing to accept. In other words, what these quantitative analyses have in common is that they attempt to develop an optimum portfolio mix. Clearly the techniques available today are much more practical and pertinent than the best efforts of only a few years back. Nevertheless, the world in which the banker operates is an uncertain and complex world, and an optimum portfolio policy will require the exercise of considerable judgment. As such then, the attainment of an optimum portfolio will be a continuous process of adjustment carried on by each individual bank under conditions of economic change, uncertainty, and risk. The actual results are likely to be optimal only in a relative sense.

.

The objective of a flexible portfolio policy is to provide an optimum portfolio balance: in other words, a portfolio containing those types and proportions of assets that would represent, at any time, a most favorable balance of liquidity, safety, and profitability. An essential precondition for an optimum portfolio balance is, of course, that the bank's excess reserves be close to zero. Therefore, the issue that is presented to the bank's management is the familiar one of maximizing well-being subject to constraints. This means that within the framework that law and official regulation set, the marginal return per asset dollar must be equated in all directions. Stated differently, management must achieve such a distribution of portfolio assets that no further gain can be attained by shifting a dollar from one form of asset into another. When this is achieved, the distribution of assets is optimum.

Developing an optimum distribution of portfolio assets is not a new issue. Portfolio management has intrigued economists for a number of years. As early as 1888, F. Y. Edgeworth, a British economist, suggested that probability analysis could prove a useful device in portfolio planning. He postulated that portfolio management by a bank was analogous to a simple game:

> ... [Imagine] a new game of chance, which is played in this manner: each player receives a disposable fund of 100 counters, part of which he may invest in securities not immediately realisable, bearing say 5 per cent per ten minutes; another portion of the 100 may be held at call, bearing interest at 2 per cent per ten minutes; the remainder is kept in the hands of the player as a *reserve* against certain liabilities. [Twenty-two digits are randomly drawn every two minutes and the difference between their sum and their expected sum, 99, is obtained.] The special object of the reserve above mentioned is to provide against demands which exceed that average. If the player can meet this excess of demand with his funds in hand, well; but if not he must call in part, or all, of the sum placed at call, incurring a forfeit of 10 per cent on the amount called in. But if the demand is so great that he cannot even thus meet it, then he incurs an enormous forfeit, say 100£, or 1,000£.[1]

Unlike Edgeworth's game strategy, contemporary economists have attempted to present a more formalized approach to the issue of portfolio management. The various analyses that have been put forward since the 1950s fall into two broad categories: those that treat the three classes of bank assets (that is, cash, loans, and securities) as homogeneous in themselves, and those that distinguish between the various assets in two of these classes (loans and securities) according to the degree of risk involved. In the discussion below, an attempt is made to provide a brief overview of the various formal techniques that have been put forward in this respect. In those cases where the literature available defies watertight classification, a classification is arbitrarily assigned.

Some of the models advanced view the problem as that of choosing a fraction of the total portfolio of assets to put into cash, loans, and securities. In these models, the three classes of assets mentioned are believed to represent the range of liquidity and earnings. Though obviously cash is the most liquid of the assets, it yields no earnings. Conversely, loans are the least liquid but yield the highest returns. Investments are at the middle of the scale of both liquidity and earnings. These models, given the probability distribution of net deposit withdrawals and the anticipated yield on loans and investments, provide a portfolio mix that maximizes the expected value of the additions (profits) to the bank's net worth. The profits from a portfolio distributed among cash, loans, and securities are determined as follows: average loan return times the dollar amount of loans, plus the average securities return, times the dollar amount of securities, minus average or expected loss on securities sold to meet unexpected cash needs.[2]

Attempts at refinement of this method have gradually led to the development of a dual criterion in evaluating different portfolio mixes. They suggest that consideration must be given to both the expected yield and the risk (that is, variance) of the portfolio. Stated differently, they advocate that the portfolio should be constructed by taking actions that maximize the expected return and minimize the variability of this return. This formula provides a trade-off between the advantages of higher returns and the disadvantages of greater variability in these returns. This dual criterion necessitates the use of a utility function to make possible the selection of an optimum portfolio in the case of more than one Pareto optimal alternative. In other words, a bank should select that portfolio whose expected return and variability have the highest utility, or that portfolio from among all possible portfolios for which the bank has the highest preference.[3]

Here portfolio management becomes basically a problem of concentrating on bank assets, determining the desirable asset structure, and treating liabilities as if they were determined entirely by forces outside bank control. New developments in financial markets, however, enable commercial banks to have some control over their deposit liabilities—a fact that has significant effects on such a portfolio model. With banks allowed to vary the rates they pay on certain types of deposits (that is, CDs) or borrow the excess reserves of other banks, their portfolio choices now are quite different from what they would be if they had no control over their deposits. Access to these forms of liquidity may allow for portfolios with much higher proportions of high-earning loans and investments, and much smaller amounts of liquid assets. Hence, portfolio management becomes a problem of determining a desired asset and liability structure rather than dealing solely with the asset structure.

The kinds of analyses referred to thus far treat all loans as equivalents of each other and all investments as equal to each other. Given these assumptions, a portfolio is then constructed that maximizes the expected return from the portfolio or an objective that explicitly recognizes both the return and its variability. Against this approach, other analysts have chosen instead to concentrate on the various types of assets within the different parts of the portfolio. One group of them believes that the main consideration in planning a bank portfolio is the determination of the maturity distribution within the different segments of the portfolio—for instance, taking loans as a class and investments as another. Much of the analytical material has, in fact, concentrated on only one of these portfolio classes—investment assets. There have been various attempts to construct mathematical models for the management of the government bond portfolio, which constitutes an important element of most commercial bank assets. These models take into account estimates of net deposit withdrawals, expected future interest rates, and bond price movements, along with bank preferences for risk and return, to arrive at an optimal maturity distribution of government bonds. Considering probable cash needs and the possible losses on securities sold to meet these needs, a distribution by maturity of government securities is chosen. The distribution selected is that which best offsets the conflict between the higher expected yields from longer-term securities and the higher liquidity of shorter-term instruments.

Thus, the purpose of this approach is to determine a maturity distribution for the government security portfolio, considering possible changes in interest rates and liquidity requirements. Thus, the conflicts are resolved between the forces of liquidity, solvency, and yield, maximizing the bank's utility. Such a portfolio has just the right ingredients of risk and return, considering the bank's trade-off between the two.[4]

Another dimension of portfolio management for which analytical techniques have been developed is portfolio variability. The variability of a collection of assets is determined by the variability of each of the assets (variance) plus an amount related to whether the variations in the individual assets add to or subtract from each other (covariance). For instance, if a portfolio is composed of two assets whose fluctuations are likely to be in the same direction, its variability of return will be more than if it is composed of two equally variable assets whose fluctuations are likely to be in opposite directions.

Here the problem has frequently been viewed as that of choosing between alternative loans so as to select the combination that most enhances the utility of the portfolio in regard to maximizing return and minimizing risk. The loan alternatives are thought to be distinguished by their respective expected yield or return,* and by their expected variances and covariances. On this basis, selection from all possible combinations of loans is made with a view either to the highest return for given variance of risk, or to the lowest possible risk of variances for given return. Once one has determined several efficient portfolios, the problem is to choose the one that offers the combination of risk and return most fitting to the bank. Using this technique, one can split the problem of portfolio composition into two parts, one being the determination of combinations that are technically efficient, and the other the selection of the single portfolio that best fits the particular bank.[5]

Several of the above approaches to bank portfolio planning are based on the assumption that the commercial banker is an investor seeking to allocate an investment fund among various investment opportunities and loan alternatives, so as to secure the highest expected earnings consistent with the degree of risk the bank is willing to accept. This may, however, be a misleading guide for policy. The particular bank does not choose among all loans on the same basis; nondepositor borrowers will be distinguished from depositor borrowers. Moreover, a bank with many depositor borrowers will have preference for cash, loans, and investments different from that of a bank that makes more of its loans to nondepositors and therefore must anticipate larger cash withdrawals.

As progress is made toward a formal analysis of the problems of decision making under uncertainty, more quantitative aids will become available in the area of portfolio selection. Clearly the techniques available today are much more practical and pertinent than the best efforts of only a few years back. In fact, individual attempts have been made to use such models as operational devices to improve portfolio performance. Yet, we are skeptical as to the effectiveness of these quantitative aids in the day-to-day management of bank funds. For one thing, none of these models could in any sense be considered comprehensive. All are bits and pieces in a framework, with numerous missing parts, and no one has yet come up with even a blueprint for the entire mechanism.

The conceptual complexity of the subject and the difficulty of predicting with any degree of precision all the relevant variables involved render extremely difficult the construction of sophisticated models for funds management. The world in which the banker operates is indeed an uncertain and complex world. An optimum portfolio policy will require the exercise of considerable judgment. As such then, the attainment of an optimum portfolio

---

*In determining the expected yield or return, allowance may be made for factors other than the loan rate of interest, that is, for bank benefits related to the attracting of new business or additional deposits.

will be a continuous process of adjustment carried on by each individual bank under conditions of economic change, uncertainty, and risk. The actual results are likely to be optimal only in a relative sense.

NOTES

1. F. Y. Edgeworth, "The Mathematical Theory of Banking," *Journal of the Royal Statistical Society* 51, part I (March 1888), p. 120.

2. On this approach see, for example: J. Duesenberry, "The Portfolio Approach to the Demand for Money and Other Assets," *Review of Economics and Statistics* 45, supp. (February 1963): 9–24; Donald D. Hester and John F. Zoellner, "The Relation between Bank Portfolios and Earnings: An Econometric Analysis," *Review of Economics and Statistics,* 48 (November 1966): pp. 372–86; S. M. Besen, "An Empirical Analysis of Commercial Bank Lending Behavior," *Yale Economic Essays* 5, (Fall 1965): 283–315.

3. See, for example: James L. Pierce, "An Empirical Model of Commercial Bank Portfolio Management," in *Studies of Portfolio Behavior,* ed. Donald D. Hester and James Tobin (New York: John Wiley & Sons, 1967), pp. 171–90; James Tobin, "Liquidity Preference as Behavior Towards Risk," in *Risk Aversion and Portfolio Choice,* ed. Donald D. Hester and James Tobin (New York: John Wiley & Sons, 1967), pp. 1–26.

4. See, for example: D. Chambers and A. Charnes, "Inter-Temporal Analysis and Optimization of Bank Portfolios," *Management Science* (July 1961): 393–410; Harry M. Markowitz, *Portfolio Selection: Efficient Diversification of Investments* (New York: John Wiley & Sons, 1959); William Beazer, *Optimization of Bank Portfolios* (Lexington, Mass.: D. C. Heath and Co., 1975).

5. See, for example: W. R. Russell, "Commercial Bank Portfolio Adjustments," *American Economic Review* 54, (May 1964): 544–53; S. Royama and K. Hamada, "Substitution and Complementarity in the Choice of Risky Assets," in *Risk Aversion and Portfolio Choice,* op. cit., pp. 27–40; Donald D. Hester, "Efficient Portfolios with Short Sales and Margin Holdings," in *Risk Aversion and Portfolio Choice,* op. cit., pp. 41–50.

BIBLIOGRAPHY

BOOKS

American Bankers Association, Bank Management Committee. *The Role of Investments in Bank Asset Management.* 6 studies. New York: American Bankers Association, 1965.

————. *Use of Senior Capital by Commercial Banks.* New York: American Bankers Association, 1967.

————, Commission on Money and Credit. *The Commercial Banking Industry.* Englewood Cliffs, N.J.: Prentice-Hall, 1962.

————, Economic Policy Commission. *The Problems of Commercial Bank Liquidity.* New York: American Bankers Association, 1957.

American Management Association. *The Dynamics of Management.* New York: American Management Association, 1958.

Anderson, Clay J. *Fundamental Reappraisal of the Discount Mechanism.* Philadelphia: Federal Reserve Bank of Philadelphia, 1966.

Anderson, Robert Bernerd. *Treasury-Federal Reserve Study of the Government Securities Market.* Parts 1–3. Washington, D.C.: Board of Governors of the Federal Reserve System, 1959–60.

Atkins, Paul M. *Bank Bond Investment and Secondary Reserve Management.* Boston: Bankers Publishing Co., 1940.

————. *Bank Secondary Reserve and Investment Policies.* New York: Bankers Publishing Co., 1930.

Bagehot, Walter. *Lombard Street: A Description of the Money Market.* 8th ed. London: Kegan Paul, Trench, & Co., 1882.

Beazer, William F. *Optimization of Bank Portfolios.* Lexington, Mass.: D. C. Heath & Co. 1975.

Beckhart, Benjamin Haggott. *Federal Reserve System.* New York: American Institute of Banking, American Bankers Association, 1972.

Board of Governors of the Federal Reserve System. *Trading in Federal Funds.* Washington, D.C.: Board of Governors of the Federal Reserve System, 1965.

————. *The Federal Reserve System—Purposes and Functions.* 6th ed. Washington D.C.: Board of Governors of the Federal Reserve System, 1974.

Chalmers, Eric B. *Readings in the Euro-dollar.* London: W. P. Griffith & Sons, 1969.

Cochran, John A. *Money, Banking, and the Economy.* 3d ed. New York: Macmillan Co., 1975.

Crosse, Howard D. *Management Policies for Commercial Banks.* Englewood Cliffs, N.J.: Prentice-Hall, 1962.

_____ and G. H. Hempel. *Management Policies for Commercial Banks.* 2d ed. Englewood Cliffs, N.J.: Prentice-Hall, 1973.

Eastburn, David P. *The Federal Reserve on Record; Readings on Current Issues from Statements by Federal Reserve Officials.* Philadelphia: Federal Reserve Bank of Philadelphia, 1965.

Goldfeld, S. M., *Commercial Bank Behavior and Economic Activity.* Amsterdam: North Holland Publishing Co., 1966.

Goldsmith, Raymond W. *Financial Intermediaries in the American Economy Since 1900.* Princeton: Princeton University Press, 1958.

Hester, Donald D., and James Tobin, eds. *Studies of Portfolio Behavior.* New York: John Wiley & Sons, 1967.

_____. *Risk Aversion and Portfolio Choice.* New York: John Wiley & Sons, 1967.

Hodgman, Donald R. *Commercial Bank Loan and Investment Policy.* Champaign: University of Illinois, Bureau of Economic and Business Research, 1963.

Homer, Sidney. *A History of Interest Rates.* New Brunswick, N.J.: Rutgers University Press, 1963.

Jacobs, Donald P. et al. *Financial Institutions.* 5th ed. Homewood, Ill.: Richard D. Irwin, 1972.

Jessup, Paul F., ed. *Innovations in Bank Management.* New York: Holt, Rinehart and Winston, 1969.

Lyon, Roger A. *Investment Portfolio Management in the Commercial Bank.* New Brunswick, N.J.: Rutgers University Press, 1960.

Markowitz, Harry M. *Portfolio Selection: Efficient Diversification of Investments.* New York: John Wiley & Sons, 1959.

Mints, Lloyd W. *A History of Banking Theory.* Chicago: University of Chicago Press, 1945.

Mitchell, Waldo F. *The Uses of Bank Funds.* Chicago: University of Chicago Press, 1925.

Monhollon, J. R., and Glenn Picou. *Instruments of the Money Market.* 3d ed. Richmond, Va.: Federal Reserve Bank of Richmond, 1974.

Morrison, George R. *Liquidity Preferences of Commercial Banks.* Chicago: University of Chicago Press, 1966.

Nadler, Paul S. *Time Deposits and Debentures: The New Sources of Bank Funds.* Bulletin No. 30. New York: C. J. Divine Institute of Finance, New York University, 1964.

Prochnow, Herbert V. *Term Loans and Theories of Bank Liquidity.* New York: Prentice-Hall, 1949.

Reed, Edward W. *Commercial Bank Management.* New York: Harper & Row, 1963.

_____ et al. *Commercial Banking.* Englewood Cliffs, N.J.: Prentice-Hall, 1976.

Robinson, Roland I. *The Management of Bank Funds.* 2d ed. New York: McGraw-Hill Book Co., 1962.

_____, and Richard H. Pettway. *Policies for Optimum Bank Capital.* Chicago: Association of Reserve City Bankers, 1967.

Rodkey, Robert G. *Sound Policies for Bank Management.* New York: Ronald Press, 1944.

Sauvain, Harry. *Investment Management,* 3d ed. rev. Englewood Cliffs, N.J.: Prentice-Hall, 1967.

Studenski, Paul, and Herman E. Krooss. *Financial History of the United States.* New York: McGraw-Hill Book Co., 1952.

Thomas, Rollin G. *Modern Banking.* New York: Prentice-Hall, 1937.

Tobin, J. "The Theory of Portfolio Selection." In *The Theory of Interest Rates,* Proceedings of a Conference of the International Economic Association at the Abbey of Royaumont, France, March 28–April 7, 1962, edited by F. H. Hahn and F.P.R. Brechling, pp. 3–51, London: Macmillan and Co., 1966.

Van Dahm, Thomas E. *Money and Banking,* Lexington, Mass.: D. C. Heath & Co., 1975.

Woodworth, G. W. "Theories of Cyclical Liquidity Management of Commercial Banks." In *Banking Markets and Financial Institutions,* edited by Thomas G. Gies and Vincent P. Apilado, pp. 155–67, Homewood, Ill.: Richard D. Irwin, 1971.

Wooster, James W., Jr. *Bankers' Handbook of Bond Investment.* New York: Harper & Brothers, 1939.

Wrean, William Hamilton. *The Demand for Business Loan Credit.* Lexington, Mass.: D. C. Heath and Co., 1974.

JOURNALS/PERIODICALS

Besen, S. M. "An Empirical Analysis of Commercial Bank Lending Behavior." *Yale Economic Essays* 5 (Fall 1965): 283–315.

Bopp, Karl R. "A Flexible Monetary Policy." *Business Review,* Federal Reserve Bank of Philadelphia (March 1958): 3–7.

_____. "Borrowing from the Federal Reserve Bank—Some Basic Principles." *Business Review,* Federal Reserve Bank of Philadelphia (June 1958): 3–9.

Chambers, D., and A. Charnes. "Inter-Temporal Analysis and Optimization of Bank Portfolios." *Management Science* (July 1961): 393–410.

Cohen, Kalman J., and Edwin J. Elton. "Inter-Temporal Portfolio Analysis Based on Simulation of Joint Returns." *Management Science* (September 1967): 5–18.

_____, Frederick S. Hammer, and H. M. Schneider. "Harnessing Computers for Bank Asset Management." *The Bankers Magazine* 150 (Summer 1967): 72–80.

Davis, Richård G., and Jack M. Guttentag. "Time and Savings Deposits in the Cycle." *Monthly Review,* Federal Reserve Bank of New York (June 1962): 86–91.

Davis, Thomas E. "Bank Holdings of Municipal Securities." *Monthly Review,* Federal Reserve Bank of Kansas City (December 1970): 3–12.

DePamphilis, D. M. "Impact of Fed Regulation on Liability Management." *Bankers Monthly* (May 15, 1974): 33ff.

Dill, Arnold. "Liability Management Banking: Its Growth and Impact." *Monthly Review,* Federal Reserve Bank of Atlanta (February 1971): 22–33.

Duesenberry, J. "The Portfolio Approach to the Demand for Money and Other Assets." *Review of Economics and Statistics* 45, supp. (February 1963): 9–24.

Hempel, George H. "Basic Ingredients of Commercial Banks' Investment Policies." *The Bankers Magazine* 155 (Autumn 1972): 50–59.

Hester, D. D. "An Empirical Examination of a Commercial Bank Loan Offer Function." *Yale Economic Essays* 2 (Spring 1962): 3–57.

_____, and James L. Perce. "Cross-Section Analysis and Bank Dynamics." *Journal of Political Economy* 76, no. 4, part 2 (August 1968): 755–76.

_____, and John F. Zoellner. "The Relation between Bank Portfolios and Earnings: An Econometric Analysis." *Review of Economics and Statistics* 48 (November 1966): 372–86.

Kelly, Daniel M. "Bank Investments in a Dynamic Money Market." *Bankers Monthly* (November 1957): 19ff.

Knight, Robert E. "An Alternative Approach to Liquidity." *Monthly Review,* Federal Reserve Bank of Kansas City (December 1969; February, April, May 1970).

————. "New Sources of Bank Funds: Certificates of Deposit and Debt Securities." *Law and Contemporary Problems* 32 (Winter 1967): 71–99.

Lindow, Wesley. "The Federal Funds Market." *Bankers Monthly* (September 1960): 20ff.

Lussey, Harry W. "Portfolio Policy Now." *Bankers Monthly* (February 1960): 17ff.

McKinney, George W., Jr. "Liability Management: Its Cost and Its Uses." *The Bankers Magazine.* 157 (Winter 1974): 19–26.

Meigs, A. James. "Recent Innovations in the Functions of Banks." *American Economic Review* 56 (May 1966): 167–77.

Moor, Roy E. "Portfolio Economics." *The Bankers Magazine* 157 (Summer 1974): 66–73.

Moulton, H. G. "Commercial Banking and Capital Formation, III." *The Journal of Political Economy* 26 (July 1918): 705–31.

Nadler, Paul S. "The Use and Mis-use of CDs." Banking (July 1965): 51–52.

Pierce, J. L. "Commercial Bank Liquidity" (Staff Economic Study). *Federal Reserve Bulletin* 52 (August 1966): 1093–1101.

Porter, R. C. "A Model of Bank Portfolio Selection." *Yale Economic Essays* 1 (Fall 1961): 323–59.

Rothwell, Jack C. "The Move to Municipals." *Business Review,* Federal Reserve Bank of Philadelphia (September 1966): 3–7.

Roussakis, E. "Postwar Trends in Commercial Banking in the United States." *Revue de la Banque,* no. 1 (1969): 75–86.

Ruebling, Charlotte, E. "The Administration of Regulation Q." *Review,* Federal Reserve Bank of St. Louis (February 1970): 29–40.

Russell, William R. "Commercial Bank Portfolio Adjustments." *American Economic Review* 54 (May 1964): 544–53.

Scheld, Karl A. "Bank Credit Cards." *Business Conditions,* Federal Reserve Bank of Chicago (June 1967): 6–9.

Staats, William F. "The Adequacy of Bank Capital is Viewed by State Authorities." *Banking* (October 1965): 43–44.

Watson, Ronald D. "Bank Bond Management: The Maturity Dilemma." *Business Review,* Federal Reserve Bank of Philadelphia (March 1972): 23–29.

ABOUT THE AUTHOR

EMMANUEL N. ROUSSAKIS is Associate Professor of Finance at Florida International University, Miami, Florida. Until 1976, he was Associate Professor at Clark College, Atlanta University Center.

Dr. Roussakis has served in a consulting capacity with banks in the United States and Europe and participated in the preliminary negotiations for Greece's admission in the European Economic Community in the area of commercial banks and banking policy. He has published widely in the area of banking and his articles have appeared in various professional journals in France, Belgium, Italy, Greece, and Germany.

Dr. Roussakis holds a B.A. from Athens University; an M.B.A. from Atlanta University; a Graduate Certificate in Advanced European Studies from the College of Europe, Bruges; and a Ph.D. from the Catholic University of Louvain.

THE FUTURE OF COMMERCIAL BANKING
edited by
Wray O. Candilis

THE ECONOMICS OF BANK CREDIT CARDS
Thomas Russell

PENSION AND INSTITUTIONAL PORTFOLIO MANAGEMENT
Martin J. Schwimmer
Edward Malca